East European Communities

HN 380.7 .A8 E256 1995
East European communities
209290

DATE DUE

MAR 20 1996

BRODART
Cat. No. 23-221

East European Communities

The Struggle for Balance in Turbulent Times

EDITED BY
David A. Kideckel

Westview Press
BOULDER • SAN FRANCISCO • OXFORD

All rights reserved. No part of this publication may be reproduced or transmitted in any form or by any means, electronic or mechanical, including photocopy, recording, or any information storage and retrieval system, without permission in writing from the publisher.

Copyright © 1995 by Westview Press, Inc.

Published in 1995 in the United States of America by Westview Press, Inc., 5500 Central Avenue, Boulder, Colorado 80301-2877, and in the United Kingdom by Westview Press, 12 Hid's Copse Road, Cumnor Hill, Oxford OX2 9JJ

A CIP catalog record for this book is available from the Library of Congress.
ISBN 0-8133-8834-1

Printed and bound in the United States of America

The paper used in this publication meets the requirements of the American National Standard for Permanence of Paper for Printed Library Materials Z39.48-1984.

10 9 8 7 6 5 4 3 2 1

To Mimi, Zachary, and Caitlin
and the children of Eastern Europe

Contents

Preface

The pace of change in East Europe is unrelenting and, to a great extent, affects publication about the region. This book, like other recent discussions of the East European transition, represents an attempt to incorporate both the currency of journalism and the reflection of scholarly research. Though the two are not mutually exclusive, they often are perceived as such, especially in publications about contemporary East Europe. However, to effectively present the extraordinary change in East Europe in a timely and substantial fashion requires not so much compromise between one and the other but rather a unity of the approaches. Each of the chapters offered here combines these forms in explicit fashion. Though the speed of events is bound to overtake these essays, and though the specifics of each chapter will vary over time, each chapter is nonetheless a clear-sighted discussion of issues that directly affect local East European life today and will continue to echo in the region for the next decades.

The transformation of East Europe has not only shaped scholarship of the region but has also influenced the career paths of scholars concerned with the region. With the increased integration of East and West and the greater accessibility of East Europe to diverse scholarly as well as other activities, those who work in the region have found themselves beset by a whole set of contradictory demands and possibilities. Many of the contributors to this volume now serve regularly as consultants to international organizations. Others are actively collaborating with colleagues in rebuilding scholarly institutions and organizations that had languished in the past years. Still others have positions of political responsibility in their respective countries. And there were even a few potential contributors who were ultimately unable to sign on due to the weight of these additional responsibilities. To each of these individuals I owe my greatest respect, admiration, and profuse apologies for my constant admonitions to put the rest of their lives on hold in favor of this project.

Aside from the contributors, thanks are also due to Kellie Masterson and Julia Joun at Westview for their encouragement and patience and also to Dinah Stiles, university assistant in the Anthropology Department at Central Connecticut State University for her extraordinary assistance and help in compiling this manuscript.

David A. Kideckel

1

Communities in the East European Transition

David A. Kideckel

The end of the highly centralized, east European socialist state is an accomplished fact. However, though wheat sheaves, oil derricks, hammers, sickles, and stars, have been ripped from the flags of the east European states, the future of the region is by no means certain. Though economic privatization is the goal toward which all allegedly move, some like Hungarians and Poles do so with dispatch while others, like Romanians and Bulgarians have adopted a clear go-slow approach. Certainly political pluralism is the watchword of the day. Still, recent socialist electoral gains in Poland, Hungary, and eastern Germany, the continued domination of centralizing politics in Romania and along the perimeter of Russia, and the growing unrest from mass migrations, ethnic conflict and the like all force the notion that social change in the region is an open question. The uncertainties of east Europe are rife with possibility, though the pictures offered are as contrasting as a burned out Balkan village and rejuvenated housing complexes from Bucharest to Bratislava. To better understand the likelihood and implications of such possibilities is the main purpose of this volume.

This book and its various contributions, written mainly by anthropologists and rural sociologists with long research and often personal experience in east European communities, addresses a number of shortcomings in our knowledge of east Europe today. Most current studies of the on-going transformation outline state level events and processes, particularly focussing on changing economic and legal systems. For example, one area within this genre concerns problems associated with the increased frequency and intensity of contact between easterners and westerners, whether in the context of economic privatization or the more personal one of the trade in infants. There are a few notable discussions of the transition's effect on the lives of real people, again mainly by anthropologists (Anderson and DeSoto, eds. 1993). However, when most observers bring discussion down to a local level such examinations still tend to focus on national phenomena such as changing class relations, emigration, or east Europe's plague of pernicious ethnicity. Local events are used only as illustration and context. When the local effects of the transition are considered, this is mainly done by journalists in quick, fairly unidimensional manners.

Thus both "macro" perspectives and journalistic descriptions tend to elide the in-depth understanding of the lives of real people in real communities who every day must make decisions based on rapidly changing circumstances and the possibilities and obstacles they provide. To better understand the transition, then, requires a finely grained local focus in addition to the more widely used macroscopic perspective. Certainly a focus on local conditions, by themselves, can not tell us about the nature of the changing east European state. However, it is the real life problems and choices that especially lay bare the structures of state life developing in east Europe today and that will ultimately shape the region's future.

To offer a balance to predominant state-level analyses, if not to actually counteract them, this volume focusses on actual communities in the east European transition and the diverse issues which people face in them on a daily basis. Community in this book is interpreted broadly. Most of the book's chapters deal with specific village communities and their experience in the transition. Particularly communities are examined in Hungary (Vasary, Hann), in Poland (Halasiewicz et al), in Bulgaria (Creed, Ivanova), and in Romania (Kideckel). Others of the chapters construe community more widely. Thus community is defined in senses of ethnic identity (Bates on Bulgarian Turks and Silverman on Macedonian Gypsies), in terms of gender (DeSoto and Panzig on east German women), as an emerging class segment (Smigielska's rural business class) or comparatively to illustrate changing social conflict (Kurczewski), agricultural privatization (Singelmann), or the transformation of inter-personal relations (Sampson). Whatever the particular spatial or topical focus, however, the volume seeks to bring the implications of national policy decisions and international influences, down to the level of local reality and, both explicitly and by implication, suggest how local populations effect the developing nature of relationships at the level of the transitional state.

In its focus on actual communities and the diversity of relations that obtain within them, the volume is organized around three major themes: 1) economic change and privatization; 2) the transformation of community social and political organization and control; and 3) changing community belief and identity systems, (including questions of class, gender, and ethnicity). In considering these questions many of the essays offer a longitudinal approach with particular communities described and analyzed from a "before and after" vantage point. In this way the actual effects of the transition can be separated out from normal expected social change and the role and effects of the socialist past and of long-standing community structures and relations can be understood.

The sub-title of the volume, "The Struggle for Balance in Turbulent Times," suggests the uncertainties and problematic aspects of local life which most of the authors define. As each chapter suggests, the jury is still out on the possibilities for east Europeans to break the strangle-hold on their lives of persistent inequality, pernicious ethnicity, and perpetual underdevelopment. The articles' focus on local life implies, then, that the primary responsibility for challenging their difficult pasts rests on community members themselves. The east European state is not only discredited and in decline (at least from the point of view of their role within and among local communities), but in some instances is in active opposition to the development of strong and prosperous local institutions. To overcome such opposition and to chart their own course for stability, equanimity, and balance, is thus a primary community task. However, it is one that must be accomplished in a social context inherited from the socialist and pre-socialist pasts that often are characterized by extreme uncertainty, if not outright acrimony and suspicion.

Community Life in the Transition

Contemporary community life in east Europe has four common features that create the context for the acting out of local life. The first three of these reflect the essential social, political, and economic reality of the last five years. These factors include the delegitimation and relative withdrawal of the state from local life, the continued influence of social relationships developed over the forty-five years of the socialist state--or what one of this book's contributors has elsewhere termed the socialist unconscious (Creed 1991), and the constant, if only implied, presence of Western society and standards of living as interlocutor, point of reference, and foil to changing east Europe. From these three grows the fourth general condition of local east European life today, the gnawing tentativeness of the present and uncertainty of the future, which can be either goads to inertia or action as people seek to plot a course for self and family.

The delegitimation of the state and its withdrawal from community life particularly affects the tenor of community relations and the development of the local economy. With centralized planning a thing of the past, communities are left to fend for themselves and develop appropriate strategies and actions for development. This, however, is made all the harder by the lack of the impartial state to adjudicate differences, and the suspicions between people generated by the rise and fall of socialism itself. As Kurczewski points out in his chapter, though there is not an increased incidence of social conflict per se in Polish communities from the time of socialism, what there is most definitely implicates changing economic practices and, to an extent, challenges the appropriateness of the private economy. This is also seen in the papers by Hann for Hungary, Creed for Bulgaria, and Kideckel in Romania.

The diminishing state role in local communities also means that economic development and social regeneration hinge on the emergence of local leadership or entrepreneurial individuals, a problematic situation indeed. When such a stratum develops, as is the case that Ildiko Vasary, Joanna Smigielska, and Radost Ivanova present, communities are energized for rapid transformation. When that is not the case, or when communities remain dependent on declining state resources, as presented by Joachim Singelmann for eastern Germany, the results are somewhat more troublesome. It is then that the inertia and frustration of the transition can especially take hold and produce the whole range of social ills that transitional communities experience.

The decline of the state has also delegitimated policies favoring the equalization of resources and supporting disenfranchised social groups. Thus, east German women (DeSoto and Panzig), Macedonian Gypsies (Silverman), and Bulgarian Turks (Bates) must seek their own sources of community, strength, and growth in the transitional state. Before the end of socialism they could rely on at least a semblance of state support. Bereft of this today, they are forced to organize themselves if their group identities, economic well-being and political strengths are to develop. As DeSoto and Panzig and Silverman point out, this is not an entirely unhappy set of circumstances. In these two cases, women in the eastern part of Germany and Macedonian Gypsies have clearly risen to the challenges posed by the transition. Though beset by economic and political challenges, the growth of their organization and common sense of purpose has served them well. In contrast, the Bulgarian Turkish minority, as discussed by Dan Bates, is beset with multiple challenges stemming from its own fractious structures and politics and a constantly threatening social context. Rather than relating to the transition in their own terms, Bulgarian Turks are in disarray, a problem directly resulting from their position in the waning years of the socialist state and persisting to this day.

Along with Bates, other observers also point out that the transition is certain to be affected by elements of the socialist past, usually said to be a latent, sub-surface factor in community life. Though this is often the case, as many of the articles point out, socialist factors are neither as hidden nor as moribund as many would have it. Instead, in many of the communities discussed here there appears to be an active, if not proactive, socialist presence in the on-going process of social, political, and economic change. Not only is socialism present in the ideas that people have about directions the transformation ought to take, but it is also the critical principle of identity that many use in developing their institutional structures, goals, and relations in transitional society. Socialism is also an active principle in the struggle for power in the transitional community. Thus, Sampson for Romania especially suggests the role of the general distrust emerging from the Romanian socialist experience and its immediate aftermath. Similarly, Hann and Vasary for Hungary, Halasiewicz, Kaleta, and Vnenchak for Poland, and Ivanova for Bulgaria point out the role of mentalities developed during socialism that channel the energies of communities today.

Each of the communities discussed here face different issues, though the similarities of the task of transition also result in certain common challenges underlying each particular case. Some of the more obvious challenges include diminishing the anger and resentment generated during socialism, recreating a vibrant economic life while restricting the growth of extreme inequality, restructuring local political life to both encourage the emergence of strong local leaders and enable effective community participation in state and regional-level decision making. Especially difficult will be the refashioning of consciousness to produce individual orientations willing to support such change or at least to give emergent social, political, and economic institutions and relations. It is this latter challenge that is made especially difficult by the nagging uncertainties of life in contemporary east Europe.

Uncertainty, of course, manifests in almost every facet of local community life. First implicated are the nagging economic questions that accompany decollectivization, privatization, and the large-scale loss of economic alternatives in the industrial turn-down. The vacuum left by these forces acting in concert is a difficult one to fill and is often met by frustration, anger, and precipitous action such as the untimely distribution of cattle Ivanova discusses in her chapter, running the mayor out of town in a wheel-barrow in Praszka, Poland as discussed by Jacek Kurczewski, or the frantic economic speculation in the Romanian village of Sampson's description. At the same time, however, uncertainty leaves great room for maneuver for enterprising individuals or those less committed to the status quo of prevailing social and economic relations.

The uncertainty of east European life especially challenges those of us who seek to understand the momentous events on-going in this part of the world. The notion of uncertainty implies movement from one social stage to another and thus generally supports the concept of transition as a way of making sense of current changes in east European life. However, as Sampson suggests, uncertainty and change in themselves are the essential realties of contemporary east Europe. Instead of an undefined movement out of socialism toward some kind of market-driven, potentially democratic set of states, perhaps the region is better seen as characterized by an articulated social form in its own right or, to paraphrase Rudolf Bahro (1978), as some kind of actually existing turbulence producing particular kinds of relationships and pressures.

If the imbalances seen in east Europe today are not transitional phenomena but comprise an actually existing social system with some potential staying power, than the instability of the region confronts us all and especially carries large implications for world geo-politics in the coming century. Though none of the articles speak at length of either the Western role in contemporary east Europe, or that of Russia, the two are constantly in the background. They are the 500 pound gorillas of the current historical moment and, people assume, so much of the future of the region depends on what these gorillas choose to do or not. To many east Europeans and outside observers the behavior of these behemoths stands as either or both savior or demon. Russian instability or its potential market can either crush or liberate community energies. Western assistance or the snare of Western dependency are likewise thought to offer the region unending toil or unlimited growth. However, the articles clearly show that the tendency to look to these giants as of ultimate effect in east Europe, is somehow misplaced. Western aid looks more and more insignificant[1] and Russia increasingly mired in her own problems. The solution, if there is one, will come with a release of regional communities' internal energies and with the conscious challenge to the forces of division and despair which stalk our times. It is my hope that these essays have helped outline what these particular forces are, even as they metamorphose in the struggle for balance in east Europe today.

Notes

1. Reworking a proverb from the socialist past, one commentator at the recent meetings of the American Association for the Advancement of Slavic Studies described the current east European futility with Western assistance in the phrase, "They pretend to help us, so we pretend to be helped."

References

Anderson, David and Hermine DeSoto eds. 1993. *The Curtain Rises: Rethinking Culture, Ideology and the State in Eastern Europe*. Atlantic Highlands, NJ: Humanities Press,

Bahro, Rudolf. 1978. *The Alternative in Eastern Europe*. London: NLB.

Creed, Gerald W. 1991. "Civil Society and the Spirit of Capitalism: A Bulgarian Critique," Paper presented at the Annual Meeting of the American Anthropological Association, November 20-24. Chicago, IL.

PART ONE

Challenges of Privatization and the Market

2

Labyrinths of Freedom: An Agricultural Community in Post-Socialist Hungary

Ildiko Vasary

Understanding the East European Transformation

Eastern Europe today is an increasingly popular locale for academic research. Pens are poised to analyze the unique transition of socialism to capitalism, democracy, and a market economy. One of the most interesting phenomena that observers have noted is the contradiction between the momentous political changes of regime and the far slower pace of actual social and economic transformation (Kolosi & Robert 1992, Agh 1992, Andorka 1992). This contrast has thus apparently contributed to a frustration among East European peoples resulting from the real possibilities of total transformation compared to the actuality of piecemeal change. Though this contradiction is rife throughout the former socialist countries, Hungary was first able to avoid it as Kadar's pragmatic style of market socialism allowed the country through the 1970s and 1980s to tiptoe away, so to speak, from much of socialist ideology and practice. The change of regime therefore, although politically and historically momentous, did not have an immediate shock effect on society. This, however, is not the case in the 1990s.

Policies unveiled by the new regime have opened up multiple avenues of change of labyrinth-like complexity[1] which the political leadership, economic advisors, and most of all society must negotiate together. The rural population, most affected by the brutal change of the human-land relationship through collectivization in 1950-1960, is now experiencing, perhaps more acutely than any other section of society, the uncertainty of freedom and the related choices that have to be made.[2] My concern, then, is to attempt to explain the diverse responses of rural Hungarians and the possible effects these responses will have on the future of rural Hungarian life.

The nature and causes of social continuity and change have always been problematic in anthropology. Both always appear somewhat random and unpredictable, perhaps because neither the fragility nor the resilience of social phenomena or processes are easily gauged. In Hungary (and throughout Eastern Europe) there are currently many factors that underlie both continuity and change. Their sources are also manifold and derive from pre-war class systems of capitalism, feudalism, traditional peasant society, and even from socialist society itself. During the decades of East European socialism, for example, peasant elements had unforeseen resilience and resurfaced in the most unlikely contexts.

In socialist Poland, for example, pre-war class relations, traditional peasant ethos and even feudal social remnants were continually reproduced. This prompted Nagengast (1991) to evaluate Polish socialism with terms such as "apparent," "chimerical," and "virtually a total failure and suggested that this system actually "veiled," and "masked" real processes going on beneath it (1991:19-20). Consequently, her assessment of present rural developments takes the period before 1944 rather than the socialist decades, as her basic point of reference.

Socialist East Europe and Hungarian Exceptionalism

Compared to Poland and the rest of East Europe, socialism in Hungary was lived differently. Rural families worked out a fragile *modus vivendi* with the regime that reconciled both collective life in the village and jobs in the second economy outside it. Most rural Hungarians worked both in a vigorous and productive private small-plot farming sector and on the collectives as well. Because of this, then, the collectivization of agriculture, albeit complete and drastic at the outset, had a number of distinguishing features which facilitated its adaptation to local community life and which differentiated it from other such organizations elsewhere in East Europe.

First, Hungarian collective farm structures were heterogenous. A number of collectives, as documented by Hann (1980) went only a small way towards true collectivization and resisted the pressure to conform to the dominant *kolkhoz* norm. Second, in the decades following their creation collectives became not more but less socialist. Thus the collectives that remained by the 1980s were a far cry from the village-based small affairs, presided over by one of the members, working with the member's horse carts and rounding up virtually all men and women at the crack of dawn for the formation of work brigades. The 1980s saw large agricultural enterprises of a regional, rather than village character, that were managed by a trained administrative and scientific staff. Most of them had developed non-agricultural production sectors and also made use of a large amount of hired wage workers rather than members in the original sense. In this production system emphasis had shifted from the primarily political nature of the original *kolkhoz* toward the purely economic goals of the late socialist organizations (Hann 1993). Elek (1991) even went so far as to speak of these organizations as examples of "tacit decollectivization (see also Donáth 1980; Hóllos & Maday 1983; Swain 1982, 1985; Vasary 1987). Last, as mentioned above, an intensive "private" sector developed alongside the collective one and became a major feature of Hungarian economy and society, on which it exerted a significant influence.

Contradictions of Policy and Practice in Agricultural Change

Immediately after the establishment of the new regime many rural citizens expressed concern about the nature of the new agricultural policy in formation. In fact, this question, had vast implications for all of society. It not only pertained to policy changes on marketing, prices, taxes, and so on, but suggested a fundamental reformulation of the human-land relationship, similar in importance to the same question raised in 1947, and again in 1959-60: the manner and extent to which individuals, collectivities and the state will share the ownership and control of the country's agricultural land. If the change of regime was to have any credibility at all, the new government had to minimally reject the principles by which agriculture had operated in socialism. But if economic continuity and productivity were to be maintained then some recognition of the former collective structures also had to occur.

The choice of policy has now been made. True to the needs of the state the new model both re-establishes the primacy of private property without actively disbanding the collectives. In order to implement this new model the "Compensation Law" was passed in 1991 which enables people to claim compensation for lands and other property lost during socialist collectivization but which places a number of restrictions on the possibilities of total compensation. The application of this law is ponderous. Applicants are issued coupons reflecting the value of their loss of either land, houses and out-buildings, or equipment and these can be used to bid at land auctions for specified plots designated for sale by the collectives. By allowing the collectives to designate land for auction they, too, are thus able to retain an unfragmented base.[3]

Considered in total, the law's significance is more than as a mechanism for partial restoration of former property rights. In fact it implicates the entire system of social structure and cultural meaning extant in the Hungarian countryside. By involving nearly everyone in the country in the choices, agonies, and contradictions of agricultural restructuring, a great variety of questions are forced out into open discourse. The Compensation Law thus forces examination of the depth of one's attachment to one's ancestral patrimony, requires evaluation of the worth of autonomy and control over one's labor, and demands individual and household decision making about the worth of agriculture and landownership as a mode of existence. In other words, it forces families to reassess what strains land places on their labor and what investments in cash and self exploitation a farm would mean. Quite ironically, the land returned under the operation of the Compensation Law may shelter one against the threat of unemployment, but simultaneously generates unemployment in the collectives by the return of land to private ownership.

Consequently, despite or because of the Compensation Law, a wholesale resurgence of traditional peasant farms or the emergence of a stratum of modern farmers is unlikely. Furthermore, a great variety of new configurations are to be expected, not least because choices will be played out in the social as well as the economic domain. Following Hann (1993), I too see that it is as much the use of land and the different meanings of property as it is the ownership of land alone that matters in determining rural social relationships. With land once again a commodity, the agricultural sector stands in a different relationship to the other economic sectors (industrial, commercial and so on). Since in Hungary rural families are involved almost without exception in many non-agricultural sectors, the new configurations will be played out at the level of family labor organization as a whole not only with reference to land ownership. In this transformation one might even expect a resurgence of socialist elements, since they have been built into collective memory and become elements of rural families' constructed identities.

The actual effects of the Compensation Law in fact depend on what real-life social practice will make of it. In particular one can expect that the new agricultural policy environment will affect people's attitudes to property, commitment to farming, and rural aspirations and attitudes towards entrepreneurialism. This last issue, remarkable for its irrelevance during socialist years, is at present the overriding concern in Hungary and, of course, the obsession of Western economies as well. Hungary presently defines its future in terms of catching up with Western Europe and, first and foremost, this finds expression in its concern to do well in "enterprise."

In rural Hungary entrepreneurial practice has a checkered history.[4] In the recent past it was fairly restricted as collectivization leveled land ownership and limited local decision making thus restricting peasant self-determination, responsibility, and work ethics. Collectively owned property came to be despised, and poorly managed and slovenly work was the order of the day. However, as sloppy as collective farm work was, a different attitude prevailed outside the collectives in what was first a half hidden sector, but which eventually grew into the powerful private small farming sector. The success of Hungarian small-farming was thus the motor for Kadar's market socialism, the

New Economic Mechanism of 1968, and a second economy of more varied dimensions. This process of "trickle-up" economics thus clearly confounded the received economic wisdom where influences are more or less seen routinely to flow from town to country, and the peasantry is considered more passive receptor than innovator particularly in the field of economics and production.[5] As Andorka (1992:234) suggests "we may consider participation in the second economy as the seed, the school of private enterprise." Though socio-political literature of the 1970s and 1980s constantly made the point that the plot farming sector was closely linked to the collectives, it must be recognized that this interpretation had a hidden agenda to protect plot farming sector by making it appear compatible with the regime's favored socio-economic structure and thus less of an ideological eyesore.

Complementary they might have been, it remains a fact that plot farming was more often hindered than helped by the collective. The latter had monopolistic power to dispense or withhold vital services and goods and they dictated the terms of marketing, which they alone could change. Land use and allocation was entirely in their control: where, how much, and who had access to land was their decision. They marked out the plot farming areas (*zártkertek*), leased or assigned plots to their members and employees, and often prescribed what could or could not be planted. It is clear from reported case histories, that seldom were these decisions made with plot farmers' best interests in mind. Still, despite all the above, it is an inescapable fact that these myriad number of small units were worked with great efficiency and sensitivity to both favorable and unfavorable economic trends.

In the peasant context, then, the meaning of entrepreneurialism differs widely from its counterpart in cash-based, capital rich urban contexts (Wolf 1966; Franklin 1969; Shanin 1990). In the latter, entrepreneurial behavior is oriented to change and transformation while in the former it is essentially conservative, at least with respect to peasant life and livelihood. As even in the most intensive years of collectivization small-plots remained under the control of peasants, they were able to amplify their use in various productive and entrepreneurial ways which in fact assisted the continuity and preservation of essential features of peasant attitudes.

Now, precise definition of what exactly peasant attitudes are is somewhat problematic, but it seems to include elements of a general nature, independent from farming itself, and of relevance to any other productive endeavor. In other words, what made the plot farming sector so successful was not some specific "peasant" farming method, but the way in which rural families related to property and production: i.e. with total commitment, initiative, and responsibility, confident of their decision making, and seeking a maximum of control. Proving this point, Hungary allowed the creation of new varieties of small enterprises, service cooperatives, and trade associations from 1983 on. It is even possible to argue that none of these would have been created had it not been for the continuous example of the achievements of small-plot farming.[6]

What with the success of peasant plot farming as well as the considerable support the collectives still attracted, a number of new issues concerning the future of Hungarian agriculture emerged with the new regime. Though a large number of possibilities were discussed the debate soon focused on three likely courses. The first supports the maintenance of a limited kind of socialist agriculture, seeing it as a more or less stabilizing force for the economy. The second envisions a return to or revival of a more "traditional peasant" agriculture, both in terms of organization and attitude. And the third supports the development of a modern, entrepreneurial farm sector. However, having such diverse possibilities is not as positive as it seems. As newspaper articles, sociological, political and economic essays and private conversations all suggest, all three courses are flawed in some way and difficult to fully implement to the point of impossibility. This will be seen in more detail as I discuss the implications of each of these different courses in the experience of one Hungarian village.

Pecsely in Transformation: 1978-1993

I did fieldwork in the Transdanubian village of Pecsely for three years between 1978-1981 and made several return visits over the last years, of which the relevant ones for the present essay took place between 1990 and 1992. In 1981 the village had a population of 600, a successful collective and a flourishing plot farming sector focussed mainly on its profitable vineyards. Pig farming and other minor types of private production were also present. As I left the field in 1981, one could discern a number of both positive and negative trends at work, but on balance the latter were more influential than the former. Such negative trends were mainly shaped by the quickening struggle of plot farmers against the reluctant and interfering officials of a distant yet overbearing collective that held a virtual monopoly over land allocation. However, they also included a poverty of local social services and cultural activities, and an aging population fueled by extensive emigration of the young. Despite these trends, however, a number of forces were at work beneath the surface of everyday life that ultimately proved to have much greater impact than one might have foreseen. For through the 1980s the village moved into an entirely different phase of development leaving behind the threatened decay of the early 1980s.[7]

On my return to Pecsely in 1990 I was impressed with the steady growth which the villages seemed to have experienced. This did not seem to be just a mere accretion in size--as in towns with bleak, makeshift housing estates stuck to the periphery in a disfiguring fashion, but seemed an unforced growth from within. Houses in a state of disrepair had been renovated to their original shape and style, often with the former family insignia restored to their front. Gardens and courtyards were no longer neglected and an entirely new street of about twenty-five houses radiated out from the village center. Altogether about thirty-five new houses were added to the existing 190, while the population remained stable at 600. This meant first that many previous aged and ailing owners were replaced by perhaps a son or daughter or, in the case of eight of the new houses, immigrants. Considering the costs required for building on that scale it was clear that the village had a prosperous decade. Now it seems more young people were opting to stay and, after having lived eight to ten years in the housing estates of the neighboring town of Fured, eight young families moved back into the village. Furthermore it appears the boom will continue for a while. Houses for sale are snatched up quickly and there is active competition to even buy derelict houses.

Community facilities had also developed. The council house, a modest three room affair, had been replaced by a spacious, modern building with a grand entrance and excellent office and assembly rooms that once served as the former headquarters of the collective. The village now also had a well stocked self-service foodstore, a restaurant and a new bar. School buildings were enlarged and improved, a dental clinic, a library, medical counselling center and a well equipped Youth Club were created as well.[8] Reading the physical aspects of the village one concludes that the more depressing trends gaining steam in the early 1980s did not, in fact materialize and today village life does not seem far behind that of a small town or suburb.

Local farming, too, has developed in different directions as foreseen by the divergent paths agricultural took in the country as a whole. On one hand, the collective farm has lost much of its local significance. After merging with other farms in the region it distanced itself from participation in village affairs and became merely one more place of potential employment, little different than the ship factory in Fured or any other regional enterprise.[9] In fact, even the collective's significance as a source of employment has declined. Only about 15 villagers actively work in the present organization which was created in 1983 by the agglomeration of 12 smaller ones. Its significance is further reduced in that its center is outside Pecsely, the chairman and administrative staff are not local, and its operations are far removed from the villages' day to day existence.

What importance it has for the village is vestigial. It still controls a sizable amount of land, has several non-agricultural sectors of production, pays out pensions to its older members, and has monetary assets of potential use for community development. It also offers marketing contracts for small farm products, farms out piglets, and so on. Compared to the collective of the 1960s we can thus suggest that a major metamorphosis has occurred with probably more change on the way. The collective still has the same chairman as before, but its operations are now reduced and rationalized under the new structure of ownership, which is similar to a shareholding system.

After 25-30 years of service, members are entitled to a share worth about 90,000 *forints* per year. In 1992, the villagers accepted this in kind, that is in wine, valued at twenty-eight *forints* per liter. Members are also issued with vouchers for the land auctions to the value of thirty golden crowns (twenty-five for employees) which they can use at the land auctions (see note 3). The essence of the change is that before all members were equal and the land, livestock, and other property of the collective was absorbed into a pool of collective assets with members only paying a nominal yearly land rent for the area they held for plot farming. However, since 1991-92 the collective's assets are, on paper, divided and allocated according to an individual's years of work and the value of the assets (*vagyonnevesites*) with which they originally joined the collective. On that basis they are issued a "wealth ticket" (*vagyonjegy*) much like a share.

It is uncertain, however, if all this will much change the day-to-day management and organization of the collectives which is much as it was before. However, even if the farm doesn't change there are now other cooperative groups of an agricultural character with which villagers can do business and cooperate so the collective will no longer have a monopolistic power in the region.

Compared to the local collective, small-plot farming has increased and diversified, even though some somber initial forecasts predicted its demise. This notion, however, was based mainly on a mistaken premise of demographic decline that assumed that the generation brought up in the traditions of peasant farming were aging and dying, while the young showed little interest to follow in their footsteps. Furthermore, related to the expansion in small-plot farming there has been a corresponding increase in stockkeeping. Where before only one or two families kept cows, now there are several with fifteen to twenty milkers apiece and far more pigs and horses are also seen throughout the village. Now, though, pigs are less often kept for household use, but instead for contractual pig farming where a typical annual household herd numbers from forty to 100 pigs. Income from the small-plots remains as much as an average wage and plots are far less vulnerable to the vicissitudes of the market. To further the efficiency of plot farming there has also been a corresponding increase in the amount of privately held agricultural machinery and at least three groups from ten to twenty members jointly own several big tractors, purchased from the collective.

With all these changes, then, the need for a regional rural banking structure is inevitable and its current lack is a large impediment to the further expansion of the market system. When created, though, it should facilitate the possibilities of small farmers to secure loans, investments for which they are now dependent on state credit agencies. Quite possibly, once the biases in favor of the collectives are eliminated in the Compensation Law, or when all collectively held land that is to be auctioned will be, local farming will be freed from any dependency on and control from the collectives and agricultural decision making will again only depend on ownership of land, large or small, by group or individuals.

Pecsely has also been lucky to escape rising non-agricultural unemployment. As before the transition, every household has one or more members in the non-farm sector and there is no unemployment in the village apart from the eight to ten people who have always been more or less unemployable, due to alcoholism or similar problems. Still, as they view events elsewhere in the country and in East Europe, unemployment is still a major source of anxiety[11] which may make people more alert to entrepreneurial possibilities or encourage their expansion of small farming activities. As "soft" factors like fears and expectations tend, in the long run, to eventually show up in "hard" facts like measurable increase in private enterprise, they cannot be taken lightly.

Social Implications of the Transition in Pecsely

Though small farming is increasingly vital it is unlikely that agriculture will return to the kind of family farming practiced more or less until 1960. All analyses point to it as irretrievably gone (Romany 1992, Rab 1992, Hann 1993) even though in Pecsely some people made sporadic efforts to reinstate it. For example, one family moved from a nearby town, used all their savings to buy a largish house and a farm and started up full time farming, concentrating on milk cows and a dairy. However, they gave it up after two years, allegedly due to lack of local support. They said that their efforts were thwarted at every step, as villagers did not buy their milk. It appears people rejected this family and their enterprise out of a sense of jealousy. As one observer remarked:

> The villagers did not hate him, but their former selves. They are no longer ready to stand up for a lifestyle from which they have been forcefully ejected. They changed their houses and holdings so that it is no longer suitable for a farming life, their entire habitus is against it. They resented this family's courage and turned against him (Bodosi 1992:16).

Of course, there were factors also at work here. The family in question was not originally from the village and suspicions towards migrants in Pecsely are still deep-seated and account in part for their rejection. But even so villagers have also internalized the negative representations of traditional peasant life promoted in socialism and hold vivid memories of the hardships of that life.

Thus, though it is very probable that small farming will continue and develop, it will not be towards some romantic re-creation of the former traditional lifestyle, but in new forms more appropriate to conditions today. As an outgrowth of plot farming, private farming may take a number of new directions. Some households will no doubt attempt to develop it into a full-time family business as in Western Europe (Rab 1992), while most others will continue small farming only as an auxiliary family activity practiced concurrently with non-agricultural employment.

Finally, let us consider the last, but perhaps the most important choice now open to villagers: enterprise. This is again one area that is related to and in some ways limited by previous social conditions with local attitudes toward entrepreneurial activity played out in a wide variety of different local events. For example, the local elections for mayor in October 1991 clearly showed villagers suspicious of such activities. In those elections two candidates came forward, both of whom had no formal political party identification though, by their platforms and previous histories were identified by villagers as supporters of one or another party. The first candidate had formerly served as the local council president for ten years. He was a local man, an agronomist, and a dedicated plot farmer. Still, though he prided himself on his non-political nature, other villagers clearly associated him with the former regime and with socialism. His platform was a rather simplistic one based on "people doing the best they could and carrying on as before." But he also put some degree of emphasis on support for small-plot farming.[12]

In contrast, this man's opponent was a young man fresh from polytechnic school, grandson of one of the village's old respected *gazdas* (private peasant head of household), and openly associated with the Smallholder Party. His program assumed that the new government would cease all support for villages and to forestall this disaster suggested that the village seek foreign investors who would bring capital into the village to set up small manufacturing centers. He talked about Austrian friends of his bringing in a shoe finishing factory and Japanese small parts factory (Vasary 1992). To most people, though, this had a positively alarming ring and, not surprisingly, he got only six percent of the vote. The over-whelming winner was the former council president. This local election thus clearly signaled the villagers' aversion towards fundamental change. They had all the change they could take for the moment and felt more comfortable with a more cautious pace.

Nevertheless, there have been several developments of an innovative kind in the village; however, they are clearly outgrowths of more predictable and traditional sorts of social relations and production activities. For example, fifteen families whose vineyards are all clustered in one hillside and are of excellent reputation formed a wine production association. Though networks of reciprocal help typically criss-crossed the village in an informal but important way, this group carried this one step further. They jointly bought several used tractors from the collective, they market their grapes together, and they give each other more than neighborly assistance. Similarly, a wine cellar association with 180 members, including some from surrounding villages and sixty from Pecsely was recently created. Each member of this group contributed 50,000 forints, and bought the cellar of the collective for seven million forints, and with government aid created a bottling plant. They are thus now a vertically integrated organization controlling production from the vineyards to the wine. In the same vein, the mechanic sector of the collective broke away from it to became a free private firm, with forty-five members, of which twenty are from Pecsely, and the others from surrounding villages. These are all men in their thirties and early forties, with professional training who now have good export connections and manufacture industrial parts for Germany. These mid-range local initiatives and enterprises are developments of the greatest promise, particularly as they happened so fast. They not only show that villagers can and do collaborate, but mark the beginning of an entirely new economic layer halfway between large scale agricultural and the backyard small-plots. This was precisely the missing economic layer in socialism!

Despite all these above activities, the economic future of communities like Pecsely still largely depend on the responses of people to the Compensation Law. It will be of great interest and social significance to see how people will use the land they receive. Currently the Compensation Law has generated remarkable reactions. Lamentations for the losses and wrongs suffered in past decades hardly figured while the change of regime was politically in the making. However, with the political transformation accomplished, they came out in full strength after the Compensation Law was passed. Only then could one hear, "I want everything back." Many feel that the compensation offered is paltry and inadequate in comparison with all that has been lost. It is as if the losses were easier to bear before. People bore them with dignity, like medals received for war wounds. The Compensation Law brought to surface how profoundly unintegrated in a psychological sense these losses have been. Stories dating back to the 1950s and 1960s are now regurgitated as if they happened yesterday. One wonders where all this sentiment was before. Of course, one could always hear it at a private level. People would come out with them during an in-depth interview, a life history or an after-dinner chat. But now we witness something different. The psychological reality is not much changed, but it has moved from the private into the social domain as people confront society with their personal history, demands, and indignation.

In 1991, when it first became possible to claim back land from the collective, interest in the matter was covert. People I talked to dismissed the possibility as of little interest. But on closer inquiry it transpired that each of them had the application for some attractive plot ready for submission. By the end of 1992, the question of land compensation is openly of interest to everyone. In this region, of course, land has great value. The region is near a popular tourist resort and land is generally of high quality. However, many villagers have not yet had their claims processed and do not have their compensation vouchers in hand.

Meanwhile the compensation process takes place at auctions where people use their vouchers to bid for plots of their choice. If there are no other offers, people may purchase more land at the lowest rate of 500 forints per acre. In competitive bidding the starting rate is 3,000 forints per acre with no upper limit on the cost. Vineyards, in particular, are likely to reach a very high rate. There has already been an auction in the village, in which seventeen percent of the available land was offered with eleven people acquiring mainly arable fields. The next auction will be held in April 1994, for seventy percent of the land and the remainder will be cleared off at the third and last auction. In Hungary as a whole, over 830,000 claims have been submitted for compensation vouchers.

It is difficult to foresee what results the restructuring of land ownership will have. Undoubtedly, land use and ownership will diverge; land leasing will increase as land becomes a commodity and object of sale. Socially, a sharper differentiation will likely develop between an emerging agrarian bourgeoisie and a landless rural proletariat. To a large extent newly acquired lands are likely to be combined with existing small-plots, but also we can expect the development of small agrarian associations, interest groups of various sports, and even independent modern farms in the Western European sense.

The Relation of the Transformation to the Socialist Past

With such considerations in mind we return to examine the extent to which the present multiplicity of options and responses represent continuities or discontinuities in relation to the socialist period. Communist politics in rural Hungary faded long ago into insignificance, but this is not to say that socialist elements were not internalized by people, including even a certain attachment to the collectives.[13] For example, the results of the local elections in October 1991 where seventy percent of former council presidents were re-elected for the new office of mayor show that an association with socialism did not deter voters from reelecting a person to office.

During the socialist decades hardships imposed on the peasantry forced them to work out strategies of a defensive kind; to seek out the smallest advantage and create opportunities for themselves where none were foreseen. To compensate for material and non-material damages in the socialist anti-peasant agenda, family and community life in villages was adjusted or even, in some respects, distorted in various ways.[14] It became common strategy to disperse a family's working members into various economic sectors (collective, industrial, services) and reconvene them after work for labor on the small-plots. Work loads were immense, but the gains substantial. Cooperation between age groups, networks of reciprocal help and the new meaning given to do-it-yourself by the sheer scale on which it operated were just some of the purely social and organization adjustments families made to counter disadvantages. The efficiency of these strategies was undeniable as, even at the time of the collapse of the regime, the rural population was holding its own economically.

Perhaps because of these hard-won successes uncertainties about the new conditions are rife. Still, as during socialism, the greatest (and perhaps only) flexible asset rural families are likely to have is their labor power. How they choose to allocate, withhold, disperse or draw it together is of crucial importance since these are the micro-strategies that will eventually show up on the economists' charts. Land, of value not only in the material but also symbolic sense, holds a promise of control, autonomy and independence and is now sought for these reasons, rather than to restore old style peasant farms. But it is only through a reshaping of the micro-strategies of family labor allocation that land now obtained can realize any of the promise it holds.

Although the prospects for the emergence of a new stratum of entrepreneurial small farms is at present unlikely, other forms of interconnections between family, community, land, and labor are at least a possibility. I refer here to the middle-range associations between small farmers, part-time farms, entrepreneurs and collectives, the development of which can already be seen. I agree with Hann (1993) that property ownership *per se* may be of far less importance than the social relations it engenders and the potential of the social over the legalistic cannot be over-stressed. Certainly such relations are confronted and shaped by new limitations of the current period: unemployment, inflation, lack of rural capital, and so on. But glancing back at the socialist period when only the social means of the judicious allocation, dispersal, and regrouping of a family's labor power made it possible for the rural population to carve an economic niche for itself, one might expect similar forces to start operating again, under the changed conditions of the present.

The present transition is undoubtedly a crisis but it is difficult to gauge its true nature.[15] Crisis, in fact, might just be a routine concomitant of the massive realignment of resources, labor, and land into a new configuration. Or perhaps it is possible that Hungary is rushing headlong towards the same problems that West European agriculture is experiencing with which we are all too familiar, if from nowhere else than from the pictures of French farmers regularly paving city streets with potatoes. The much vaunted family farmers in the EC survive at the cost of vast state subsidies and concessions which Eastern Europe at present cannot afford. Perhaps the transformation of Hungary and Eastern Europe at large is not so much a dash to the riches of agriculture in a market economy but rather its troubled waters, which might be closer than expected.

Notes

1. This metaphor is a recurring one. In socialist times there was also talk about "the maze effect," which referred to the difficulty for people to foresee where any chosen path might lead since the rules were prone to change without warning, causing immense insecurity and caution in all undertakings (Baric 1965).

2. The number of people involved in agriculture represent a staggering proportion of the population and the choices made will be of more than passing interest. Although only 35,000 full time agriculturalists were counted in 1991, about 1.5 million in the adult population are involved with small-plot farming.

3. The system is of course more complex than that. Vouchers may be claimed for lands, buildings or equipment, by original owners or their direct descendants. The vouchers may also be used to buy other types of privatizing shares or traded, but in both cases their value is diminished. The primary use of vouchers is in land auctions. Lands for auction are designated by collectives, and there is also a Land Claims Committee in each village and several legal advisors at the auctions. Land is graded in terms of the pre-war standard of "golden crown" (*aranykorona*). The better the quality of a plot, the more g.c.s it is worth. One hectare of medium quality land is worth 15 to 20 g.c.s. Vineyards are worth 3 times as much. The baseline value of one golden crown at the auctions is between 500 and 3,000 *forints* with no upper ceiling set for bidding.

4. Of 1.4 million part-time farmers, only about 39,000 are considering going into full-time farming, mainly of a specialized kind (fruits, grain, paprika, etc). Employee-based farming enterprises are negligible at present; only 9,905 are private employed in farming set against 2.3 million helping family members (Agricultural Statistics 1991, Romany 1992).

5. It is a further interesting feature that plot farming originally practiced by the rural and poorer section of Hungarian society has gradually spread upwards and is increasingly practiced by the more educated strata (Andorka 1992:242-250).

6. This may explain the rapidity with which a top echelon of entrepreneurs came into being in Hungary since the change of regime. In 1990 the private sector overall was a mere 4.2 percent and by 1991 it jumped to 17 percent, with 44 percent of the population declaring to be ready to have a go at some private enterprise (Andorka 1992:242).

7. This also seems to have been the case in villages far from Pecsely and the Transdanubian area and with entirely different developmental histories (Hann 1980, 1993).

8. Changing times brought about some intriguing transformations. The former Protestant parish and prayer room has been turned into an inn and a bar of dubious reputation and the bar counter stands where the altar used to be. It is, no doubt, more frequented than before. On the other hand, the former communist party's premises have been turned into a Catholic prayer room and the former Protestant pre-school is now a library.

9. The collective has also retreated from agriculture and reduced several production branches, like stock-farming and viticulture while at the same time developing non-agricultural sectors such as gravel mining, a small chemical plant, and manufacture of mechanical parts.

10. Last year, for example, it contributed heavily, constructing an unpolluted water main to each village house. However, this seemingly socially responsible behavior was actually forced on the organization since it was proved responsible for the pollution of all groundwater and wells by excessive use of pesticides and fertilizers.

11. These fears have risen sharply. In 1986 only seven percent contemplated the possibility, but in 1991 as many as forty-seven percent. But popular fears of impoverishment are supported by facts. The TARKI survey shows that in 1989-1991 incomes remained unchanged in real terms, but this is perceived as falling behind. Income differentials go wider, in the sense that the richer strata gained over the middle stratum. In real terms the pensioners are the group that fell behind (Kolosi & Robert 1992:1-15).

12. One of his ideas, for example, was to run electricity to the hillside wine cellars.

13. "We forced people to do what was good for them," one collective chairman said in a typical commentary. But ordinary members, too, feel profoundly demoralized at the prospect of the passing of the collectives (Rab 1992:62-87). Indeed, even in Pecsely the possibility of extracting their part from the vast regional collective of which it is now a fraction and restore a truly local collective, as it had been until 1973 (and quite successful at that) proved economically inviable. On the other hand, in the neighboring village of Szentgal a new collective was indeed formed in 1992.

14. The balance of daily work hours is very revealing. In 1988, a man spent on average 231 minutes/day on his main job, ninety-eight minutes on small-plots, and a further thirty-four minutes on building, do-it-yourself etc. Women worked 150 minutes/day on a main job and a further 58 on the small-plot (Andorka 1991:242-50). Adding almost a third to a normal working day speaks of exceptional self-exploitation.

15. Total collapse of the agrarian structure is forecast regularly in both newspapers and sociological analyses (Sipos and Halmai 1991:33-44). Crisis management is reckoned to be essential but suggested interventions are contradictory: modernization, but avoidance of overproduction; labor saving mechanization, but without loss of jobs; more export westward, while it is well known that Western European markets are burdened by market saturation of their own. Agriculture, it would seem, has become too efficient for its own good. But what has been learned cannot be unlearned. A stricter ecologically oriented organic farming may offer some solutions but is not yet politically nor socio-economically viable.

References

Agh, A. 1992. "The Year of Structural Stalemate." *MOPE,* pp. 17-35. Budapest.

____. 1990. "Mit Kell Meghallani 1990-ben." *Kozgazdasagi Szemle* 37(10):1194- 1220. Budapest.

____. 1992. "Social Changes in Hungary in the past Years." *MOPE,* pp. 242-251. Budapest.

Baric, L. 1965. "Traditional Groups and New Economic Opportunities in Rural Yugoslavia." In R. Firth, ed., *Themes of Economic Anthropology,* no. 6 pp. 253-277. London: Tavistock.

Bodosi, Gy. 1992. "Vagyainkat Terelgessuk Legalabb!" *Vaszpremi Naplo*, July 16, p. 4.

Bourdieu, P. 1977. *An Outline of a Theory of Practice.* Cambridge: Cambridge University Press.

Donath, F. 1980. *Reform and Revolution--Transformation of Hungary's Agriculture, 1945-1970.* Budapest: Corvina.

Elek, S. 1991. "Part Time Farming in Hungary: An Instrument of Tacit Decollectivization." *Sociologica Ruralis* 31:82-88.

Franklin, S.H. 1969. *The European Peasantry: The Final Phase*. London: Methuen.

Hann, C.M. 1980. *Tazlar: A Village in Hungary.* Cambridge: Cambridge University Press.

____. 1993 "From Production to Property: Decollectivization and the Family-Land Relationship in Contemporary Hungary." *Man* 28:1-22.

Hollos, M. and Maday, B., Eds. 1983. *New Hungarian Peasants: An Eastern European Experience of Collectivization.* Social Science Monograph. New York: Brooklyn College Press.

Kolosi, T. and P. Robert. 1992. "A Rendszervaltas Tarsadalmi Hatasai." *Valosag* 2: 115.

Nagengast, C. 1991. *Reluctant Socialists, Rural Entrepreneurs.* Boulder: Westview.

Rab, L. 1992. "Melyszantas." *Valosag* 8: 62-87.

Romany, P. 1992. "Fold Ember Falu." *Valosag* 6:11-23.

Shanin, T. 1990. *Defining Peasants.* Oxford: Blackwell.

Sipos, A and Halmai, P. 1992. Az Agrar Politikai Celok Alternativai es Dilemai. *Valosag* 9:33-44.

Swain, N. 1982. "The Evolution of Hungary's Agricultural System Since 1967 in Hungary." In P. Hare, H. Radice, and N. Swain, eds. *A Decade of Economic Reform*, pp. 225-251. London: Allen & Unwin.

____. 1985. *Collective Farms Which Work?* Cambridge: Cambridge University Press.

Vasary, I. 1987. *Beyond the Plan: Social Change in a Hungarian Village.* Boulder: Westview.

____. 1990. "Competing Paradigms: Peasant Farming and Collectivization in a Balaton Community. In C.M. Hann, Ed. *Market Economy and Civil Society in Hungary*, pp. 163-182. London: Frank Cass.

____. 1992. "Silent Processes of Transformation in a New Regime." *Teres Tarsadalom* 2-3:151-159.

Wolf, E. 1966. *Peasants.* Englewood Cliffs, NJ: Prentice Hall.

3

An Old Song in a New Voice: Decollectivization in Bulgaria

Gerald W. Creed

When I returned to the village of Zamfirovo in northeastern Bulgaria in the summer of 1992 I was engulfed by political commentary. Despite not having seen me for nearly four years, my village friends could scarcely get through the most superficial pleasantries before launching into analyses of current village developments. While some villagers supported the changes, many more, including the most vocal ones, were highly critical.

Emotions were particularly inflamed as I arrived during the early stages of decollectivization. The dominant local interpretation of this project quickly emerged in the form of a Bulgarian aphorism: "an old song in a new voice." During the time of my stay this adage was invoked repeatedly by a variety of villagers. For some it constituted their entire commentary on the issue of decollectivization; for others it provided a pithy syntheses at the beginning or end of a longer discourse. From the latter the meaning of the saying became clear: these villagers somehow saw post-socialist land restitution as a reprise of communist collectivization.

What could collectivization and decollectivization possibly have in common? As ostensibly opposite processes, the charge of similarity was paradoxical to say the least. In what follows I attempt to account for this paradox. I begin with a description of the decollectivization program with particular reference to the village of Zamfirovo. From this it becomes clear that the similarity between collectivization and decollectivization was not in their antithetical objectives, but in the parallel ways their divergent goals were pursued. The subsequent section of the paper discusses these similarities, pushing the folk model beyond the intentions of villagers who invoked it to reveal a series of continuities. These similarities testify to a continuing legacy of socialism which I refer to as the "socialist subconscious."

The continuities, however, have temporal limits; a year later in the summer of 1993 I rarely heard anyone refer to decollectivization as "an old song in a new voice." Thus, the expression not only reveals much about the early nature of decollectivization, its diminished applicability signals changes in agrarian politics. This progression, in turn, reveals much about the general trajectory of the so-called transition in Bulgaria.

Decollectivization

Given the extreme politicization of everything in eastern Europe after 1989, it is not surprising that the early outcome of agricultural reform in Bulgaria was shaped predominantly by political developments. The first free Bulgarian elections in June of 1990 resulted in a slim victory for the Socialist Party (BSP)--the new name of the old Communist Party. They received 47.15% of the popular vote which factored into a parliamentary majority of over 52% of the seats. This outcome provoked an extended period of noncooperation by the other major parliamentary block, the Union of Democratic Forces (UDF), which was essentially a coalition of varied interest groups and parties, united by their anti-communism.

Ironically, the ensuing parliamentary impasse was created on one level by the relative confluence of BSP and UDF objectives. Both parties claimed to want political democratization and capitalist-style economic reforms. Since their intentions were apparently similar, the struggle revolved around initiative--who would acquire the capital (symbolic, political and economic) associated with making the transition? The UDF apparently decided not to risk allowing any of it to go to the socialists even if this meant delaying progress toward some of their own goals. Such a strategy stymied early legislative progress but proved extremely effective. By December the socialist Prime Minister Lukanov had resigned. He was replaced by Dimiter Popov, a judge who was not a member of either party.

On another level the nature of post-communist politics generated distinctions between the BSP and UDF conceptualizations of change. The BSP constituency included many old "hard liners" who could not be alienated if the party hoped to maintain significant political influence, so commitments to transition had to be balanced by concessions, such as support for a slower pace of change. At the same time, the constitution of the UDF as an anti-communist coalition required its representatives to continually define themselves in opposition or distinction to the socialists.[1] Thus, during the period of the socialist dominated government, the legitimacy and popularity of the UDF was potentially enhanced by recalcitrance and diminished by cooperation. This combined with the limitations imposed on the BSP by part of its constituency to heighten differences and constrict practical progress.

The situation is illustrated well by the history of land reform after 1989. Technically, land had never been nationalized in Bulgaria, and thus remained the property of cooperative farm members. During and after collectivization, however, the state usurped ownership rights so that cooperatives ended up operating more or less like other state enterprises. Maya Keliyan (1991:2) captures this duplicity by referring to the collective farms as "pseudo-cooperatives." Consequently, the objective of land reform after 1989 was technically not the return of property or "privatization," but simply the restitution of property rights to official owners. Colleagues who were generally critical of the decollectivization program never failed to correct me when I referred to the process as one of "privatization." Supporters of the UDF were less concerned about the distinction, reflecting, I assumed at the time, their different interpretation of collectivization as de facto nationalization.

Even if the essential objective of agricultural transition was simply the restitution of ownership rights, the first reforms fell short. When the "land law" (shorthand for the Ownership and Use of Farm Land Act) was actually passed in the spring of 1991, many of its articles constrained the exercise of certain property rights, a fact the UDF attributed to the dominant influence of the BSP, which still controlled parliament if not the Prime Minister. The quantity of land an individual could own was limited to 30 hectares at most, and reduced to 20 hectares in areas of intensive cultivation. Owners could not sell land within the first three years of reclaiming it from the collective farm and they were explicitly required to use it for agricultural purposes. Even after the three-year waiting period, sale was restricted to either relatives, leaseholders, neighboring landowners or the state and municipalities.

All of these restrictions seemed to perpetuate the attraction of existing cooperative arrangements. Their appeal was further enhanced by the law on cooperatives which came out in the same year. "New" agricultural cooperatives were allowed to register. They would be responsible to the owners of the land who would have ownership rights, receive dividends for their land contribution, and have the option of withdrawing from the cooperative. The anti-socialist opposition saw this as a ruse to continue the old collective farm system. Old managers would be able to simply reregister their farms as new cooperatives, often after plundering them of their technology and other moveable resources for either personal benefit or the benefit of the new cooperative which they expected to manage. Their control of the new farms would then perpetuate their political influence in the village. Subsequent events supported elements of this interpretation as several "new" cooperatives were registered and complaints surfaced about suspicious economic dealings. At the same time few people seemed interested in reclaiming land for private cultivation.

Actually there was very little time for the new policy to have any effect as parliamentary crises provoked new elections for October 1991. This time the UDF won, and although they lacked a clear parliamentary majority, they were able to govern for a time more or less in coalition with the Movement for Rights and Freedom (MRF), the party of the Turkish minority, which was the only other party to achieve the threshold of votes necessary for parliamentary representation.[2] One of the first actions of this new government in March of 1992 was to amend the land law, eliminating what were perceived as its socialist vestiges. The limits on the size of holdings were abolished as were the restrictions on who could buy and sell land. Owners were also given more latitude in the use of restituted agricultural land. Cooperatives registered under the new cooperative law were disallowed and a radical system designed to *eliminate* all existing collective farms.

The system devised to achieve this goal is what I refer to as decollectivization. The program was organized around two networks of committees set up throughout the country. The first type were called "land commissions." They received claims and supporting documents from all families who had given land to the cooperative farms during collectivization. The commission decided how much and which land people were entitled to receive. Some commissions were responsible for a single village, but others operated at the district level.[3] In the case of Zamfirovo the requisite land commission was located in the district center of Berkovitza and was responsible for twenty-one surrounding villages. The commission consisted of a president and five members, including three land surveyors and two agronomists. Members were nominated by the district council, but had to be approved by the Ministry of Agriculture which retained all rights for appointment and dismissal of commission members. Financial support for the work of the commission also came through the Ministry of Agriculture. I was shocked at the technology of the commission compared to that which generally characterized Bulgarian bureaucracy. The commission had two computers, one with a color monitor, and two printers, one a laser variety.

One of the deadlines for submitting land claims was approaching during my stay in the summer of 1992. Despite the fact that many villagers said they were not interested in farming the land, they had all filed their claims for restitution. According to one village advocate of decollectivization, "those who said they did not want the land were the first to submit their claims." The national deadline for claims had to be extended several times to accommodate the volume of requests and to allow time for people to locate documentation. The commission based its decisions primarily on old tax registers and the records of the collective farm from the time of collectivization when contributions were supposedly itemized. The former, however, were not meticulously maintained in the interwar years and the latter were not exactly accurate.

Prior to collectivization villagers often relied on common community knowledge of boundaries and ownership rights. Major disputes over land usually concerned inheritance, which involved the creation of new boundaries and divisions rather than disagreement over the existing boundaries of the plot to be divided; the latter was generally agreed upon by neighbors. Thus, many villagers treated the official registers used to calculate their tax or requisition burdens as manipulable. People could understate their holdings or contributions for the purpose of reducing these burdens without endangering their land claims, which were communally recognized. As an added precaution they protected and saved other documents such as deeds and land transfers, some dating back to the acquisition of land from Turks at the time of liberation from Ottoman control. The latter documents, however, did not necessarily assure that the land had not been sold to someone else prior to collectivization. Consequently, tax registers and collective farm inventories carried significant weight, and villagers who underreported their holdings on these reports often lost claims in the restitution process.

If such reports could not be found, however, claimants could use witnesses, ideally owners of neighboring lands, to verify their prior ownership. The commission also used local elders from the various villages who remembered which land belonged to whom. Given the dependence on communal knowledge described above, it is likely that this was a useful resource. As the president of the land commission said to me, "you would be surprised how much older villagers remember."

Still, the problems faced by the land commission were legion. Multiple claims for the same land; claims for land that had been flooded by irrigation reservoirs; disputed claims by descendants of deceased owners, were but a few of the more recurrent problems. The president said the biggest problem she faced was the lack of records regarding construction over the last forty years. "We have no idea if the land being claimed by somebody has been built on by the farm or state, and this affects whether or not the land can be returned in its original borders."

The commission managed to proceed by relegating most of these problems to the judicial system. According to the president of the Berkovitza commission they attempted to resolve conflicts over land, such as multiple claims, but if they were unable to reach an acceptable solution they simply referred the case to the courts. They made no attempt to deal with the issue of inheritance at all. Land rights were restituted by the committee to the former owner, living or dead. In the latter case the legal inheritors had to devise their own settlement and have it legally approved in order to receive land rights. If they could not agree, the case would have to go to court. People who contested the commissions's decision, such as those who lost land due to past underreporting, also had to take their complaints to court. The president of the land commission said it could take two years for people to get answers on such matters.

The land commission also sidestepped the problem of land that had been built upon by distinguishing two categories in their restitution decisions: land that could be restituted in its "real" borders (i.e. those existing at the time of collectivization), and land that could not. The latter consisted of land that had been built upon or otherwise altered, including land currently within the large blocks cultivated by the cooperative farm. People could take possession of land restored in its original boundaries, but rights to other land were restituted in principle only. In other words owners received a document saying the land was theirs, but they were not allowed to take it over for cultivation or sale. For example, a memorandum from the Ministry of Agriculture was posted on the door of the land commission stating that only land that had not been planted by the old collective farm could be taken over for use by owners when restituted.

Most land in the country did not qualify for restitution in its real boundaries. According to 1992 data from the Ministry of Agriculture, land which could be restituted directly amounted to less than 12% of all land nationwide. In Zamfirovo the amount appears to be much greater. Based on a sample of 200 owners the amount of land that could be restored in real boundaries accounted for nearly 27% of their total landholdings. Zamfirovo's advantage in this regard may be due to the location of the village in the foothills of the Balkan mountains, where significant stretches of forests and steep terrain were not incorporated into collective farm blocks. Of course these plots are also not very attractive for private cultivation.

Even desirable land available in its original boundaries was sometimes not accessible because someone else was using it for their "personal plot." As is well known, members of collective farms usually retained access to a plot of land for their own subsistence. In Bulgaria these plots were usually limited to half a hectare, although villagers usually found ways to extend their acreage. In Zamfirovo the plot was typically divided between grain acreage, a vegetable garden and a vineyard. These plots may have been part of a family's private property prior to collectivization, but they may have been allocated subsequently by the cooperative farm. The latter was particularly likely for households established after collectivization. If someone had been allotted such a plot and had planted a vineyard or small orchard, the former owner could not simply reclaim the products of someone else's labor, but he/she could claim the actual land.

The Ministry of Agriculture is expected to issue guidelines for financial compensation to vineyard owners by landowners in such circumstances, which will clear the way for restitution. As of July 1993 no guidelines had been issued and I witnessed a rather heated argument between two villagers as a result. The landowner wanted to reach a financial agreement immediately, saying they did not have to wait for the state guidelines. He was clearly hoping to acquire legal right to harvest the fall crop of grapes himself. For the same reason the owner of the vines was insisting that transfer could only occur after ministerial guidelines had been issued.

Such difficulties illustrate the chasm between the decisions of the land commission and the actual restitution of land. This gap accounts for the completely antithetical responses I received to queries about the process of land restitution in the summer of 1993. Some villagers said it had not made any progress at all, while others said it was virtually complete. The latter were referring to the legal documentation of the rights to land, the former to the reality of private cultivation.

Still and all, the work of the land commission can be seen as fairly straightforward compared to other elements in the process of decollectivization. Reportedly, another set of commissions has been assigned the responsibility of coming up with regionally specific plans for the restitution of land rights which cannot be restored in original boundaries. Their objective is to find a way to return land to former owners without recreating the system of scattered mini-plots which characterized the pre-socialist period. Even if they manage to keep the bulk of land for each owner together, the outcome will still represent a system of relatively small plots since the average holding in Zamfirovo is only 2.8 hectares. Furthermore, whatever plan they might conceive is certain to result in even more litigation.

While all these problems are being settled the work of agriculture is being carried out by the second group of actors in the decollectivization drama, the "liquidation committee." The March amendments to the land law directed regional governors to dispatch committees of four to six members to every cooperative farm in their region. These committees replaced the old farm management and were assigned the somewhat schizophrenic tasks of managing agricultural activities while liquidating the collective farm. As their title suggests, the latter objective took precedence.

One could hardly have designed a program with more potential to alienate villagers. Even villagers who despised the cooperative farm management in their village, or who had little if any connection to the farm itself, could hardly countenance "liquidation." It is certainly true that the cooperative farm was not truly cooperative in any sense, but this does not necessarily mean it was not seen as a *village* institution. Even if it was only a village branch of a larger state system, the farm was still a village entity. This belief had been evident in the resistance to consolidation programs following collectivization, including resistance to the agro-industrial complex (Creed 1992:102-3; 109). Villagers wanted farms that corresponded to the land of the village, even if authority ultimately rested with the state.

Given the association of the village with its land and by extension the cooperative farm, the idea of "liquidation" struck a sensitive chord. A retired village woman who had worked most of her adult life for the collective farm seemed to capture the ambiguity. "We worked in the fields from sunrise to dark and got paid next to nothing. And it was all manual labor, there were few machines in those days. It was awful. All that work to build the cooperative farm, and for what? Only to have it liquidated." She saw the liquidation process as the destruction of all that she had given her life to build, but her argument was constructed with accounts of the difficulties she endured working for the early cooperative farm, which in another context could have been construed as a critique of collectivization. In other words, the affront of decollectivization did not depend upon a benign interpretation of collectivization or socialism. Many villagers found liquidation offensive.

The use of the word "liquidation" was certainly a factor in village reactions. Various villagers commented on the word, pointing out its exclusively destructive connotation and asking rhetorically why it was necessary to destroy everything. A common analogy was made to construction processes--"it is very easy and quick to tear down a building, but not nearly as easy to build something from scratch." The obvious insinuation was that the government was only doing what was easiest, with little concern for the monumental task of rebuilding. Unfortunately the choice of the word "liquidation" cannot be explained as simply the public relations gaffe of the century: it correctly reflected the various objectives of decollectivization. The ostensible goal was in fact to eliminate collective farms by transferring all of their financial resources to would-be private producers. The term was also appropriate in political terms. The eradication of collective farms was intended to undermine the economic foundation of old communist leaders in the villages and thus liquidate the continuing support for the BSP.

The UDF, which lost the first election and won the second by a small percentage, was by no means secure in its political position. Leaders knew from election results that their support was particularly weak in the villages. There are many reasons why village residents favored the BSP in large numbers (Creed 1993), but UDF leaders, many of whom had shown themselves to be fairly uninformed about the countryside, apparently decided that the rural population voted socialist primarily because they were still in the grip of local communist leaders, whose continued power came in large part from their control over the village economy through the cooperative farm system. Thus, President Zhelev is reported to have made the statement that the only way to get rid of the Communist Party was to get rid of the collective farms. Ironically, this argument lends further support to the idea that the cooperative farm had some village significance apart from the centralized authority provided by the communist system, since if it relied solely on the communist system farm leaders would no longer have had such purported power in 1992. This, in turn, is consistent with my prior contention that the cooperative farm was never completely conceptualized by villagers as a local arm of the state agricultural system--it remained a symbol of the village itself. Thus, it is not surprising that these units were assumed to benefit from the de facto decentralization of political power after 1989.

The liquidating committee took over the Zamfirovo cooperative farm in June 1992. The committee consisted of two men from the village, one from the district town of Berkovitza, and the chairman from Mihailovgrad, the regional capital. The chairman was born in the village, but migrated to town when he was young. As elsewhere in the country the composition of the committee was the next bone of contention for villagers already unhappy about the liquidating process in general. First, committee members were accused of being unqualified, that is, they were not agronomists or experienced farmers. This complaint was generally valid because the vast majority of Bulgarians trained in agronomy or related occupations were part of the old cooperative management structure which the UDF was trying to purge. In addition, two of the members of the Zamfirovo committee were not village residents and this further diminished their suitability in the opinion of many villagers. These same villagers, however, assessed the two local members of the committee to be even less capable, having been chosen solely for their support of the UDF, so it is hard to imagine that anyone could have satisfied village critics. Still it is true that officials did not attempt to diffuse potential resentment in their appointment of the committee.

The major criticism of the chairman regarded his political history as a Communist Party member, leading villagers to interpret his rabid anti-communism as hypocritical and/or opportunistic. Still, villagers seemed to respect his higher education, even if it was not in agronomy, and he still had relatives in the village, which seemed to mitigate his status as an outsider. Thus, when I arrived in June of 1992 villagers were taking a "wait and see" attitude toward him. As one of the most severe critics of liquidation put it, "we can work with him." The chairman also benefited early on by association with the new agricultural policy allowing villagers to take over designated areas of cooperative farm land for their own use, which amounted to a lifting of the limits on personal plot acreage. Some villagers took over plots they expected to have returned to them, others were granted temporary rights to other cooperative farm land until such time as it was returned to prior owners. Nearly every village household took on additional land through these arrangements in the summer of 1992. Typically, this land included small plots near water resources for intensive vegetable cultivation, and much larger plots of meadowland. Additional meadowland was particularly attractive since it allowed villagers to expand their household livestock operations and increase highly valued meat and milk production without a proportional increase in labor. Still, every increase required additional work and it seemed that everybody in the village was making hay in the summer of 1992.

These possibilities kept early attitudes toward the liquidating committee somewhat benign. Before I left the village at the end of the summer, however, the situation had reversed and villagers were increasingly critical and vocal. At one slightly drunken dinner party toward the end of my stay there were even suggestions that someone should do the chairman physical harm. In the summer of 1993 I found even more pervasive criticism of "the liquidators," as the committee had come to be known.

The turning point followed immediately from one of the first actions of the chairman. He sold the bulk of the cooperative's young sheep which had been designated as reproductive stock. This diminished the ability of the cooperative to reproduce its sheep flocks. Villagers who hoped to establish a new cooperative saw the holdings of the existing cooperative as their future resource base and interpreted his action as a preemptive strike against them. Even villagers who seemed less committed to a future cooperative believed that sheep should be returned to villagers rather than being sold. Of course, the chairman was just doing what his position dictated, liquidating the farm. By the summer of 1993 there were no sheep left in the cooperative. Some had been returned to villagers and the rest sold. The same process was well underway with cattle as well, though some of the farm's dairy enterprises were still operating due to political changes I will discuss later.

Resources from the sale of farm goods were used to pay the operating expenses of the farm. Many factors conspired to increase these needs and thus fuel the pace of liquidation. Agricultural subsidies which underwrote the cooperative farm system were reduced or withdrawn, making it necessary for the farm to come up with more of its own resources. The lame duck situation of the cooperative farm made it nearly impossible to secure loans from banks for the costs of planting, so in many cases cash had to be generated up front. At the same time, prior debts of the farm also had to be paid off, and expenses such as salaries continued as usual. Thus, the seemingly schizophrenic objectives of the liquidating committee actually fused into a singular devouring persona: the committee financed the continuation of agricultural production through the liquidation of farm resources, so that continuing cultivation itself provided the motivation for ever more liquidation.

Villagers were sensitive to this strategy as they saw village resources trickling away in the process. One villager said they could pay off the whole farm debt by selling one piece of machinery, "why don't they do that instead of chipping away at everything?" Of course there was the issue of finding a buyer for the old expensive machinery, which would probably have been more difficult than finding a buyer for a bunch of sheep or calves. Also, selling machinery may have been equally devastating for villagers in the long run.

Defense of this process by the chairman of the Zamfirovo committee echoed ideas I heard from UDF supporters in Sofia. He insisted that just letting people leave the cooperative farm or reclaim their land was insufficient. As he put it "The main thing is for people to develop a sense of private property. To get a piece of paper and know that the land is theirs and they have to decide what to do with it. This is a very difficult idea to instill. Someone came by the office the other day and asked me for something from the farm for his sheep. He has no conception that those sheep are solely his responsibility. This we have to change." Furthermore, he continued, "the old cooperative leadership was basically a family affair, one group of kin and their connections controlled everything. They had to be removed from power before any real cooperative could be possible. Besides they had no understanding of how to run a farm for profit. They were only concerned about pleasing their superiors. They had to be removed so that capable people can take leadership positions and individual farmers will feel free to make their own decisions." In other words decollectivization was necessary to instill ideas of private property and eliminate communist control, which should eventually result in a more productive agriculture.

Of course, in the meantime, one could only expect agricultural production to decline as the system of production was liquidated. Thus, in one of the most perverse repercussions of decollectivization, declining production became a reflection of the success of farm administration. If one of the goals was to liquidate the collective farm what better evidence of success could there be than diminishing output? The decline in output meant that farms had progressively less income, which necessitated further liquidation to meet expenses or pay debts. So declining production not only verified the progress of liquidation, it drove the process ever further along.

Not surprisingly, then, Zamfirovo production declined significantly under "the liquidators." They took over in the summer of 1992 after much of the planting had been done, so output in that year was relatively stable, but the following year large blocks of land went unplanted, and perennials such as grapes and strawberries were neglected. The strawberry crop, once the pride of Zamfirovo and a source of hard currency, was negligible in 1993. The chief culprit was the complete lack of irrigation. Zamfirovo has three reservoirs with irrigation pumps and in 1985 the farm irrigated over 600 hectares. In 1993 no land was being irrigated because the equipment had not been maintained and workable parts had been looted. The committee chairman explained that they had not bothered to maintain irrigation equipment because they were originally told that the liquidation process would be completed in a year, so they never expected that they would still be managing the farm in the summer of 1993.

Given the complexity of the process, the one-year time frame was clearly unreasonable from the start, but it was further jeopardized by a political crisis in October 1992. A vote of no-confidence in the government of Filip Dimitrov resulted, two months later, in the appointment of Liuben Berov as Prime Minister. Under the new government, which was nominated by the MRF, but received the tacit support of the BSP, two changes were evident in regard to decollectivization. First there was a softening of the official antipathy toward cooperatives. Whereas in the summer of 1992, officials dismissed cooperatives as a communist legacy, in the summer of 1993 most seemed reconciled to the necessity of some form of cooperative cultivation.

Perhaps this lay behind the other major change, a moratorium on the sale or distribution of cooperative livestock. The possibility of personal profiteering through sale of cooperative livestock had been a lightning rod for rural anxiety from the beginnings of the transition. The liquidating committees became the focus of such accusations after they took control of the farms, but communist managers of collective farms had been accused of similar offenses prior to 1992. The moratorium attempted to defuse this volatile concern, but it also reflects the changed attitude toward cooperative arrangements. As cooperatives became a more acceptable outcome of the agricultural transition, there was greater concern to protect potential cooperative property from dissipation.

A new cooperative registered in Zamfirovo with 546 members in October 1992, the same month that the government fell. Since members generally joined for the entire household this represents a decided majority of the village's approximately 700 households. With the establishment of a new cooperative village critics of liquidation quickly changed their tune. Whereas they had opposed liquidation in the summer of 1992, they were hurrying the process along in the summer of 1993. They hoped that the new cooperative would be able to acquire the remains of the old one, and as we have seen, the longer the liquidation process continued the more resources it consumed, leaving less for its successor.

The new cooperative, however, will have to share the remaining wealth of the farm with villagers who have not joined the cooperative. According to a member of the liquidating committee these 200 or so households have as much land between them as the 546 new cooperative members. In fact, according to its chairwomen, the new cooperative farm included 1,000 hectares of worked land, which is only about one-third of the amount worked by the old collective farm in the 1980s.[4] In other words, the largest land holders did not sign up at the start. They may be waiting to see what possibilities exist after the auctioning of cooperative property. The calculation of shares with which villagers can bid for existing cooperative property includes compensation for the use of land throughout the communist era as well as for equipment originally contributed to the cooperative farm. Thus, some of the larger landowners may expect to be able to compete individually in this auction. Still, there are very few large land owners in Zamfirovo.[5] How this event unfolds will have a significant influence on the ultimate result of decollectivization.

Parallels

From the preceding description we can begin to see why villagers in the summer of 1992 drew comparisons with the 1950s.[6] In both periods an agricultural arrangement sanctioned, indeed sanctified, by the state was forcibly implemented in the village with limited attention to local conditions or desires. As many villagers saw it, decollectivization was just another attempt by the state to dictate agricultural arrangements. Far beyond the mere restitution of property rights, which would have allowed villagers to do as they chose with their land, they interpreted liquidation as an attempt to foreclose the cooperative option altogether and install private cultivation in its place. The non-agricultural enterprises in the country were already faltering under the pressures of the transition and villagers saw the concomitant determination of the new government to return land to private control as an ominous confluence: a way to force the newly unemployed into full-time agricultural labor.[7] Interestingly, this suspicion replicated interpretations I heard of the communist government's tightening of migration restrictions in the 1980s.

Given village suspicions about the underlying agenda of decollectivization, the previously mentioned differential response of UDF and BSP supporters to my use of the term "privatization" becomes more significant. I originally assumed that UDF supporters did not protest my use of the term simply because their view of collectivization was more akin to nationalization, making the term more appropriate. Village interpretations, however, suggest that "privatization" was in fact the real objective of the UDF. The comment of a UDF supporter in Sofia verifies this conclusion. Upon my suggestion that some type of continued cooperation in agriculture might be necessary, he responded with a question, "Where in the developed world do they have cooperative cultivation?" Before I could even respond he provided his own revealing answer, "Nowhere!" Clearly, cooperatives were not an option. As one village grandmother put it, "First the communists made us give up our land, and now the UDF is making us take it back. It is like getting slapped on both sides of your face." She illustrated her point by turning her head from side to side as if she had received successive blows to the face.

Actual physical force may not have been used in the decollectivization of Zamfirovo, but it was a clear and present threat, just as it was during collectivization. The latter was achieved with very little force because local leaders effectively employed financial, political, and psychological means to coerce villagers to join the cooperative. The decollectivization program required little or no activity from villagers themselves and thus minimized the likelihood of any resistance. In both cases, however, no one doubted that force would be used if necessary. There were numerous examples from elsewhere in the country of physical coercion and threats in the collectivization process (see e.g. Brisby 1960:40, Gyurova 1989, Jones and Jankoff 1957:304, and Dobrin 1973:45). Similarly, the use of force to insure decollectivization gained national attention when the villagers of Zalapitsa in south central Bulgaria occupied their town hall and refused to let the liquidating committee take over the farm. Police were dispatched and the committee forcibly installed.

Thus, the rhetoric of decollectivization as the restitution of property rights allowing villagers to do as they pleased with their land probably struck villagers as analogous to the communist concept of "voluntary collectivization." Yes, most people in Zamfirovo joined the collective farm voluntarily, but not until private cultivation was rendered virtually impossible or extremely difficult through higher requisition rates and lack of access to rationed goods. Similarly, the decollectivization program allowed owners to reorganize cooperatives, but only after they had legally taken possession of the land. By then, the barriers to organizing new cooperatives would be nearly impossible to overcome without legal supports from the state. How, for example, would cooperatives reconsolidate the fragmented land contributions of members without access to state pressure? Moreover, what would be left to consolidate after the liquidation program? Thus the option of forming new cooperatives appeared in 1992 much like the continuing option of private framing in the mid-1950s; theoretically possible, but practically impossible.

Of course in both cases representatives of the state were present to insure that state objectives triumphed over any local resistance. During collectivization, there was a state representative sent to advise the cooperative, but the program proceeded primarily by tapping sympathetic villagers and training them in "Party schools" to carry out the Party program. By the time of decollectivization, democratization had rendered local officials less reliable as executors of central plans. This accounts for the use of committees which were appointed or approved by higher levels as vehicles of state control. Additionally, as Kideckel (1992) astutely notes, the conflicts generated by the process of decollectivization perpetuated local reliance on the state as the ultimate arbiter. So, albeit through different mechanisms, the central government directed collectivization and decollectivization, and both projects enhanced state control.

This brings us to a broader parallel: the continuing politicization of agriculture. While one could argue that agriculture is always politicized, it has certainly been more so in eastern Europe than many other areas, and Bulgaria typifies this extremism. Since the inter-war period agriculture has at times been less an area of policy concern and more a facet of political identification, with various regimes and political parties presenting particular agricultural platforms as part of their self definition. Once a particular agricultural arrangement becomes part of political definition, agriculture ceases to be open to negotiation or innovation. This association occurred with both collectivization and decollectivization.

Collectivization of agriculture was already associated closely with the communist system due to the Soviet precedent.[8] The Bulgarian decision to follow suit after the Communist Party consolidated its control further fixed the association between the two. The identification was also assured by the dominance of agriculture in Bulgaria at the time of communist ascension. Subsequent changes were viewed against this agrarian backdrop which directed attention to agricultural changes. Thus, collectivization became a metaphor for the communist transformation in general. Since the idea of cooperative agriculture was so closely identified with communism, an anti-communist agenda was by default anti-cooperative. The association also explains why the UDF thought that eliminating communist power in the villages required the liquidation of cooperative farms.

The politicization of decollectivization was also evident in the appointment and actions of the constituent committees. Whether outsiders or locals they were often selected for their commitment to the new political ideology of anti-communism. My interviews with the liquidating committee in Zamfirovo, for example, were peppered liberally with anti-communist jokes and complaints. In fact, the chairman claimed that in districts where communists were on land commissions, nothing had been accomplished whatsoever. The president of the Berkovitza land commission testified to the extensive politicization of the process with a negative example. She bragged in the summer of 1993 that the Berkovitza commission had the distinction of not having had any members replaced since it started working the previous year. As she put it, "many commissions in the country have had to be replaced because the members were chosen for political reasons and were driven by political motives, which caused problems. We are professionals and this has not been the case here." The point is that both collectivization and decollectivization were driven strongly by political interests.

At the same time, I do not want to reinforce the misconception that collectivization was solely an ideological operation. As I have argued elsewhere (1992), the attraction of collectivization was that it addressed so many issues simultaneously. It provided a potent symbol of communist transition and a mechanism for central control of the countryside, but it also addressed the economic problems of agriculture, which included a desperately fragmented, relatively unmechanized, small-holding cultivation. Here again, the strategic similarity with decollectivization is significant. Decollectivization also promised to accomplish multiple goals. Symbolically, it provided a definitive signal of the de-communization of society. Politically, it was to undercut the power base of the BSP in rural areas. Economically, it was an important step in establishing private agricultural production and consequently, if one accepts the ideology of capitalism, increasing production. Noticeably absent from the motivations of both collectivization and decollectivization were the wants and concerns of rural residents themselves.

This deficiency was due in large measure to the centralization of both programs and the rigidity of their objectives, which limited local-level input. This does not mean, however, that the monolithic program worked out the same in every place. What is fascinating in terms of the parallel between the two programs is the degree to which both were colored by local factors, despite being centrally fashioned and dispensed. Kideckel (1982) has made this point effectively for Romanian collectivization and it holds for Bulgaria as well. We have already provided an example of such variation in discussing the use of force. While some villages required forceful means to achieve collectivization others did not. The difference depended significantly on the varied abilities of local leaders in charge of the process.

Local leadership was even more significant in the early outcome of decollectivization. During the summer of 1992 I surveyed ten different villages in the south central region of Bulgaria to compare their decollectivization experiences with that of Zamfirovo. In some villages the chair of the liquidating committee was committed to eradicating cooperative structures. At the other extreme were liquidating committee members who were concomitantly members of new cooperatives, despite the fact that the latter were technically illegal. In between these extremes were villages where the liquidating committee simply overlooked the continuing operation of new cooperatives. In some such cases there were several cooperatives operating simultaneously. The local agronomist in one village told me that villagers were organizing two cooperatives: one for UDF supporters and one for socialists. Even though UDF supporters in the village apparently deviated from their party's preference for private production, they would not cooperate with farmers who were socialists.

Members of liquidating committees may have allowed cooperatives to operate unofficially for personal profit, especially when they were members of both a new cooperative and the liquidating committee. Several informants expressed such suspicions, saying that those who wanted to restore the cooperatives were just trying to find a lucrative niche for themselves.[9] Perhaps the most balanced observation was from a women in Zamfirovo who called up the cooperative farm office and volunteered this analysis: "There are two crazy people in this village--the man who wants to liquidate the cooperative and the man who wants to start a new one." Still, discussions with liquidating authorities who were allowing cooperatives to function in 1992 convinced me that some of them were driven by a desire to maintain the village economy. Since liquidation was likely to leave the village with no functioning agriculture of scale, and villagers lacked the means to take over the job privately, cooperatives seemed like the only game in town. Where the chair of the liquidating committee had no such concern or interest, agriculture declined along with the cooperative structures and fueled village anxiety. As one person put it when I asked about the process of decollectivization in 1992, "every village is a different story."

A final similarity between decollectivization and collectivization was the role played by local communal resources. Whether the objective was a state system of cooperatives consolidated from private holdings or a system of private ownership and cultivation, communally held village land would technically remain outside these structures. Both projects, however, incorporated these resources to facilitate the installation of the system and to assure its dominance. During collectivization communally held land was sometimes simply incorporated directly into the cooperative farm. More surreptitiously, it was often used to compensate owners whose land obstructed consolidation of land contributed by cooperative members. A private landowner who did not wish to join the cooperative but whose land separated the plots of other members was required to hand over his/her land in exchange for land elsewhere. Often the land he/she received in return was communal land, and it then entered the collective farm when everybody joined.

Communal property was also targeted by the decollectivization program as a potential solution to the expected shortfall of land for restitution. The land law specifies that state and municipal land can be used both to compensate owners whose land cannot be returned and to provide land for cooperative farm workers who were previously landless (Articles 20-1, 10b-1 and 26). The law also states however, that municipalities shall be reinstated in ownership of farm land of which they were dispossessed. So it is unclear which article will take precedence. The director of the land commission in Berkovitza said that communal land would be restituted directly to village councils. Still, given the legal opening, it is likely that officials in districts faced with more severe shortfalls of land will use communal property to meet individual claims. This may be more devastating to the household economy under decollectivization than it was under collectivization since villagers often continued to exploit cooperative land more or less communally during the socialist period.[10]

Conclusions

Some of the parallels drawn here go beyond those intended by villagers claiming decollectivization was "an old song in a new voice." Most of those who invoked the adage did so with only the broadest similarity in mind--that both programs were attempts by the state to force villagers into radically different agricultural arrangements. Given the continuing association in Bulgaria between agriculture and the village, both were seen as attacks on the village itself. Collectivization was an attack by communists in the name of a proletarian working class; decollectivization was an attack by urban intellectuals in the name western oriented capitalist entrepreneurs. While both promised to eventually improve agriculture and village life, this idea seemed far from the central rationale of either program.

Viewed from this vantage point the early decollectivization campaign is a perfect manifestation of what I refer to as the "socialist subconscious" (Creed 1991). With this term I attempt to capture the extent to which, perhaps unknowingly, early post-communist reformers replicated programs or strategies characteristic of the socialist system. Reformers were determined to create the antithesis of socialism, but in the early years of the transition they often used methods and programs that struck many, including people in these societies, as absolutely socialist in character. The idea of the socialist subconscious is not a psychological explanation of this development, but rather a psychological metaphor for a sociological phenomenon.[11] It is an attempt to reveal the continuity of subtle ideas and behaviors routinized during socialism, what Bourdieu (1977) might call the "habitus" of socialist "practice." Such behavior is not as easily discarded as a defunct ideology.[12] The official ideology of socialism was clearly defined and thus easily rejected by anti-communist reformers. However, aspects of political culture which were improvised during the socialist era to help actualize or shore up the formal ideology were not necessarily seen as elemental to it, and they survived the anti-communism of the early 1990s.

Some would argue that the continued utilization of old methods and approaches was not *sub*conscious at all; anti-communists employed these methods consciously after 1989 precisely because they had proven successful in the past. This is possible, but the corollary to this is that the anti-communists saw their actions as mere political strategies rather than as elements of the socialist system which actually produced these tactics. If so, this is further testimony to how aspects of socialist practice could be normalized and externalized, which is the essence of the socialist subconscious.

The apparent waning of anti-socialism as the sole issue in the east European transition has focused attention on various issues and programs in their own right, which has helped to diminish the evident influence of the socialist subconscious. Thus unlike collectivization, the extreme version of decollectivization described here was checked somewhat after October 1992. We can see, then, that the process of decollectivization provides a sort of microcosm of the early transition in general: a dominant anti-communism, which was ironically manifested in ways revealing the socialist subconscious, gradually gave way to more moderate perspectives.[13]

Thus, the interpretation of decollectivization as a reprise of collectivization does not hold over time. It also does not imply that the programs were completely identical from the start, clearly there were differences. Furthermore, this interpretation was by no means a unanimous perspective in Bulgaria even in 1992. The different village experiences with decollectivization mentioned above resulted in different interpretations. Zamfirovo had a less than amiable experience, and was also a village with a strong socialist tradition, which no doubt further biased village interpretations. Even in Zamfirovo, however, there were supporters of the program who advocated any means necessary to purge the village communists. For them the fact that collectivization had been enforced by the Communist Party whereas decollectivization was carried out by the elected UDF, made all the difference in the world. However, by 1993 the same aphorism only needed a slight adjustment to fit their opinions as well. They accused the *new* cooperative formed in October 1992 of replicating old communist structures. During my meeting with the chairman of the liquidating committee in 1993, he kept referring to the new cooperative as the "TKZS," the most commonly used term for collective farms in the socialist era. He made a special point to explain to me why he used the old term: "they are the same personnel, working the same way as before," in other words, an old song in an *old* voice.

Notes

This research was made possible by a faculty incentive grant to Hunter College, CUNY from the Joint Committee on Eastern Europe of the Social Science Research Council and the American Council of Learned Societies. I am grateful to the villagers of Zamfirovo and to colleagues at the Institute of Sociology in Sofia for their assistance. Thanks also to Daniel Bates and Trenholme Junghans for comments on an earlier version of this article.

1. Perhaps this was even more the case in Bulgaria, where the opposition was fairly united. Elsewhere in eastern Europe the opposition was fragmented early on and thus involved in processes of distinction that were more than simply degree of anti-communism.

2. For more information on the Turkish minority and the Movement for Rights and Freedoms, see Bates, this volume.

3. The land law (Article 33) specified that land commissions should be established at district levels, but also provided for the establishment of village-level commissions at the request of district councils.

4. The uncertainty of tenure and the continuing operation of the old cooperative make the current amount of land worked by the new cooperative an insufficient indication of actual land that the cooperative might eventually access through its current membership.

5. The average land holding in Zamfirovo at the time of collectivization was 2.78 hectares, and there were only four villagers with more than 10 hectares.

6. Collectivization began in the late 1940s and was completed in 1956. Space does not permit a detailed description of that process and subsequent agricultural reforms here. For those interested in this history see Creed (1992). For comparative material see Bell (1984); Kideckel (1982, 1993); Humphrey (1983); Salzmann and Scheufler (1986); Swain (1985); and Verdery (1983).

7. If the Hungarian case provides any comparison this suspicion may have been grounded. Szelenyi and Szelenyi (1991:16) point out that the Smallholders Party used this argument in advocating the restoration of the 1947 landholding system. They suggested that labor intensive small-scale agriculture could employ the masses who lose jobs due to the rapid restructuring of other sectors of the economy.

8. Shanin (1971) actually suggests that the Soviet precedent was the sole motivation for collectivization, but this is too extreme.

9. Kideckel (1992:72) describes nearly identical suspicions in Romania.

10. In a provocative analysis Ellen Comisso (1991) suggests that property rights under socialism were in fact communal even though defined as cooperative or state ownership.

11. In this sense it is similar to what Verdery has characterized as the phantom limb syndrome (quoted in Kideckel 1993:227) or part of what Jowitt calls the Leninist legacy (Jowitt 1992:284-305).

12. Herein lies a clue to the power and of Vaclav Havel's (1985) resistance. His insistence on "living in the truth" can be seen as an attempt to limit the internationalization or routinization of behaviors he saw as undesirable responses to a distorted system.

13. This same general outline is detectable in descriptions of agricultural reform elsewhere is eastern Europe. Skalnik (1993:224) suggests that Slovakian discussions of the new Land Act in 1991 included the possibility of "dissolving from above," but Pollak's (1992) description of a single Slovak village more than a year latter, shows that some collectives continued successfully as revamped cooperatives. Kideckel's (1992) account of decollectivization in Romania shows a similar softening of anti-collective attitudes on the part of the ruling National Salvation Front.

References

Bell, Peter D. 1984. *Peasants in Socialist Transition: Life in a Collectivized Hungarian Village*. Berkeley: University of California Press.

Bourdieu, Pierre. 1977. *Outline of a Theory of Practice*. Cambridge: Cambridge University Press.

Brisby, Liliana. 1960. "Bulgaria's Economic Leap Year," *The World Today*. 16:35-46.

Comisso, Ellen. 1991. "Property Rights, Liberalism, and the Transition from 'Actually Existing' Socialism," *East European Politics and Societies* 5(1):162-188.

Creed, Gerald W. 1991. "Civil Society and the Spirit of Capitalism: A Bulgarian Critique," Paper presented at the Annual Meeting of the American Anthropological Association, November 20-24. Chicago, IL.

____. 1992. *Economic Development Under Socialism: A Bulgarian Village on the Eve of Transition*, Ph.D. Dissertation, CUNY.

____. 1993. "Rural-Urban Oppositions in the Bulgarian Political Transition," *Südosteuropa* 42:369-82.

Dobrin, Bogoslav. 1973. *Bulgarian Economic Development Since World War II*. New York: Praeger.

Gyurova, Svobada. 1989. "Trudnosti i greshki pri masovoto kooperirane na selyanite v Plevenski okrug," *Istoricheski Pregled* 45:56-67.

Havel, Vaclav. 1985. "The Power of the Powerless," *In* John Keane, ed., *The Power of the Powerless*. Armonk: M.E. Sharpe. pp. 23-96.

Humphrey, Caroline. 1983. *Karl Marx Collective:Economy, Society and Religion in a Siberian Collective Farm*. Cambridge: Cambridge University Press.

Jones, B.D. and Dimiter A. Jankoff. 1957. "Agriculture," *In* L.A.D. Dellin, ed., Bulgaria. New York:Praeger, pp.287-312.

Jowitt, Kenneth. 1992. *New World Disorder: The Leninist Extinction*. Berkeley: University of California Press.

Keliyan, Maya. 1991. "Selskostopanskata kooperatsiya," *Sotsiologicheski Pregled* 4:1-9.

Kideckel, David A. 1982. "The Socialist Transformation of Agriculture in a Romanian Commune, 1945-1962," *American Ethnologist* 9:320-340.

____. 1992. "Once Again, the Land: Decollectivization and Social Conflict in Rural Romania," *In* Hermine G. DeSoto and David G. Anderson, eds., *The*

Curtain Rises: Rethinking Culture, Ideology, and the State in Eastern Europe. Atlantic Highlands, NJ: Humanities Press, pp. 62-75.

____. 1993. *The Solitude of Collectivism: Romanian Villagers to the Revolution and Beyond.* Ithaca, NY: Cornell University Press.

Pollak, Janet. 1992. "Rye Whiskey, Plum Candy, Tourist Hotel and Restaurant: Cooperative Success in a Slovak Village," Paper presented at the Annual Meeting of the American Anthropological Association, San Francisco, December 2-6.

Salzmann, Zdenek and Vladimir Scheufler. 1986. *Komárov: A Czech FarmingVillage.* Prospect Heights, IL: Waveland Press.

Shanin, Teodor. 1971. "Cooperation and Collectivization: The Case of Eastern Europe," *In* Peter Worsley, ed., *Two Blades of Grass*. Manchester: Manchester University Press, pp. 263-274.

Skalnik, Peter. 1993. "'Socialism is Dead' and Very Much Alive in Slovakia: Political Inertia in a Tatra Village," *In* C.M. Hann, ed., *Socialism: Ideals, Ideologies, and Local Practice.* New York: Routledge. pp. 218-226.

Swain, Nigel. 1985. *Collective Farms Which Work?* Cambridge: Cambridge University Press.

Szelenyi, Balazs and Ivan Szelenyi. 1991. "The Social Impact of Agrarian Reform: Social and Political Conflicts in the Post-communist Transformation of Hungarian Agriculture." *The Anthropology of East Europe Review* 10(1):12-24.

Verdery, Katherine. 1983. *Transylvanian Villagers: Three Centuries of Political, Economic, and Ethnic Change.* Berkeley: University of California Press.

4

Two Incidents on the Plains in Southern Transylvania: Pitfalls of Privatization in a Romanian Community

David A. Kideckel

Privatization: East and West Compared

Agricultural privatization and the related phenomenon of decollectivization are two of the most significant influences on rural East European communities today. However, to understand the nature and significance of privatization we need to delve beneath the very different meanings of the process as conceived in the West and lived in the East. Western development agencies, on one hand, consider agricultural privatization more as an end point of a process, i.e., the operation of a full-fledged system of private agricultural production (World Bank 1990, 1993), but pay less attention to the manner by which it unfolds. In particular, issues that develop in communities after land has been privatized are disregarded except as they impact on the amortization of aid debt. Furthermore, reflected through the rose-colored haze of end-of-communism triumphalism, Western observers tend to consider East European privatization a universal good because it is thought a necessary concomitant of a free market, a harbinger of civil society and democratic politics, and one more factor easing the adversarial relations of the Cold War.

Where Westerners bother to note the problems with the process they consider them as temporary and more a condition left over from the unrealistic economic relations and practices of the now-defunct socialist states. For Western institutions and individuals involved in the distribution of aid to East Europe, it is simply a matter of developing the right mix of laws and policies for privatization to succeed in unmitigated fashion. Furthermore, Western programs of privatization often tend to ignore local and national differences and emphasize large-scale cross-national similarities (Wedel and Kideckel 1993). To the aid community, then, to paraphrase Gertrude Stein, "private property is private property is private property."

For East Europeans, who must live with the consequences of schemes often hatched elsewhere, privatization is more the process than the result and, as such, is recognized as the mixed bag it really is. While there are many positive features recognized in the process, privatization is not cost-free but entails a great number of compromises and contradictory decision making. Furthermore, as East Europeans are quick to recognize, if only implicitly and by actual experience, the implementation, subsequent practice, and adjustments to privatization implicate the on-going tenor of local social relationships. Thus the process itself is of great significance not only for the economic prospects of communities and constituent households but also for the quality of local social life and the development of a strong and vibrant civil society at the local level.

Given the multi-vocal significance of privatization for East Europeans, our challenge is to understand what the meaning of this process is for different communities and individuals and how its actual implementation affects local life. This essay focusses on one seemingly small event in the overall process of privatization in a Transylvanian Romanian community subsequent to decollectivization. It details the division and distribution of jointly-worked, though privately held land from two local agricultural associations to local family households for their own private production. On the surface, this two day event which brought together representatives of about forty households, was an apparently inconsequential moment in the overall process of Romanian and East European privatization. However, as I show, the act of land division conjured up a variety of key symbols and meanings and thus aroused many of the contradictory pressures in these communities present from before collectivization and left unresolved with privatization. In the playing out of this land division, then, new social fault lines were exposed, other social principles challenged, and new ways of relating created and put into operation.

Romanian Privatization: Laws and Goals

The significance of the events recounted below can only be explained within the context of the recent history and political economy of Romanian agriculture. Romania was one of the most collectivized countries in Eastern Europe when Ceauşescu fell in December 1989. Almost immediately after the December "events"[1] rural communities everywhere began to reappropriate their land in spontaneous acts of decollectivization. However, given the importance of agriculture for state export and the new Romanian government's uncertain political identity, the government sought to restrict such actions. In many instances, in fact, decollectivization was also opposed by numbers of local citizens who supported the collectives for diverse reasons (Kideckel 1990, 1993a).

As pressure for economic restructuring mounted, however, the Romanian Land Law (Law 18) was passed in February 1991 which formally recognized the informal decollectivization and reappropriation of property ongoing since the fall of Ceauşescu. Though Law 18 formally ended collectivization, it was filled with loop-holes and half measures that protected state property and it also recreated a number of problems that had plagued Romanian agriculture before collectivization. A summary of its major provisions suggests some of its related problems. First, the law was far-reaching in its land distribution, providing about 80% of Romania's agricultural land to former owners, their heirs, or to landless folk who worked a required amount of time on the former collectives. Given the large number of people reappropriated, a land tenure system was created that was dominated by small holdings of one to three hectares distributed in a number of dispersed parcels. For example, in a survey of 500 villages, a team from the Romanian Academy of Agricultural and Silvicultural Science found the land tenure structure described in Table 4.1 where 49.3% of surveyed households owned from one to four hectares in about seven different parcels. Second, because land was returned indiscriminately, many of the reappropriated were either older people expropriated during collectivization or their urban-based heirs. The resulting demography of land ownership left 43.1% of owners resident in cities, 39.1% pensioners or salaried or wageworkers, and only 17.8% actual peasants physically capable of working their land.

Another issue of Law 18 concerns land location. In plains areas, where socialist state construction and land "improvement" was most pronounced, land was returned in large plots and redistributed to former owners on a proportional basis. For the most part (with some exceptions) this policy retains large parcels of land for subsequent use in some kind of associative farming. In hill zones, however, the land was returned according to how it was formerly distributed, resulting in a system of strip farming with parcels oriented from hilltop to lowland. Though this makes economic sense to land-poor hill peasants who worry about adequate rainfall, slope, soil fertility, etc., it also recreated many environmental problems extant before World War Two (Dicks 1993).

To remedy problems related to Law 18, ameliorate the lack of agricultural capital, technology, and traction,[2] and maintain economies of scale wherever possible, the Romanian parliament also passed Law 36 enabling formation of production associations of private peasants, of which there are two types: (1) those with legal personhood, or "societies of a juridical type," and (2) family societies, with no formal statutes nor recognition as legal persons. Owing to the difficulties of private, non-associated farming and state support of the juridical

Table 4.1: Number of Rural Households by Size of Holding and Number of Parcels (500 Village Sample).

Land/ House- hold	Hsehld #	Hsehld %	Avg. Ha. Tot/ Hsehld	Avg. Ha. Arable per Hsehld	Avg. # Parcel per Hsehld	Avg. # Arable Parcels
	671	2.5	0.0	0.0	0.0	0.0
0-.5 ha.	2431	11.9	0.2	0.1	1.3	1.8
.5-1 ha.	3022	14.0	0.7	0.5	2.3	1.7
1-2 ha.	4551	20.9	1.4	1.1	3.5	2.5
2-3 ha.	3640	16.8	2.4	1.9	4.5	3.3
3-4 ha.	2481	11.6	3.4	2.7	5.1	3.8
4-5 ha.	1619	7.7	4.4	3.5	5.4	4.2
5-10 ha.	2710	13.1	6.6	5.3	6.4	4.8
10 + ha.	263	1.5	10.5	7.5	6.6	4.6
Tot.	21388	100.0	2.5	2.0	3.9	2.9

Source: Bulgaru et al. 1992:16

societies both types have grown steadily in number and size. In July 1991 there were 267 juridical groups and 239 family societies. By November 1991 they had increased to 1,586 and 4,817 respectively and by February, 1992 numbered 2,641 and 9,207 (Ianoş 1992:25). Currently there are about 11,500 family societies with a total of 720,000 members (sixty-three members/society) that farm an average of 156 ha. and 4,050 juridic societies with 780,000 members (or about 200/society) that farm an average of 494 ha.

The distribution of each type of society is hardly amenable to prediction, and varies from region to region and even from community to community. Rural communities rarely have no associations, some have only juridic or family groups, and still others have multiple numbers of both. Some of the more important factors determining formation, size, distribution, and organization of the societies include: (1) the history of community-collective farm relations (where mainly positive, juridical societies tend to dominate; where not family groups or individualized private agriculture is more apparent; (2) regional ecology (plains regions tend to have more juridical societies than hill zones and both juridical and family groups farm larger amounts of land in the plains than in hill zones); (3) the production profile of the former collectives (juridical societies predominate among former collectives that had diverse production profiles and generated income from non-agricultural activities); and (4) idiosyncratic factors like the persuasive powers of former farm technicians or the recalcitrance of one or another individual householder.

The production profiles of the societies also differ. Family societies are mainly oriented to basic crop production and rarely even keep livestock in common. Members of a typical family society provide a portion of their land to the society to produce crops that benefit from economies of scale (grains, sugar beets, fodder) and retain the rest of their land for subsistence. Though my data are impressionistic it seems that family societies consult less often with agricultural extension (*Camera Agricole*) agents and utilize fewer inputs (fertilizers, pesticides, etc.) than juridic groups. Labor is also less mechanized in family groups and its internal organization and decision making is more or less consensual. Remuneration in the family groups is strictly according to the amount of land entered by each constituent family, minus the cost of purchased or leased inputs. So far as I know, family groups do not hire others' labor. Though nominally "family" groups, they are comprised not only of kin, but also of friends, neighbors, work colleagues, ritual kin, etc. This quality of their membership articulates them well with the diffuse social relations that characterize Romanian villages.

Juridic societies are often the direct heirs of the agricultural production cooperatives (CAP), and were literally often formed on the heels of the CAPs. In some instances, for example, CAP specialist cadres who lost their jobs during decollectivization spearheaded the formation of juridic groups by convincing local peasants to contribute capital and/or land to the society. As heir to the CAPs juridic societies often retain a similar production profile. Though they specialize in field crops they occasionally have other production activities such as stockkeeping and vineyard and orchard management. These resources are contributed directly from individuals who received them from the former collectives or, in some instances, were purchased from the liquidating CAP.

In juridic associations, the owners and dominant members are those whose capital forms the society,[3] though not necessarily those whose land is farmed by the society. Other individuals participate in juridic societies with only land and still others give both land and labor. Juridical groups also hire occasional day labor, though much of their labor is performed by people with land (though not necessarily capital) in the society. According to one estimate, a total of 26% of these societies hire some types of labor: 8% permanent, 7% during peak production periods, and 11% some kind of temporary day labor (Brooks and

Meurs 1992). The profit from the work of the juridic society is apportioned only to its actual share holders. However, with increased profits the evaluation of work norms for those people who work in the society also increases, thus providing a degree of economic co-interest to ensure the quality of production.

The Romanian government clearly favors the juridic groups because of their economies of scale, their role in maintaining the fixed capital of the former collectives, the greater coordination of their production with perceived regional and national needs, and their more frequent consultation with extension agents. Consequently, credit is much easier obtained for juridical societies, inputs more widely used by them, and there even seems to be a degree of economic coercion for peasant households to join or stay in them though, for the most part, the association of peasant households in both forms of society is voluntary. Still, despite this pressure and the fact that juridic societies are more the direct heirs of the former collectives (often their leaders are the same people that headed up the collectives), entry in them is positively viewed by its members and many of those who provide it with land. Because of their more mechanized profile (and fewer requirements of manual labor) the juridic groups are particularly attractive to absentee land owners and old and infirm individuals who essentially rent their land to the groups. Paradoxically, the largest of local landowners also enter these groups more often than family ones as they have the leeway to place a share of land with the association and leave part totally under private cultivation.

The potentially great variation in agricultural organization gives any Romanian local community wide latitude in developing its own agricultural production system. However, it also encourages potential friction as diverse community interests seek to define that production system to their advantage. Furthermore, the different mix of production organizations adopted by any community also serves as a window into the prevailing structures and sets of social relationships that define that community and the relationships between its constituent households as well as its relationship with the state. Below I examine one event in the life of a Romanian community to consider the relation of agricultural production to community organization, to analyze the development and resolution of social tensions that develop in the process of privatization, and the implications of the process for the future of local political economy and the growth of a vibrant and productive market-based democratic system.

The Incidents Observed

During fieldwork in October 1992 in Hîrseni commune in southern Transylvania one of the most talked about events was the division of a ten hectare parcel of formerly collectively farmed land into a number of private family plots. The land was to be divided by forty-four households that previously owned land in this area. The households were now members of the two juridic associations in the village which currently farmed the land. The land parcel, locally termed "the upland meadow" (*lunca din sus*), was located on the village's southern perimeter on the road to the Carpathian Alps. Because of its proximity to the village and quality soils,[4] owning land here had always been particularly desirable. Decollectivization and the growth of a subsistence agricultural economy made it more so. In the early phase of decollectivization this plot was earmarked for associative farming and in the 1992 growing season was used for maize production by both associations. Still, because it was defined as hill land it nonetheless could be divided according to boundaries registered in earlier agricultural registers and cadastres. Thus, the division of land (*împărţirea pămîntului*) recounted below was a matter of some local consequence.

The two associations, of eighty-five and forty-seven households respectively, dominate the local agricultural scene. As in Romania generally, they have access to cheaper inputs and state credit, their land is concentrated in a few large and more easily worked plots and, in particular, they make much more economic sense in the mixed agro-industrial economy that characterizes the region.[5] The larger of the two associations, the "Transylvania Agricultural Society," was the first formed after the breakup of the Hîrseni collective farm and originally comprised all households involved in associative farming. Subsequent to the 1991 agricultural season, however, sixty or so households split off to form the "Cringurele Agricultural Society," named for a parcel of land north of the village considered by villagers the most fertile and productive local area. Since then the "Transylvania" membership increased slightly while that of Cringurele steadily declined. In fact, participating in the parceling out of *lunca din sus* were three households that had decided to quit Cringurele and strike out on their own as fully private producers. The Transylvania group would divide its share of the land among its members who previously owned land here on one day and Cringurele and the privatizing three the next.

Day One

Parceling out the land on this first day was a fairly easy process. According to some of the people present, it reminded them of the way that the former collective farm divided land for household use plots every spring. Thirty-five households of the Transylvania Association were slated to receive parcels of land of about twenty are in size. The *lunca* land could have appropriately been divided according to where each family held land previously. However, the Transylvania group decided to distribute their plots according to a random lottery. They considered the land fairly uniform in quality, though it is slightly more fertile and easily worked the closer in to the village.

The day's events had hardly begun when I showed up at 8 a.m. to observe lottery preparations at the home of the Transylvania Association president. Mrs. Marciu, the president, was the former head bookkeeper of the local collective farm and, according to many, was both the brains behind and chief organizer of the Association. Given her reputation it was somewhat incongruous to watch this remarkable woman in nightgown and bare feet preparing breakfast for her family as she ordered her daughter to prepare slips of paper numbered to thirty-five in preparation for the lottery. Mrs. Marciu and her daughter were assisted by Mrs. Munteanu, the new head bookkeeper of the Transylvania group, who also had been a collective farm office worker. The three women were incredibly efficient. Mrs. Marciu sent her daughter off to make sure that some Association men would show up at the parceling with a horse and a two meter measuring stick[6] to facilitate the process. Subsequently, she and her colleague prepared a registry listing each of the Association families with land at the *lunca*, and the amount of land to which they were entitled.

At the *lunca* things proceeded fairly smoothly. As is their way, villagers showed up in small groups of two or three, some few with horses, carts, and plows, but most on foot. After about an hour Mrs. Marciu called a roll to make sure that representatives from all participating households were present. She then informed people about the lottery procedures. Each household would be called in turn to select a numbered slip of paper from a bag held by Mrs. Marciu. The number corresponded to a plot of land that would be measured out on the *lunca*. The lower the number, the closer the parcel to the village and the better its perceived quality.

As orderly as the day had been, as the lottery began there was a breakdown in democratic procedure. Clearly people were not used to such practices because, when Mrs. Marciu asked people to select their numbers, there was a mad rush to reach for the bag and pull a number. The disorder was incredibly funny and the participants laughed and joked with each other about it. One older woman seemed to pull a number she didn't like. She looked at it, made a face, and then put it back to draw another. Even I got in to the act as my host's grandson pushed me forward when it was time for their household to draw. Mrs. Marciu said I couldn't participate, but the people surrounding her shouted her down, some claiming that I'd be bad luck for the family and others saying the opposite.[7]

After the draw was over, and Mrs. Marciu had duly registered each household's plot location, people set about marking off the plots, first measuring their perimeters, then plowing furrows to demarcate each. Given that this land was now being converted to private use I was surprised at the lack of concern for precision in measuring the plots. Those using the *capra* occasionally lost count and plowing was so haphazard that every furrow meandered unevenly across the *lunca*. Still, no one complained. As one older woman said:

> Before we cursed those who made the collective farm. Now we do the same to those who give us our land back. We don't have tools, tractors, diesel fuel, let alone titles, so we can't worry too much about every little bit of land.

Day Two

The following day, the Cringurele Association had its turn, its practices starkly contrasting the Transylvania group before it. Early in the morning at the home of the Cringurele leader, Gheorghe Simion, things were in total disarray. As he ate breakfast in his pajamas, two other members of the group stood near him and discussed the day. One, Ion Dascalescu, was the now-elderly son of one of the largest pre-collective village landowners, and the other a neighbor from across the street. The Cringurele leaders were at first uncertain how many families would participate in their lottery (fourteen households was the final figure) and took no steps to record names of participants, fill out lottery slips, or attend to any other preliminary tasks. However, they continually emphasized how their group comprised the largest pre-collective landowners in the village and how, because of their better stewardship, their agricultural production was better than the Transylvania association. They were also rather bitter about what they saw as discrimination against their group. They said it was short-changed by the local land commission on the amount and quality of land they received in the recent land distribution.

The Cringurele day proceeded in a disorganized manner. By the time he dressed, gathered pencil and notebook, and spoke with colleagues, Mr. Simion did not get to the *lunca* until about eleven a.m., two hours after he was supposed to be there. Even so, when he arrived there were only a few people present and none with horse or plow to mark plot boundaries. One man was sent into the village to get them so this delayed the process another hour. Finally after all the people and requisite materials were assembled the division was ready to begin. However, where the Transylvanian group set about this task with all ready speed, paying little attention to precise boundaries, the Cringurele group immediately began to try to identify the location of the boundary between their plot and that of the households going private. Their concern that it be defined as precisely as possible produced the first of many arguments. This focussed on which of two rocks at the side of the road was the appropriate boundary. For over an hour people debated the merits of each rock as boundary marker, referring to their size, shape, relation to nearby trees, and other qualities as evidence of each rock's status. As absurd as the debate seemed, it particularly mattered to the three families leaving the association who were there to receive their final allotment of land in the *lunca.*

The arguments about the rocks became so furious that Mr. Simion requested someone return to the village to bring one of the agents of the state cadastral service. The current cadastre service is run by county government. Though ostensibly independent, because some cadastre offices were implicated in what some villagers see as inequitable land divisions, they are suspicious of the service and its agents. Nonetheless, the local agent, a young woman recently graduated from university, dutifully left her office to come out to the *lunca* and offer her advice on the boundary squabble. This took another half hour as she sat by the ditch at the side of the road with cadastral documents and intense Cringurelese around her. Finally, when all agreed where the boundary was, the three privatizing families separated from the rest of the group to mark their plots with horse and plow. Since there was a need for the other plots to be measured a cry went up for Mr. Dascalescu to do it. However, he demurred as he turned to me and said:

> They asked me to do this before and now they ask me to do it again. But I don't want to be responsible for the measuring because everyone will criticize me even if I do it honestly.

With the hour now growing late and no one yet assenting to do the measuring, the assembled group began to break up and agreed to return the following morning to try it again. As people wandered off, in the distance one saw the three privatizing families beginning to burn off the wheat stubble on their new fields.

"Inside" Privatization: Land Tenure, Production, and Daily Life

On the surface "Transylvania" and "Cringurele" are similar organizations with similar goals and statutes. However, as is apparent from their land division activities, there are compelling differences between the two groups. To account for such differences we must look beneath their surface reality to consider the structural basis of their variation. To aid this we can use structural linguistic notions of *parole*, surface reality, and *langue*, the actual structure of a particular speech event or analogously, the notion of "inside baseball" discussed by sports aficionados in the United States. This suggests that the rules and play of the game are really only a surface reality actually dependent on the deep structures, histories, and local knowledge brought to any game situation. So, too, land division in this Olt Land community; so, too, privatization throughout East Europe.

"Inside privatization" in Hîrseni shows a range of differences between the two associations that account for the divergent land division experience. At the base is a slightly variant orientation to the organization and remuneration of agricultural production. To the outsider such variation is barely perceptible, but to the inside player makes all the difference in the world. In fact, such variation has implications for everything about the associations from their names to their integration into community life and the political relationships they produce and destroy.

The range of association differences are summed up in Table 4.2, below. However, the linchpin of variation is the greater commitment of the Transylvania group to principles like those of the former collective farm compared to Cringurelese greater concern for private agricultural ownership and production. Locals of both groups summarize the collectivist-oriented Transylvania approach by referring to it as an "old system association" (*asociaţiă de tip veche*). However, by "old system" people mean very different things, and the idea of "association" itself also has very different significance depending on one's interpretation of it. To Transylvania members and their sympathizers, "old system" refers exclusively to their organization of production and remuneration. Thus, this association mainly produces field crops on land contributed by members, seeks to be fully mechanized in production (but where not assigns members oversight responsibilities on land contributed), and pays members thirty percent of production in cash and kind, pro rated according to the amount of land a household contributes. The other seventy percent is used to defray costs of inputs, administration, and the like. This system is similar to that referred to as *acord global* (Cernea 1974, Kideckel 1993) or the "contract payment system" previously practiced by the CAPs. Furthermore, this system also allows those unable to work the land, like the elderly and infirm and urban-based land owners, to contribute it to the association and receive ten percent of the amount of production on a proportional basis.

When Cringurelese speak of the "old system" they refer as much to a political idea as they do to an economic one. Thus, to Cringurele members and others oriented to private agriculture, the "old system" of the Transylvania association refers to its bureaucratic and collective-like structure. Cringurelese, in fact, caricature the Transylvania group as mainly comprised of former leaders of the now-defunct CAP who created the association to save their sinecures and order other people around. They jokingly call the Transylvania group the "Asociaţia Saddam Hussein" after the Iraqi dictator. This attitude was summed up by the leader of Cringurele who said of the Transylvania group:

> Our agriculture works much better than (theirs). We were the richest people before collectivization and thus the hardest workers. The other associationists were on CAP salaries and learned only to command and eat for nothing.

To avoid any taint of collectivism themselves, the Cringurele group returns the full amount of production to its members. After the cost of inputs and the like are subtracted, production is divided according to the amount of land a household registered with the society. Individuals who register land with the association must work for the association, and Cringurele makes no provision for those unable to do so. Whereas Transylvania members will engage in some joint production (e.g., manuring field crops), Cringurelese only use their association as a kind of service cooperative through which households gain access to machinery and other inputs.

Table 4.2: Characteristics of the Hîrseni Associations

Names	Transylvanian Agricultural Association, *Asociația Saddam Hussein,* Old System Association	Agricultural Society "Cringurele," *Associația a lui Simion, Asociația Jacques Cousteau*
Size	85 households and increasing	47 households and declining
New Members	Open with approval of general assembly	Membership closed
Leaders	CAP leaders and local officials with leading role	Former large landowners with leading role
Managerial Pay	Managers receive small amount of grain for work	Managers unpaid and voluntary
Labor Structure	Joint labor in all activities, except personal plot	Some joint labor in field crops; Individual labor in potatoes
Pay Structure	Paid @ 30% of production per hectares contributed	Production in field crops divided per hectares contributed
Non-working Members	Some excused from work with reduction to 10% remuneration	All members expected to work

Out of this basic distinction, then, grows attitudes to property and labor expressed in the divergent experience of land division. Whereas the Transylvania group is organized to a fault, at the same time it is less concerned about small amounts of land and rigid boundaries. In contrast, the Cringurelese are more worried about personal property and private right than about the needs of their organization. Even the name "Cringurele" shows this orientation. In this community Cringurele refers to a parcel of high quality land where some association households previously owned plots. Most of this area, however, was owned by the wealthiest pre-World War Two landowner who died in jail during the early years of the collectivization campaign. Thus, by calling themselves

Cringurele, they especially draw a contrast with the more collectivist-oriented Transylvania group and seek to provoke sentiment and memory.

The Transylvania group's nickname for Cringurele is more humorous than political. They call them the Jacques Cousteau Association, because of the uncanny resemblance of Mr. Simion to the famous French oceanographer. Nonetheless they find much to criticize about Cringurele. Above all, they blame them and other privatizers for the sorry state of community agriculture. For example, the Transylvania group president said:

> Agriculture today gives such poor results because we (Romanian villagers) were taught to be led and to listen to strong leaders. Nowadays, everyone wants to be heard and this is not good. Though we were held tight in the past the work went well. What the Communists did for agriculture these people (i.e., private farmers) will never be able to do in a million years.

Aside from their differing political economic organization other specific local conditions like ecology and history also influence association practices. The extent of their influence should give pause to those who propose national level policy. For example, one critical factor is the heterogeneity of local land resources. Where land is of fairly homogenous quality, privatization (and appropriate land use patterns) is easier to achieve than in heterogenous zones, like Hîrseni. Here private householders vie for access to lands of the best quality and make short term, often ecologically unsound, land use decisions to make the best of their difficult inheritance (cf. Dicks 1993). For this specific incidence of land division, because the land elsewhere in the community is of such mixed quality, those going private felt they had to be concerned with every centimeter in the *lunca*, resulting in their fevered attempt to define the boundary between their and Cringurelese lands.

The history of local agricultural collectivization and the quality of local social relations that derive from it can also aid or confuse privatization. Thus, in the Olt Land region during collectivization in the 1960s some people lied about the amount or quality of the land they deeded to the collectives in hopes they could retain control over their own resources by legal ruse (also see Creed, this volume). This original lie backfired when people sought to re-claim their land with privatization. As the originally falsified registers were the only documentary proof of ownership, people had to rely on the testimony of neighbors to attest to their rightful possessions. Where these relationships had grown tentative due to the depredations of the socialist years, they were unable to prove their claims. Similarly, questionable land documentation enabled cooperating groups of relatives or neighbors to conspire to falsify land claims for their own benefit. Together these legal uncertainties have perpetuated the suspicions and petty acrimony of the socialist period.

Privatization and the Social Future

What, then, do these events mean for future economic and political developments in this Olt Land village and, by extension, the rest of rural Romanian society? Right now, the jury is out. To some variation in agricultural forms and the differential support and concerns of village social groups--the demands of the Transylvania group for greater organization and leadership and the struggle of the Cringurelese for their few bits of earth--have only positive portends. In this interpretation, though privatization processes are somewhat messy, they encourage democratic practice by forcing recognition of and action on self- and group-interest. For example, the expansion in numbers of conflicts and hearings about land is said to encourage greater local understanding of legal process and individual rights and responsibilities. Reviewing the transition in Tázlár, the Hungarian village he has studied intermittently over two decades, Chris Hann (1993) suggests that "comrades have turned into lawyers," but considers this change to offer hope for a democratic future.

An economic argument also supports this interpretation. Thus, those favoring the outright and unrestricted privatization of agriculture see such developments as necessarily preliminary to the freeing of the rural economy from the control and oversight of an oppositional state. Simultaneously the diversity of agricultural forms and practices available to this local population enable all manner of individuals and households to be integrated within the private agricultural economy despite their different socio-economic and demographic situations. Furthermore, the debate over land use as expressed by the two associations can only help renew, clarify, and deepen local knowledge of appropriate agricultural practice that was lost due to the centralized decision making of collectivization.

Still, despite these more sanguine views of events like the Hîrseni land distribution, other of their aspects have quite opposite implications. They are readily seen when these events are considered in relation to the over-all political and economic context in Romania (or elsewhere in East Europe, for that matter). Romania today, like so much of the East, is characterized by rapidly increasing unemployment and inflation, an abdication of state responsibilities to local communities, and an unsettled politics at every level of society. To an extent these uncertainties are fueled by the head-long rush to privatization demanded by external aid-granting institutions like the World Bank and the IMF.[8] Given the anguish of the over-all political economy and the lack of economic alternatives, the turbulent land situation only breeds difficulties at the local level. Such mundane conflicts like the Hîrseni land division thus have outsized negative implications on people's relations with their neighbors and their attitudes toward society as a whole.

For example, underneath the more detached attitudes of the Transylvania group is an increasing land hunger and growing competitiveness for agricultural resources. The attempt by privatizers to extend their ownership has not been missed by anyone in the community where, today, agriculture is the only secure source of a minimal income. Away from the humor of the lottery Transylvania members speak bitterly of the destruction of the wealth represented by the CAP. In contrast to this, the slightly favorable access of the Transylvania group to mechanized means of production is the focus of great bitterness by Cringurelese. To them, the fix is in and it favors only those who continue to support a quasi-socialist political economy.

Though both these extreme views are unrealistic, they are intensified by the competition and suspicion that activities like the land divisions engender. As they become part of the received wisdom of the transitional community, they facilitate further social and political breakdown. Thus, to a person, the Transylvania group members see the greed and self-centeredness of the Cringurelese as responsible for the dissolution of local agricultural production while the Cringurelese suggest the Transylvania-ites and their supporters are behind the unfair limitation of Cringurele lands. Where before there were factions on the collective, and before collectivization a universe of private farmers competing economically but cooperating socially, now there are only separate "mafia," each attempting to have its way at the expense of the other, no matter the social cost.

In closing, it is clear that agricultural privatization is not yet the panacea for local rural economies that it is thought to be in the West. Though its promise is large, its process is a convoluted one sure to strain the social and political possibilities of local communities for some time to come. This is not to say that the effort to extend privatization in the Olt Land, Romania, or elsewhere in East Europe need be limited. To the contrary, these incidents clearly suggest that, if anything, it requires a redoubling of effort and the provision of an even greater resource base to facilitate it. Above all, the case of the Hîrseni land division also suggests that the process of privatization ought be given as much attention as its end goals. Only in this way will the fledgling private agricultural systems of East Europe literally and figuratively get off the ground.

Notes

Research for this chapter was supported in part by a grant from the International Research and Exchanges Board (IREX), with funds provided by the Andrew W. Mellon Foundation, the National Endowment for the Humanities, and the U.S. Department of State. None of these organizations is responsible for the views expressed.

1. The circumstances behind the political actions that toppled Ceauşescu are still murky and the source of rumor in Romania. Because of the quick rise to power of former communists, many Romanians now consider the dictator's fall to have been a coup d-etat, and no longer speak of the December 1989 actions as a revolution, but merely the "events."

2. It is estimated that there is only one draft animal (oxen or horses) for every three private peasant households and in order to purchase a tractor a private peasant must show documentation that they have access to forty hectares of land to cultivate.

3. According to statutes a juridic association needs a minimum of ten individuals each with 10,000 Lei as the basic fund of capital..

4. This parcel was considered by locals the second most fertile area of the lands surrounding this particular village.

5. There is also a family association in the village but it is comprised of only four households, and is of marginal economic and social relevance.

6. This device, called a *capra* (goat), is so-named as it vaguely resembles a goat's horns.

7. Actually, I pulled a low number and then receded into the crowd as people joked about how Americans always have good luck.

8. The recent debate about the responsibility of IMF policies for the Zhirinovsky and Communist vote in the Russian elections is a case in point (Erlanger 1993).

References

Brooks, Karen M. and Mieke Meurs. 1992. "Romanian Land Reform in the Earliest Period of Restitution, February-August, 1991: New Patterns of Land Holding and Use. Unpublished ms.

Bulgaru, Mircea et al. 1992. *Probleme de Baza ale Agriculturii României*. Bucharest: Institute of Rural Economy and Sociology of the Academy of Agricultural and Silvicultural Sciences.

Cernea, Michael. 1974. *Sociologia Cooperativei Agricole*. Bucharest: Editura Academiei.

Dicks, Michael. 1993. "The Environment." In Vol. 2, *Romania: A Strategy for the Transition in Agriculture*. pp. 273-91. Washington, D.C.: The World Bank.

Erlanger, Steven. 1993. *New Yeltsin Moves May Signal Easing in Economy Reform*. New York Times, December 18, 1993, pp. 1, 6.

Hann, Chris. 1993. "From Comrades to Lawyers: Continuity and Change in Local Political Culture in Rural Hungary", *Anthropological Journal on European Cultures* 2(1): 75-104.

Ianoş, Ioan. 1992. *Romanian Agriculture in Transition.* Typescript. Bucharest: Institute of Geography.

Kideckel, David A. 1990. "The Politics of Decollectivization in Romania After Ceauşescu." *Working Papers on the Transitions from State Socialism*, No. 90.9. Ithaca, NY: Cornell University Center for International Studies.

_____. 1993a. "Once Again the Land: Decollectivization and Social Conflict in Rural Romania." *In* H. DeSoto and D. Anderson, eds. *The Curtain Rises: Rethinking Culture, Ideology and the State in Eastern Europe*. Atlantic Highlands, NJ: Humanities Press, pp. 88-106.

_____. 1993b. *The Solitude of Collectivism:Romanian Villagers to the Revolution and Beyond.* Ithaca: Cornell University Press.

Nagengast, Carole. 1991. *Reluctant Socialists, Rural Entrepreneurs: Class, Culture, and the Polish State*. Boulder: Westview Press.

Parliament of Romania. 1991. *Lege Nr. 36 din 30 aprilie 1991 privind societăţile agricole şi alte forme de asociere în agricultură.* Bucharest.

Wedel, Janine R. and David A. Kideckel. 1993. *Foreign Aid as Ideology and Culture: The Case of Transitional East Europe*. National Science Foundation. Research Proposal. Typescript.

World Bank. 1990. *An Agricultural Strategy for Poland: Report of the Polish European Community, World Bank Task Force*. Washington, D.C.: The World Bank.

5

Agricultural Transformation and Social Change in an East German County

Joachim Singelmann

The year 1989 witnessed a major realignment in Eastern Europe. Beginning with the events in Poland and Czechoslovakia, all Eastern European countries set out to transform their societies from state socialism to parliamentary democracy, and their economies from central planning to market principles. In the process, the military boundaries of the post-World War Two period were redrawn, so that the term East once again has became congruent with its geographic meaning.[1] It brought the Cold War to an end and gave Europe a new form of stability. However, the disappearance of the cold war also brought to light regional and ethnic tensions previously hidden by the all-encompassing East-West conflict.[2] The civil wars in the territories of the former Yugoslavia and USSR are illustrations for this new instability.

East Germany is a special case of political and economic change in Eastern Europe, for no other East European country had a Western counterpart with which it had the option to unify. As such East Germany offers a unique opportunity to examine the consequences of the transformation from state socialism to liberal democracy. It is the purpose of this chapter to discuss the consequences of this transformation for the agricultural sector in one Eastern German county. To that end, this chapter (1) provides a brief summary of the process of German unification; (2) describes the locale of the research; (3) examines the organizational change resulting from the restructuring of the agricultural collectives; (4) discusses the implications of these changes for agricultural production and employment; (5) summarizes the change in employment and living standard in the community since unification; and (6) closes with a discussion of the broader context in which agricultural change takes place.

The Process of Political Unification

On October 4, 1990 the German Democratic Republic (GDR) ceased to exist. This step was the culmination of events that began during late summer and fall of 1989: the decision by the Hungarian Government to open its border with Austria to East Germans, the flooding of East Germans into the West German embassies in Prague and Warsaw, the weekly demonstrations in Leipzig since September, the ill-fated 40th anniversary of East Germany in Berlin, the replacement of Erich Honnecker, President of the GDR, and the opening of the Berlin Wall on 9 November 1989. The fall of the wall presented two options to East Germany: (1) its continued existence as a democratic socialist society, or (2) unification with West Germany. Two other possible developments preserving the existence of East Germany were never realistic options: the continuation of dominance by the communist party (SED), and the formation of a democratic capitalist society.The disappearance of the East German borders, the lack of support for the old regime by the USSR, and the total discreditation of the legitimacy of the SED completely ruled out that party's continued leadership, even as a reformed party. And the creation of a democratic capitalist society would have raised the issue of its *raison d'être*: what would have been the purpose of two German countries with the same political system?[3]

There is general agreement that East German opposition groups such as *Neues Forum* (New Forum) and *Demokratischer Aufbruch* (Democratic Beginning) had as their aim the democratization of East Germany, including freedom to form political parties and to travel abroad (Neues Forum Leipzig 1990; Schüddekopf 1990; Jarausch 1993). At the early protests, little if any mention was made of political unification with West Germany. However, when the number of refugees reached the levels existing immediately prior to the build-up of the Berlin wall in 1961, with the SED-leadership--despite Gorbachev's prodding--showing no signs of liberalization during the 40th anniversary festivities, the issue of unification slowly emerged as one of the demands on the part of East German opposition groups (cf. Reich 1992). Yet it was far from being clear on November 9, 1989 which path the political change in East Germany would take.

If anything, the initial expectations were that the new political forces in East Germany would try to reform their country (Knabe 1989; Naumann 1990). Besides the opposition movements, many intellectuals like Christa Wolf and Stefan Heym encouraged people not to go to West Germany but, rather, to help to rebuild their society (Scheuch 1991). Early opinion polls showed the Social Democratic Party (SPD) in a strong position, with some surveys placing the SPD in the lead with over 50 percent of the vote (Stern, 1990). Soon after the opening of the wall, however, the SPD became much more cautious in calling for unity than did the Christian Democratic Party (CDU) and, especially, its chairman Helmut Kohl, the West German Chancellor.

Two things appear to have changed the balance between the two possible paths, i.e. unification or a form of democratic socialism: (1) the very strong and personal support by Kohl who, for a variety of reasons, made unification the main goal of his Administration (Kopstein and Richter 1992); and (2) the economic lure of the West German currency for the East German population (cf. Luft 1991). As soon as the wall fell, Kohl set upon a relentless campaign in the East for unification. Although the East German CDU was (almost) as much part of the old regime as the SED, his personal support for the new leadership of that party steadily turned popular support away from the SPD towards the CDU. The strategy was simple: Kohl declared that no one will be worse off, and many will do better. "In another memorable phrase he predicted that eastern Germany would soon be transformed into a 'blooming landscape' of prosperity and social justice (Kinzer 1994:22)." His goal clearly was unification, while there was great uncertainty among the ranks of the SPD about the proper steps to take. He took part in the election as though he himself was running for office. Kohl was, in effect, running, for his timetable set German unification at a date prior to the West German election scheduled for December 1990. In that case, the December election would become an all-German election, and Kohl was confident to become the first Chancellor of the united Germany.

Kohl's personal engagement greatly impressed the East Germans. The calls by many intellectuals to reject the economic and political unification were quickly discredited when it was pointed out that many of them who called for independence from the West had been able to travel to the West, when most people were confined to the Eastern-block countries. Moreover, the various activist groups (*Bürgerinitiativen*) were never able to form a joint program as an alternative to unification. With Kohl pushing for unification and holding up the German Mark as incentive, a majority supported his position at election time in March 1989, when the Christian Democrats clearly became the dominant party in East Germany, winning absolute majorities in many districts. Despite Kohl's cautionary remarks immediately after the successful East German election that the costs of unification are high and that East Germans would have to contribute their part to it, the Christian Democrats won the subsequent local and state-wide elections.

The newly-elected CDU-led East German government then signed a treaty with West Germany that set the terms for the currency union of 1 July 1990 and the political unification of October 4, 1990 (Insel 1990). Although the difficulties for East Germans associated with unification had already started with the currency union in July, the support for the Christian Democrats did not decline much at the first all-German election in December 1990. When I queried people in Eastern Germany in the summer of 1991 why they voted for Kohl, most gave the following answer: "He told us that he would help us. He said that nobody would be worse off." Two things help explain their belief in the Christian Democrats even in the face of adverse experiences: (1) they trusted Western politicians the more that they mistrusted East German leaders, and (2) they were still part of a system in which some people had the power to act while others were assigned to watch (or look away).[4] That mentality is slowly beginning to change and the new reality has begun to set in. Current opinion polls have the Christian Democrats in the lead in only one state (Saxony).

Locale and Data

The location of the research project reported on in this chapter is the Schloßberg[5] county in southeastern Thuringia.The county is located in the triangle formed by the cities of Leipzig, Gera, and Jena. It has a population of around 25,000 persons, of whom about 16,000 live in the town of Schloßberg. In addition to Schloßberg, which is the county seat, the county has two other small towns.

In 1989 agriculture accounted for 17% of total employment, manufacturing 42% , construction 3%, trade 9%, and education and other social services 16%. There were two major industrial employers (a metalworks factory and a furniture and piano enterprise) in this county prior to 1989, but only the metal-works factory can be considered a large-scale establishment. The furniture and piano enterprise consists of many small units that were combined into one administration by the socialist party. Historically, manufacturing in this county was characterized by small companies and *petit-bourgeois* production, and current development point to a return towards that production structure.

The topography of Schloßberg is similar to that of Frankonia in northern Bavaria which is the neighboring region about 60 miles to the South. It has rolling hills and relatively poor soil. Agriculture therefore largely concentrates on dairy farming and meat (beef and pork) production. In fact, the district of Gera (to which Schloßberg belonged during the East German era) in 1989 had the second-highest number of cattle and milk cows per 100 hectare of agricultural land in East Germany (Staatliche Zentralverwaltung 1989). Until 1989, the county had thirteen agricultural collectives[6] and two state farms which together employed about 2,500 persons.

The information providing the basis for the discussion of organizational change in agriculture and its implications for employment was collected during several weeks of fieldwork in that county in each year since 1991. During that time I interviewed all major policy makers and key bureaucratic officials of the county, and I conducted a survey of the collectives in 1991 concerning changes in production and employment.[7] I am also conducting an annual panel survey of school children and their parents and teachers every January since 1992. This survey started with all students in the 7th and 9th grades, and it follows them (and their parents) as they pass through the school system and beyond.[8]

From Collectives to Cooperatives

Before viewing the restructuring of the agricultural collectives after unification, below I briefly review the emergence of collective agriculture in eastern Germany.

The System of Collectives

During the latter part of the 1950s farmers were pressured into forming agricultural collectives. At first, these retained a strong cooperative character, as they were limited to joint cultivation of land and sharing private production assets like tractors and harvest combines. Land, agricultural equipment, and buildings remained private property. This form of collectivization resulted in Agricultural Production Collectives (APC) Type I.

Soon after the completion of this phase, further pressure was exerted on farmers to intensify collective production. The goal of this campaign was to bring not only land but also equipment and buildings under APC control. This form of collectivization was termed APC Type II. Here farmers retained title to their land, and the value of equipment and housing transferred to the collective was duly recorded. However, the key point is that farmers lost complete control over production, including its schedule, mix, and return. While they still made the entrepreneurial decisions and received profits in the APC Type I, they now became de facto employees of the APC Type II. Although the by-laws of these APCs provided for the election of a chairman and leadership collective, no person could be elected to those posts without the endorsement of the local party leader. This structure of agricultural production was completed in the early 1960s.

One consequence of the agricultural collectivization in East Germany was the disappearance of the occupation of farmer. Workers on the APCs, even those who brought in their land and equipment, were organized along industrial principles of the division of labor: some become tractor drivers, others milkers, and so on. With the aging and retirement of the previous family farmers, the expertise of how to run a farm became more and more concentrated in the hands of the APC leadership, i.e. those persons whom the political leadership approved of (if it did not outright appoint them). Only the APC chairman and some of his deputies had the opportunity to acquire knowledge (formal training and on-the-job experience) of how to run a farm. As in virtual all other spheres of the East German society, political approval was a key to occupational advancement.[9]

By 1970 the East German government decided to further industrialize agriculture by separating crop and animal production. All land was transferred to newly-created crop APCs, with three to five animal APCs allocated to each crop APC. This restructuring resulted in the APC Type III (see also Pryor 1992:146-47). In the county of Schloßberg, two crop APCs and one crop state farm were formed, which together were linked to twelve animal APCs.

East German collectivization was the most comprehensive among the East European countries; APCs in East Germany produced around 90 percent of total agricultural output, far above countries like Poland or Bulgaria where at least one half of agricultural production came from privately held plots. The problem with the reorganization of agriculture into Type III APCs was, however, that animal APCs lost all control over crop production and, thus, over their most important production input: feed. They could neither influence the allocation of land to certain crops nor the availability of crops at specific times. Frequently the allocation quotas given to the crop APCs by the political leadership were more in the interests of other organizations than the animal APCs that were linked to the crop APCs. This had a negative impact on the productivity of the animal APCs. Moreover, the division of labor between crop and animal production required a substantial expansion of administrative overhead, for the transfer of feed crops between the two forms of APCs became transactions between independent firms requiring staff time for selling, purchasing, quality evaluation, and bookkeeping.

Dismantling the Collectives

Shortly after the monetary union between East and West Germany on July 1, 1990 the separation between crop and animal APCs was revoked. The animal APCs were able to reclaim their original land, and the crop APCs were abolished. All employees of the crop APCs were transferred to the animal APCs, unless they chose retirement. This reorganization of the collectives resulted in ten APCs and one state farm in the county of Schloßberg. The combination of the animal and crop APCs immediately showed positive results. The renewed control over crops to produce the correct feed in sufficient amounts by itself increased the yield of milk per cow by 60-80%, without any other changes in production factors.

The unified Germany meant the end of the state farm in Schloßberg, as all state enterprises were either put up for sale or closed by the *Treuhand.* Its prized possession--a large hog-raising farm--was sold to a large Bavarian company, with the former chairman of the state farm as the new director. The last (and only) freely-elected East German parliament passed a law specifying the mandated reorganization of the APCs. This law stipulated that all APCs would cease to exist on January 1, 1992, unless they took prior steps toward reorganization. APCs can choose from among three alternatives: (1) the formation of a cooperative (according to the German Cooperative Law of 1896); (2) the formation of a limited partnership or public corporation; and (3) dissolution of the APCs, with the net profits to be distributed among the persons who brought land and other assets into the APC. The amended law proposed by the united-German administration and passed by parliament specifically states that the claims of property-owners have priority over possible claims by workers who may have contributed their labor power to the growth of the APC but who never owned any assets that were transferred to the APC. This law is consistent with the general approach towards restructuring of the economy in eastern Germany. It is a top-down strategy (in contrast to the bottom-up strategy followed in Czechoslovakia) which gives priority to capital.[10] Accordingly, the office in charge of privatizing state companies (*Treuhand*) typically subsidizes investments rather than wages, which has resulted in very substantial job losses.[11]

By January 1992, the ten APCs in Schloßberg county made the following decision regarding their new organizational structure: seven formed cooperatives (*e.G.*), two are now limited partnerships (*GmbH*), and one decided to form a public corporation (*AG).* All ten APCs have had free and confidential elections to elect a new director. Workers in eight of the ten APCs re-elected their past chairman. Two factors account for the high proportion of management retention: (1) the previous chairmen were trusted, and their possible political engagements did not overshadow their technical expertise. On the contrary, some political activism of the chairman was viewed as something positive, for it may have increased the investments by the state in the APC and thus put it in a better competitive position today. In this sense, even those members of the APCs who were politically neutral or opposed to the previous regime benefitted from the political connections of their chairmen. (2) The previous regime tightly controlled access to education and vocational training. It discouraged the operation of family farms and thus did not provide any opportunity to the rank and file members of APCs to acquire the formal skills necessary to run a farm enterprise. Thus there were few personnel alternatives to the previous leadership of the APCs.

For the vast majority of agricultural land, the ownership question was solved quickly, and Schloßberg county was no exception. Farmers had never lost title to their land (they had only lost the land-use right), and East Germany kept very good records. Who owned what land was therefore clear as early as Spring 1990. The only uncertainty involved property left behind by refugees who went to West Germany, or other abandoned land.[12] By Spring 1991, the ten APCs in Schloßberg could lease all the land they wanted.

Perhaps the main point distinguishing APCs from state-owned agricultural or industrial enterprises is that APCs were permitted to form financial reserves. Agricultural collectives were the only economic organizations in East Germany allowed to retain financial reserves; state farms and other state enterprises had to transfer all net profits to the state at the end of each fiscal year. The reserves held by the APC were crucial for their survival after July 1990, when they were exchanged for West German currency at the very favorable rate of 2:1; the last market rate prior to the currency union on 1 July 1990 was five East German marks for one Deutsch mark. This hard currency--which ranged from about 100,000 to about 500,000 Deutsch marks per APC--enabled the APCs to make investments in machinery and seeds when commercial credits were not yet available because of the unclear property and fiscal situation immediately after the currency union.

For the past three planting seasons (1991-1993), the ten farms in Schloßberg have signed lease contracts covering about 70-90% of the land they previously cultivated. This shows that almost no landholder is willing (or able) to start a family farm.[13] The few exceptions are often special situations. The absence of plans for family farming in this county are, in part, related to the same factor as the reelection of the APC chairmen: during the previous regime, few people had the opportunity to acquire farming skills. Those who had private farms prior to collectivization are now too old to start over.[14] Younger farm workers, even those with land, are unwilling to commit all their assets to the family farm, given the current economic uncertainty and their inexperience with the market economy (or European Community rules). If their farm were to fail, they would lose everything they own, but if the cooperative fails, they would still have their land. Many others have long moved away from the land and hold only title to it; they have no interest in farming. While many of them would prefer to sell their land rather than leasing, there are still few takers. For some, the best hope is the establishment of an industrial park planned by many communities. Where such plans exist, agricultural land would be turned into commercial property.

Production and Employment

Given the current lease arrangement, the ten agricultural enterprises cultivate between 1,000 and 2,000 hectare (about 2,500-5,000 acres). As noted above, the success of these enterprises is based on dairy and meat production. The prices for both commodities declined drastically between 1989 and 1991, but they have since stabilized. The key factor for the continued economic viability of the farms is the milk quota assigned to them. Since 1990, that quota has been set at 70% of each farm's output in 1989. For most of the ten farms, that means a quota of around 900 liters per hectare per year. Thus, the new farms are facing the exact reversal of their previous problem: while the low quality of inputs made it very difficult for the collectives to fill the quota given to them prior to 1989, the new agricultural units now have to reduce their animal holdings because the superior inputs lead to overproduction. According to European Community (EC) laws, farms exceeding their milk quota are being penalized by losing part of the price support for their quota. However, since they already reduced their animal holdings from the 1989 level, any further reduction would put into question their ability to economically survive. Furthermore, the milk quota given to this region is less than 50% the quota given to farmers in northern Bavaria, a region with similar agricultural conditions.

Although the APCs initially expanded their payroll substantially in the aftermath of the combination of crop and animal collectives, total agricultural employment soon went down, for many agricultural workers chose retirement. This decision was facilitated by the fact that the government, in order to reduce the growth of unemployment, made it possible for workers in Eastern Germany to retire at age fifty-five with a pension set at 63-69% of their previous salaries. Given the relatively small differential between agricultural and industrial wages in the former East Germany, that incentive was sufficient to have induced many agricultural workers to chose early retirement. In this case, the age structure of agricultural employment also helped the farms, for a far greater proportion of agricultural workers than of industrial workers were either at retirement or pre-retirement ages. Thus, an analysis of the employment data for the 10 farms shows that they were able to substantially reduce their payroll without having had to fire many employees. Another factor contributing to the relative ease of payroll reduction has been the changing functional requirements of agricultural employment. During the previous regime, APCs had to keep a group of construction workers on their payroll to help maintain and rebuild the many old buildings, for such workers could not be obtained from anywhere else. The new opportunities to start up private businesses made it no longer necessary to keep these workers. On the other hand, most of these workers easily found other and usually better-paid employment, thus reducing the social and individual costs of dismissal.

A comparison of agricultural enterprises with industrial enterprises in Eastern Germany shows that the former have several advantages as they enter the new economic system. For one, as noted above, former agricultural collectives were entitled to build financial reserves;those with sizable reserves are likely to survive at least the first few years. Second, the fairly old age structure of employment in agriculture has been, in this case, an advantage over industries with a more youthful labor force, for it permitted quick and relatively painless reduction of the agricultural payroll. In addition, the new economic system made many non-agricultural positions in the former collectives superfluous; these persons could easily let go because their skills (brick layers, carpenters, plumbers, etc.) are in great demand, owing to the rebuilding of the infrastructure in Eastern Germany. Third, since the ownership of title to agricultural land was never in question, the legal basis for the continued operation of the agricultural enterprises was quickly resolved. In most cases, there are little economically viable alternatives to the continuation of these enterprises in the form of either cooperatives or limited partnerships.

The current size of the cooperatives/partnerships in Schloßberg county would make them competitive with many farmers in Western Germany. The main obstacle faced by the new agricultural enterprises of eastern Germany is the fact that agriculture—in any economic system, socialism or capitalism—is only a limited market activity. In fact, if the cooperative farms were able to produce at capacity, they might well show a higher productivity than many of the small family farms in the West. Herein lies one of their problems. The agricultural enterprises in eastern Germany, as agriculture throughout the Western world, are subject to government regulation of production quotas. While the former East German government set quotas that the collectives had to meet if not exceed, the EC sets quotas that cannot be exceeded without penalties.

The national governments in western Europe allocate the quotas given to each country within their jurisdiction. It appears that the current agricultural policies in Germany are aimed more at protecting West German family farmers than ensuring the competitiveness of East German agriculture. While these policies state that all forms of incorporation are open, the preference of the CDU is the family farm.[15] For example, if someone wanted to start up a family farm in Schloßberg county, s/he would be allocated a larger milk quota than that given to the former agricultural collectives. This presents the following paradox: for the industrial sector, the basic policy position is that any company that cannot produce competitively in comparison to western Germany should be closed and not subsidized, for a short and severe shock will lead to less pain in the long run than a slow and drawn-out reduction of production that is artificially continued through wage subsidies.[16] If that same approach were followed in the agricultural sector, the government would rather attempt to reduce the number of small farms in western Germany than attempt to break up the relatively competitive agricultural cooperatives in the east. This policy inconsistency reinforces the impression that many steps taken in conjunction with unification were at least as much for the benefit of western Germany as for eastern Germany. The public image that is cultivated, in contrast, paints a picture of steady transfers of funds from the west to the east.

Over the past two years, however, even the Christian Democratic legislators and officials in Schloßberg have recognized the value of the cooperative form of agricultural production.In fact, the county administrators in charge of agriculture now predict that the cooperatives in Schloßberg are more likely to succeed that the limited partnerships.

Social Change in the Community

Schloßberg, like most parts of eastern Germany, has changed more in the past four and one-half years than during the two preceding decades. The most visible change is the virtual makeover of the entire infrastructure, from new natural gas heating systems to new streets and telephone lines. Few streets remain that don't spot at least one house with a new roof or new windows, which are two of the first improvements to the housing stock. Tar paper was difficult to obtain in the GDR, and the new double and triple pane windows are becoming essential to keeping the rising energy costs in check. The facades of the houses show the improved quality of the paint: GDR paint typically did not bind and peeled off within months after application. The switch from high-sulfur coal to natural gas, in conjunction with the gradual disappearance of two-cycle cars like the *Trabbi*, has greatly improved the air quality in the town. This is especially noticeable during winter times when in the past one could literally taste the soot on one's tongue.

Many other physical changes are readily apparent. While it used to often take over one-half hour to wait in line for gas, there is now twenty-four hour service at a multi-pump gas station. Supermarkets and discount stores are replacing the individual retail stores, automatic teller machine dispense cash twenty-four hours a day, and computer, fax, and copying services are readily available. It was only ten years ago that, when I inquired about the possibility to make photocopies, I was told that the woman in charge of the copy machine had been sick for two months, and no one knew when she would return. It then took visits to three other towns to finally find carbon paper that saved me from having to type a legal document four times over.

While many business have closed down, others have expanded and some major new firms have located in the town. The most visible new factory is a brick-making company situated at the Schloßberg *Autobahn* exit employing about 250 workers. While there have not been many new industrial firms in Schloßberg, many new crafts (e.g. carpenter, plumber, electrician) businesses have been founded, especially with the start of 1991. During the period July 1990 to June 1991, for example, thirty-six new crafts businesses were registered, with seventeen closings. The growth of new businesses has been even more dynamic in the retail sector, with 109 new registrations (and fifty-three closings). Most of these business employ family labor or, at most, a couple of wage workers, but these business starts show that people are willing to start out on their own, in contrast to family farming, as discussed above.

The introduction of markets is challenging the business skills of those small proprietors (mostly craftspeople and small shop keepers) who were allowed to have their own firms in the GDR. They had a protected niche that allowed them to make a good and predictable living, for they were able to trade goods or services for others in short supply. The case of the only automotive tire retail and repair shop in Schloßberg during GDR times illustrates this point. This establishment had to carry only two different types of tires for passenger cars, it had short opening hours, and the proprietors carried no debt. Now, the business has to stock well over 100 different types of tires, it has to keep a close eye on promotional activities by discount stores and service stations, and its financial liability amounts to over one half million dollars to cover investment in new machinery and to carry the large inventory. It is too early to tell if this family business can survive, but the proprietors had little choice; their business would not have any chances for survival without these massive investments.

There is nary a sphere of community life that has not changed. While vital statistics data are not yet available for Schloßberg (owing to a change in the registration system), data for eastern Germany show a 40% decline in the birth rate and a 50% decline in the marriage rate from 1989 to 1991 (The Week in Germany 1993a). In Thuringia, the birth rate dropped from 11.6 per 1,000 population in 1989 to 5.7 in 1992 (The Week in Germany 1993b). There is little reason to believe that Schloßberg is an exception to this trend. In fact, one of the immediate changes that struck me in 1990 was the virtual absence of pregnant women in the town, compared to the 1970s and 1980s when families with baby carriages were a very common sight in the streets. Two factors contribute to this abrupt fall of the birth rate: (1) pro-natalist policies in the GDR resulted in much earlier family formation than was common in the West. The end of these policies after unification removed the incentive to marry and have children in the late teens and early twenties; (2) with so many uncertainties existing in peoples lives, they are postponing family formation. These factors also show, however, that the extremely low level of the current marriage and fertility rates is likely to go up once the pattern of life course transition becomes more similar to the western pattern and the labor market conditions improve. Results from my annual survey among high school students show that over 90% plan to have children, and that two children remain the modal category.

Another change affecting every young resident of Schloßberg is the restructuring of the school system. In GDR times, students had at least eight years of schooling.[17] Students desiring vocational training to become skilled craftworkers would go on to complete the tenth grade. University-bound students would complete twelve years of schooling in order to pass the *Abitur* (high school exit examination required for university studies). About 15-20% of my Schloßberg sample completed the eighth grade, 60-65% the tenth grade, and about 20% had the *Abitur*. Women are more likely than men to have completed the 10th grade and the exit exam. The key characteristic of the GDR school system was that all students would go to the same type of school through the eighth grade. Unification introduced the western German school system, in which parents have to decide after the fourth grade whether their children will go to the *Gymnasium* (university preparatory) or to a vocationally-oriented school. Those choosing the latter school type are split once more after the sixth grade into those graduating after the ninth grade and those staying through grade ten. These choices are not merely tracks but involve going to different schools. Not surprisingly, students in the vocationally-oriented schools come from families with lower socioeconomic status. Immediately after unification, a multi-million dollar renovation was begun in the *Gymnasium*, including state-of-the-art sports facilities. The vocationally-oriented schools, in contrast, received very little in assistance. Most of the instructional material and furniture has remained, and the physical plant continues to deteriorate. Many students in these schools are feeling left out of the new developments. Several indicators reflect the alienation of students and parents: teachers find it almost impossible to get parent participation in school matters; the response rate to my surveys is significantly lower than it is in the *Gymnasium*; and most of the respondents sympathizing with right-wing radicalism are students and parents from these schools. More (and visible) government support for these schools would likely be an effective counter-measure to the growing shift of students in these schools to the right fringe of the political spectrum.

The area of most concern for many people, of course, is employment: its security for those already employed and the availability of jobs for those entering the labor market. During my visit shortly after the currency union between East and West Germany on July 1, 1990, I noticed that the first West German federal agency to set up office in Schloßberg was the Employment Office.[18] I was also struck by the intensity of the discussion about unemployment. One thing people never had to worry about before was the availability of a job. Now, unemployment was the prevalent topic of discussions in the cafés and bars. People passed forms and instructions around and consulted with each other about what steps to take.

Although the currency union exposed the East German economy to the full competition of the West, unemployment in Schloßberg remained below 5% during the third quarter of 1990. However, it gradually rose, passing 10% in the first quarter of 1991 and reaching its highest rate of 17.5% in the first quarter of 1992 (Arbeitsamt Jena 1993). The unemployment rate has since stayed around 15%. These relatively low unemployment figures are the result of extensive labor market measures taken by the federal government to retrain workers and ease the transition to the market economy. Without those measures, the unemployment rate in Schloßberg would have been around 40%. The overall unemployment rate also masks substantial sex differentials. Shortly after unification, women had only a slightly higher likelihood to be unemployed than did men. However, many more women than men lost their jobs during 1991 and 1992. By the end of 1992,women made up two of every three unemployed workers, and this ratio remained unchanged March 1994 (the latest month for which unemployment figures are available) (Arbeitsamt Jena 1994). One problem women are encountering in the job market is that government employment agencies use different standards for men and women. Men available and looking for work are accepted as unemployed and thus eligible for unemployment compensation (depending on their work experience), regardless of family status. Employment agencies, however, do not consider mothers without jobs to be available for work unless they can show proof that they made arrangements for child care. This has created a Catch-22 situation for mothers. Without a job, many cannot afford day care, but they need day care to be eligible for help from the employment agency in finding a job. Unification for many women thus has brought a substantial loss of financial independence.

On balance, the residents of Schloßberg consider themselves to be better off after unification than before. Over 60% of the respondents in the panel study state that they prefer unification over a separate eastern Germany, with less than one fourth expressing preference for a separate eastern Germany. Over half of them said that they are better off than they were in 1989, compared to 15-20% saying they were worse off. Similarly, one half of the respondents stated that the situation in their part of Germany was better than it was in 1989, while less than one third viewed the situation to be worse. Fewer women than men said that they were better off, reflecting the greater economic loss on the part of women.

The trend data, however, show a growing discontent with the pace of development in eastern Germany. By January 1994, the percentage of respondents saying that their part of Germany was better off than in 1989 had fallen to 49% from 67% two years earlier. Similarly, preference for unification dropped from 78 to 63% among the respondents, and there also has been a moderate drop in the percentage of those saying that they are better off than they were in 1989. These survey results are very consistent with the views residents express to me about their situations in the new Germany. What comes through in these conversations is an intense mistrust of any policy originating in the western part of Germany.

The Political Economy of Eastern German Development

Viewing existing agricultural policies, the restructuring of education, as well as many other changes that have taken place, it is clear that the key to understanding the situation of eastern Germany is the recognition that unification is more properly viewed as a process in which East Germany joined West Germany. After all, it was only East Germany which ceased to exist.[19] As is always the case when someone joins an organization, s/he is subject to the by-laws of that organization. In that sense, the problem is not so much that Kohl was wrong when he stated that most people would do better in a united Germany. Economically most people indeed have improved their situation, with two major groups probably experiencing a decline in their standard of living: those graduating from school who are unable to find apprenticeship jobs, and persons aged forty to fifty becoming unemployed, for they are too old to find new employment and too young to qualify for early retirement.

The major problems for the true unification of the German population appear to exist more on the non-economic level. The gulf that exists between the two populations is less the result of the economic gap between East and West but more due to the way policies are implemented. All too often, East Germans are told in no uncertain terms that they have to catch up to the West through hard work, thus negating everything they worked for during the past forty-five years. At the heart of the gulf is the problem of eastern Germans to find a new identity. While many had difficulties answering the survey question, "which specific laws, institutions, or ways of life would you want to bring into the united Germany?" most persons clearly revealed an identification with East Germany as a nation, although not as a regime. The task for West Germans thus is to facilitate the new identification of the population in eastern Germany.

The transformation of East Germany is unique in Eastern Europe because by joining West Germany, it immediately benefitted from the West German welfare legislation and is receiving about $60 billion yearly in infrastructure funds. In 1992 alone, the net west-to-east transfer of public funds amounted to about $110 billion (The Economist 1992). This advantage, at the same time, also presents a special problem: the reference point for East Germans is no longer the standard of living that existed in East Germany, but Western Germany's standard of living. Thus, although my annual community survey shows that most respondents stated in both 1992 and 1993 that they were better off than in 1989, they still felt relative deprivation because they are not as well off as are western Germans. Since the East-West gap in the standard of living will likely persist for many years to come, so might be the relative discontent of eastern Germans.

The annual survey results in Schloßberg clearly indicate a growing disillusion with the new political and economic system. Questions aimed at tapping support for liberal democracy, for example, show a substantial skepticism about democracy and its ability to solve Germany's problems. About half of all respondents were not sure that democracy in Germany was the best political system, and twice as many people expressed preference for a different system than for the current one. Similarly, less than one third of the respondents believe that the democratic system can solve Germany's problems, and an increasing number of persons (36% in 1992 and 44% in 1994) said that democracy cannot solve the existing problems. While these statements are not yet reflected in strong electoral preferences for non-democratic parties, the Schloßberg survey results show growing support for the right-wing *Republikaner* party. In 1992, less than 2% of students expressed party preference for the Republicans. In 1994, 10% of all student respondents would vote for the Republicans in the general election; that percentage is 13.5 for students from the vocationally-oriented school.

The socio-political situation in Schloßberg--as in many parts of Eastern Germany--thus is one of ambiguity. Many people are able to develop private initiatives and are prospering. Those with jobs—especially in the state sector and in financial services—are doing very well. Not surprisingly, these developments have sharply increased the socioeconomic differences in the community.This stratification occurs along many dimensions:home ownership, employment, schooling, and gender. Women's unemployment, for example, is twice the level of that for males.[20] A critical milestone for the trajectory of the new system is coming up later this year when many of the labor-market measures taken by the government to ease unemployment will expire. If the economy by then does not create sufficient demand to absorb these retrained workers, the current discontent is likely to intensify. Four of the five eastern German states will have elections in 1994, and the national election is set for the fall of 1994. There is no doubt that the CDU will be turned out of office in most of the eastern German states (with the likely exception of Saxony).[21] What is unclear is whether former CDU supporters shift to the other centrist party--SPD--or to the political fringes. If the latter happens, it is far more likely that Germany's political spectrum shifts to the right than to the left, in contrast to other formerly communist countries where there is a resurgence of support for former communists.

Notes

Revision of a paper presented at the annual meetings of the Rural Sociological Society, State College, PA, August 1992. This research was supported by grants from the German Academic Exchange Service (DAAD) and the Humboldt Foundation. I also gratefully acknowledge financial support from the College of Arts and Sciences and the Agricultural Center, Louisiana State University.

1. On this new political map, Prague is again a more western city than Vienna.

2. The ignorance and/or unwillingness to deal with these problems is perhaps the major shortcoming of the geo-political design that guided U.S. policy from 1968 to 1989.

3. While many persons outside Germany have several reasons for the existence of two German nations, those reasons would not been persuasive for Germans themselves.

4. This mentality still remains with many people. I observed the following situation in Thuringia in July 1991. A family entered a restaurant and was not seated by the waitress (people typically choose their own table in German restaurants). After a while the man complained that they had not yet been assigned, where upon the waitress answered: "haven't you noticed that the system has changed?" Similarly, I usually had great difficulties explaining why I was in Eastern Germany to do research. People always wanted to know for whom I am doing the work, who pays for it, and who assigned me to this task. The notion that a person could design a research project by himself and try to find funding for it seemed very foreign to them.

5. This is a fictitious name to protect the identity of the respondents. Since the project will continue for another two years, including two more waves of the panel survey, revealing the real name of the county might influence the outcome of the project.

6. The literal translation of the German term *Landwirtschaftliche Produktionsgenossenschaft (LPG)* is Agricultural Production Cooperative (APC). However, these APCs have more the character of a collective than a cooperative as the latter term is understood in the United States or West Germany.

7. I am currently conducting a second survey of the agricultural enterprises to analyze the changes that have taken place since 1991.

8. The third wave in January 1994 for the first time surveyed an entire class of graduates from the vocational schooling track who left school in the summer of 1993 and are now working (as apprentices) or looking for work/apprenticeships.

9. This does not mean, however, that political activism was required in all cases. There were a number of university professors (although not at the highest levels and less in social sciences) who never belonged to the SED. Similarly, the degree of political activism required depended on the level of the position. The leadership of the agricultural collectives under consideration here did not have to be strong activists and not even party members. The important issue was whether they were trusted by the political leadership of the county.

10. A related law stipulates the principle that in cases of property claims, the return of property has priority over compensation. This principle continues to provide an obstacle to new investments, for investors will not provide new funds until the question of ownership for specific projects is cleared up.

11. Current estimates point to a reduction of employment by over 25%, with unemployment rates approaching 30% .

12. Since land had little value and could not be privately used, many persons who inherited land did not transfer the title to their names.

13. The decision against family farming is typical for all of eastern Germany (cf. Luyken 1991, Hamburger Abendblatt 1992).

14. It is also difficult to calculate the value of buildings and other property on the former APCs. Much of this property is technologically outdated, and many buildings need costly repairs. Thus, much of the "value" of the APCs depends on their continued operation; their breakup and distribution of property among the APC participants could well imply a distribution of negative net value.

15. When I asked several CDU politicians and administration officials in 1991 to comment on such an interpretation of the law, they responded that they would not disagree with that interpretation. (See also the statements by the German Minister of Agriculture in The Week in Germany, 22 November 1991.)

16. This position has most recently been criticized by a group of economists from the University of California at Berkeley who show that wage subsidies, tied to wage rises, would cost minimally more than the current approach, yet would prevent people from going through the pain of unemployment.

17. Students leaving after the eighth grade are not dropouts but received a complete curriculum.

18. It ironically occupied two floors in the former headquarters of the SED.

19. The official German term in many documents for the territory of former is Germany is *Beitrittsgebiet*, which translates as joining territory.

20. For an example of how women are paying a higher price for unification than men in eastern Germany, see Ferree and Young 1993.

21. Fewer than 14% of the Schloßberg respondents said in January 1994 that they would vote for the CDU in the general election.

References

Arbeitsamt Jena. 1993. *Jahresbericht 1993.*

____. 1994. *Der Arbeitsmarkt.* March 1994.

Economist. 1992. "A Survey of Germany." 23 May.

Ferree, Myra Marx, and Brigitte Young. 1993. "Three Steps Back for Women: German Unification, Gender, and University 'Reform'." *PS: Political Science and Politics* 26:199-205.

Hamburger Abendblatt. 1992. "Ostdeutsche Bauern scheuen die Selbständigkeit." 2 March.

Jarausch, Konrad H. 1993. *The Rush to German Unity.* New York: Oxford University Press.

Kinzer, Stephen. 1994. "A Climate for Demagogues." *Atlantic Monthly* 273 No. 2:21-34.

Knabe, Hubertus (ed.). 1989. *Aufbruch in eine andere DDR: Reformer und Oppositionelle zur Zukunft ihres Landes.* Reinbek: Rowohlt.

Kopstein, Jeffrey, and Karl-Otto Richter. 1992. "Communist Social Structure and Post-Communist Elections: Voting for Reunification in East Germany." *Studies in Comparative Communism* 25:363-380.

Luft, Christa. 1991. *Zwischen Wende und Ende.* Berlin: Aufbau Verlag.

Luyken, Rainer. 1991. "Was für Bauern braucht das Land?" *Die Zeit* 12 July.

Insel. 1990. *Der Vertrag zur deutschen Einheit.* Frankfurt: Insel Verlag.

Naumann, Michael (ed.). 1990. *Die Geschichte ist offen: DDR 1990—Hoffnung auf eine neue Republik.* Reinbek: Rowohlt.

Neues Forum Leipzig. 1990. *Jetzt oder Nie: Demokratie Leipziger Herbst '89.* München: C. Bertelsmann Verlag.

Pryor, Frederic L. 1992. *The Red and the Green: The Rise and Fall of Collectivized Agriculture in Marxist Regimes.* Princeton: Princeton University Press.

Reich, Jens. 1992. *Abschied von den Lebenslügen: Die Intelligenz und die Macht.* Berlin: Rowohlt.

Scheuch, Erwin K. 1991. *Wie Deutsch sind die Deutschen? Eine Nation wandelt ihr Gesicht.* Bergisch Gladbach: Gustav Lübbe Verlag.

Schüddekopf, Charles (ed.). 1990. *Wir sind das Volk! Flugschriften, Aufrufe und Texte einer deutschen Revolution.* Reinbek: Rowohlt.

Staatliche Zentralverwaltung für Statistik. 1990. *Statistisches Taschenbuch der Deutschen Demokratischen Republik 1989.* Berlin: Staatsverlag der DDR.

Stern. 1990. "DDR-Wahlen: Modrow und SPD vorn." Issue 10 (1 March):277.

The Week in Germany. 1991. "Minister: 10,00 Private Farms in Eastern Germany." 22 November.

____. 1993a. "1991 Statistics Show More Single Households, Fewer Births." 15 October.

____. 1993b. "Eastern Birthrate Drops Dramatically." 12 November.

6

A Polish Village in the Process of Transformation Towards a Market Economy

Andrzej Halasiewicz, Andrzej Kaleta, and Dennis Vnenchak

Introduction

Before analyzing selected social processes in rural Poland that began in 1989 with the destruction of real socialism in central and eastern Europe we must indicate that at the beginning of this historical change, Polish villages were in quite a different situation from elsewhere in the former Soviet bloc countries. Unlike in Russia, Lithuania, Hungary or East Germany, Polish villages were dominated by individual, private farms and these three million or so family farms produced a majority of food for the Polish market (see Smigielska, this volume). Attempts to collectivize Polish villages in 1956 had failed, and from that time the economic, social, and cultural conditions of the Polish village were dominated by a reasonably stable private sector.

Still, despite the fact that about 75% of all arable land belonged to family farms, all infrastructure belonged to the state. Until 1970, compulsory deliveries of agricultural products were in effect, which meant that each Polish farmer had to sell a given amount of grain, milk, or meat to state-owned trade companies for the price established by the state, and prices were usually set very low. After compulsory deliveries were abolished in 1970, Polish farmers certainly did not gain any privileged economic or social position in the state, but they functioned in a relatively stable environment allowing them to sell all their products. However, this relatively good situation changed with the January 1990 economic reforms, the so-called Balcerowicz plan. At that time prices were freed, internal exchange of devalued Polish currency begun, the market opened for Western goods and cuts in spending were introduced. Such cuts mainly diminished subsidies for unprofitable companies and social welfare, but also limited agricultural subsidies as well.

The social costs resulting from the 1990 economic transformation have been very high. In the first half of 1990, there was a 30% fall in production and 38% fall in real earnings (Kolodko 1991). All this was accompanied by an increase in unemployment (a phenomenon unknown in real socialism) and a decrease in spending on social welfare. Despite the improvement in the availability of a consumer goods (one of the main problems of the socialistic economy), an increase in the value of currency, and a decline in inflation, the living conditions of the majority of Polish families still eroded. It seems that the extent of the social costs of the transformation were not foreseen. Rather there was a naive hope that with the declaration of a free market, production and income would automatically increase.

Even though all social groups in Poland are paying the costs of the transformation from the centrally planned economy to the free market , it seems that Polish villages, which contain about one-third of the Polish population have been hit especially hard. In 1992, there were two million individual farmers owning 72% of all arable lands, about 1,500 state-owned farms with 19% of arable land, about 2,000 collective farms with 4% of the land. Altogether, these three separate production types cultivated about 18.5 million hectares of land. An additional 1% of the land was farmed by about 1.7 million people, on plots smaller than one hectare. Finally, the remaining 4% of the land is controlled by the State Land Fund and awaits someone to work it. Such a large number of farmers working relatively small areas of arable land means that the average size of an individual farm is less than six hectares and the average employment in individual farming is twenty-five people per 100 hectares while in collective farms it is thirteen per hundred hectares and on state farms eight. Overall, the number of people employed in agriculture is estimated at about 4.5 million or about 27% of all active labor force in Poland. These numbers suggest the scale of the problem classified as the "crisis of village and farming" as well as the extent of the economic and social transformations necessary for the "restructuring of village and farming." Before outlining the strategy we feel necessary for rural Poland, we will suggest various dimensions of this crisis.

Socio-Economic Dimensions of the Polish Village Crisis

Despite the fact that Polish farmers had some previous experience in a market economy (during "real socialism" they were able to independently make decisions about production and sales), of all Polish social or occupational groups they felt the impact of the transition to a market economy most intensively. This results from a number of interrelated factors. First, starting in 1990 the internal demand for food products went sharply down caused by an abrupt fall in real wages and a decline in state spending on social welfare. In addition, in the initial stages in the transformation of the political system the restructuring of prices took place. As a result of doing away with government subsidies, the prices of many industrial goods became relatively lower while prices of food became relatively higher. It is estimated that because of this, the amount of food purchases went down by nearly 20% (Balcerowicz 1993). The decline of demand in the internal market was followed by the collapse of markets in all the former socialist states (especially the former Soviet Union) and by opening the Polish market to cheap food products from Western Europe.

The second major cause of the current economic problem in Polish farming has been very high interest on loans. Multiple increases in interest rates on loans (up to 70 to 80% per year) hit various parts of the Polish food industry very hard. Food processing plants, which in 1990 had no revenues, had to take expensive credits that placed them on the verge of bankruptcy. Thus many of them were forced to limit their purchase of farm products, which in turn, worsened the situation of farmers (Szot 1993).

Along with the declining demand for food products, the new phenomenon of massive unemployment has also had negative effects on village life. The first group to be let go by factories in trouble were the so-called farmer-workers, owners of small farms who in addition held jobs in industry. Many inhabitants of rural areas also had to quit their jobs in towns because of their employers' bankruptcy or the high cost of transportation, which in the socialist economy was heavily subsidized by employers. The numbers of unemployed in some villages neared 40% of the work force. Furthermore these ranks are fed by graduates of various types of schools who have fewer chances for employment than their contemporaries in towns.

The problematic market for farm products along with unemployment are the external factors influencing the situation of villages and farmers. However, there is also a range of problematic factors within farming itself. We have already mentioned the fragmented agrarian structure and the relatively low productivity of Polish agriculture relative to the high percentage of workers per hectare. Without government subsidies, such conditions prevent intensive farming. It is also difficult to compete with the very productive and heavily subsidized Western farm industry. Thus this mixture of unfavorable external and internal factors has led to a dramatic decline in living standards for the majority of rural families. Their situation is bad because they lack money, but also is made worse because they lack the skills necessary to function in the new social-economic realities that have replaced the ineffective but benevolent centrally planned economy.

The Socio-Cultural Dimension of the Polish Village Crisis

The deep socio-economic crisis that hit Polish villages in early 1990 was followed by an equally deep socio-cultural and ecological crisis. It is manifested by: (1) demographic change, including de-population of peripheral areas, especially in the eastern part of the country; (2) a weakening of local economies and the liquidation of communal infrastructure, followed by a decline in local employment, income, and standards of living; (3) elimination of traditional family farming along with its socio-economic, cultural, and natural environment functions; (4) progressive devastation of the natural environment (contamination of soil, air, water, impoverishment of fauna and flora); (5) an obliteration of the specific characteristics of regional cultures and the physical destruction of the landscape and village architecture; and (6) a widening of social pathologies like crime, alcoholism, drug addiction.

The cause of these distressing phenomena lies in the largely inappropriate development strategy of Polish village and agriculture, elaborated throughout the nearly fifty years of socialism. This strategy was directed toward so-called socialist industrialization and the urbanization of rural areas. We must add that this policy in almost unchanged form is still being carried out by the consecutive governments chosen in democratic Poland after 1989. It was based on North American and West European development strategies based on so-called modernization. This doctrine manifests itself in mechanical implantation of solutions from industry to the problems of agriculture and socio-cultural solutions of the city to the problems of village. Accordingly, villages were treated as something that were not quite towns but, with progress and the equalization of life opportunities, should become them.

The politics of socialist industrialization and village urbanization also led to deep changes in the consciousness of rural inhabitants that provoked: (1) a departure from the pre-1945 predominant agrocentric value system which focussed on land, work, and local community, in favor of the acquisition of urban values; (2) the dissolution of traditional social bonds based on personal prestige and respect for family and community values towards those of a public nature, with their roots in occupational roles; (3) the elimination of traditional folk culture from the lives and consciousness of village inhabitants and replacing it with mass culture; (4) a weakening of the abilities of rural inhabitants to define their own separate life styles, articulate their own value systems, and influence decisions concerning their living environment.

Local Dimensions of the Crisis: The Example of Lucim

In the two previous sections, the global dimensions of the Polish village and farming crisis were outlined and we analyzed their aspects from a general perspective of all rural areas. These areas, however, consist of thousands of villages inhabited by millions of people who, with increasing uncertainty if not fear, look towards the future. To focus our analysis in a more local perspective, we will use data collected in the village of Lucim located in Koronowo district, on the border of historic Kujawy region (about twenty-three kilometers northeast of Bydgoszcz). In this village for the last several years, with money provided by Polish Committee of Scientific Research and European Commissions, the Sociology Department of Nicolaus Copernicus University in Torun has been conducting research on the complex revitalization of rural areas. Lucim is a small village of 1,454 hectares and about 600 inhabitants. The first mention of the village dates to 1323. However, it was not until 1359 that Lucim received its tenement privileges. From 1772 to 1920 the village was under Prussian control. From September 1939 until liberation by the Soviet Army in 1945, Lucim belonged to the Third Reich. Thus, nearly 180 years of Germanization almost entirely wiped out the local cultural tradition.

Despite the above, the village managed to preserve many features of its medieval spatial organization. Now it is divided by the national road that links Bydgoszcz with Koszalin. Its bigger and older part lies to the west of the road; while the eastern part of the village was developed after the creation of the road. Architecturally, the village is dominated by modern, "block"-type construction that have nothing to do with traditional local architecture and are glaringly out of place in the local landscape. The rest of the local lands consist of small farm fields, pastures, a cemetery, orchards and small gardens that are usually surrounded by traditional fences. The central part of the village is occupied by an old, devastated manor with adjoining arable lands and a row of 19th century buildings which, since the end of World War Two, were occupied by workers of the local state farm. The view of the manor is spoiled by a four story apartment building erected in 1970 by this farm. Except for one school with classes through the fourth grade, a diary products collection center, and several small shops, the village has no communal infrastructure. A few historic buildings (an old pub, historic cottages and larch manor) require restoration.

The village's environment and landscape are its most promising resources to potentially attract both wealth and tourists. Compared to similar areas in western Europe, the Lucim area is still relatively undeveloped and in a natural state. The wealth of the natural environment allows for the presence of various species of plants and animals which are disappearing in other parts of Europe. Sustaining this variety and reconciling growing land use needs with those of natural environment and landscape protection is not easy. Lucim's splendid natural environment is threatened by various factors. For example, lack of a sewage system and a sewage treatment plant have already caused contamination of a pond in the center of the village. Contaminated liquids from an unauthorized landfill have penetrated the soil and caused, in turn, contamination of water. In another part of the village, sand excavation has caused a degradation of a glacier hill which, in this region, constitutes one of the most important historical environmental features. Protection is also required for the water table and for the numerous area lakes and ponds. It is needed not only because they are an important part of the landscape but also because they constitute a living environment for many species of fauna and flora. Though, in the near future the biggest threat will come from drought and lowering the level of ground waters, human activities are also a factor. Thus, because of the digging of a new drainage ditch two major water reservoirs were depleted. Their existence is also threatened by the burning of canes and bulrushes and the location of summer cottages which cause degradation of their banks.

The biggest threat to the natural environment in Lucim seems to be the ever increasing use of machinery and chemicals in farming which leads to impoverishment of the environment and its natural ecosystems. If this process is not replaced by the introduction of natural farming, the effective protection of what is still left should be undertaken. It should begin with connecting natural living environments by special "corridors". It is especially important to connect water reservoirs in this manner and protect fields against erosion by the use of hedges.

Lucim is inhabited by about 600 people in about 150 families. The majority of the population are under forty. Though young, however, their economic potentials are limited by their generally low level of education. People between the ages of twenty to thirty-five (the group that under "real socialism" had the best opportunities for education) have mostly elementary technical training (over 60%), and only a few have secondary technical education (12%). High school diplomas are held by 2%, and university diplomas by 6%. It is not necessary to add that such an educational structure weakens the local population's ability to compete on the job market and constitutes one of the biggest causes of local unemployment. When it comes to social-occupational structure, farmers (65%) and workers (about 25%) predominate. Office workers constitute a very small group, and a local intelligencia is almost non-existent (1.4%).

The main source of income in Lucim has always been work in the approximately 100 individual farms and in the small state farm. A small number of people had been commuting to work in the nearby towns of Koronowo or Bydgoszcz. As mentioned earlier, the collapse in the demand for farm products (limiting job opportunities in rural areas) and recession (followed by layoffs in industry) led to dramatic declines in the living conditions of Lucim families. In 1990 an average Polish salary was 1,029,637 zl (or about $108 USD) and 1,436,807 zl (or about $151 USD) in the fourth quarter of the same year. However, only every tenth family in Lucim made over one million per month. In other words, the financial situation of only one in ten Lucim families could be classified as decent and only a very few as good. The rest have been in quite a difficult situation. In 30% of local households the income was below 500,000 zl. The worst financial situation has been shared by the unemployed which now number 30% of the potentially active work force population.

The problem of unemployment, especially the unemployment of youth, is undoubtedly the most important social issue in Lucim. It began in the early 1990s as a result of the privatization of the state farm and the layoff of farmer-workers from industry in the surrounding towns of Koronowo and Bydgoszcz. Research conducted in Lucim in September 1991 showed that there were no farmers among the unemployed (Borowicz 1993). For a majority of the unemployed, who are mainly young people, loss of work is associated with a narrowing of their perspectives. Their chances for employment are much lower than those of people in cities. This is a result of their low level of education and lack of qualifications as well as the specificity and scarcity of work places in the rural areas in general.

Along with the above economic changes the transformation of the political system that began intensively in 1990 had a variety of other effects. For one, it weakened the significance of traditional factors of social stratification. Thus criteria such as age, education, profession, place of employment lost their meaning as indicators of social differentiation in rural communities. Generational differences also lost their significance for the differentiation of value systems, though one could detect this process as early as the late 1970s and early 1980s). Thus, today, the value systems of both people under thirty-five and those over fifty seem to be quite similar. They are oriented towards what we call a "small-scale stabilization." That is, they see their main source of social support and interest as located in small, localized groups like family and friends. In contrast, they have very tenuous connections with both values and relationships that are played out in such macro structures as county, region, and nation.

It is as difficult today as it was during real socialism to consider education and occupation as factors differentiating Lucim citizens. One of the reasons for this is the lack of correspondence in Poland between the criteria which constitute high social status (e.g. education and professional qualifications) and the extent of income. People with the best education and professional training, who held or hold high positions in a social hierarchy have little ability to determine and shape the lives of others had, apart from their moral influence. What is even worse, the income of socially prominent individuals like teachers and doctors is lower than those with less education and professional training. In other words, education and professional qualifications have value to only a small number of Lucim citizens and most members of the community interviewed saw their real significance only as a potential aid to achieve other, more desirable values.

There is no doubt that a factor strongly differentiating individuals and actively creating interest groups in the post-socialist community is financial status. Growing financial differences have clearly divided the groups of people we analyzed into a relatively small sub-group of ten to fifteen families who are well-to-do and differentiated them extensively from the rest of the village population some of whom, as in the case of the unemployed, quite often have difficulty in fulfilling their basic food needs. Thus, we can observe the creation of two distinct social groups with separate political and economic interests in a process which can only minimally be traced back to divisions present in real socialism.

Despite the above, more generally it can be noted that the first four years of transformation have actually resulted in decreased inequality in Lucim, though this fact is not accepted by the majority of Lucim inhabitants, especially those who consider themselves economically worse off. They manifest their disapproval of current conditions first by their large scale refusal to participate in elections. Thus, almost 60% of them did not participate in local elections in June 1994, while those that did vote did so for political forces that promised to level differences between the poor and rich. It was thus communities like Lucim that were responsible for the great electoral successes of leftist parties in the recent parliamentary elections. This, however, does not mean the acceptance of the old communist maxim "from each according to their ability, to each according to their need," but rather attachment to a just maxim that people deserve access to resources "depending on their achievements." Lucim citizens do not condemn becoming richer through honest, well organized, and socially useful work, but they do not accept fortunes that developed by extra-legal means.

Most citizens of Lucim closely identify with the village as they were born there (about 50%) or because they are employed in Lucim or its vicinity (another 20%). Over half of the population also identifies with the natural environment and local landscape. They claim that in Lucim, which they term their "little motherland," they feel at home. Only every fifth citizen of Lucim declares that he or she could as well live somewhere else. The majority despite the actual reality, consider their living environment as well-organized and having little effect on the natural environment or the local landscape. Only every fifth person has a more critical view on this matter, pointing to the advanced devastation of landscape and environment. Asked how they see their role in the revitalization of the environment, 60% see no or limited possibilities for themselves, 70% cannot even say what actions should be undertaken, and only 5% sees the necessity of acting (e.g. building sewage treatment plant). A majority (80%), however, declares their readiness to act towards improvement of the living environment. All of this leads to the conclusion that in Lucim there is a rather favorable climate for actions towards protection and improvement of living environment. However, without local leaders to motivate them, this potential may go untapped. It seems that Lucim citizens are at the first stage of an ecological awakening. More and more of them are beginning to realize that this process is essential; that without the ability to prevent imbalances in the natural environment, there will be no improvement in the conditions and quality of their existence, no matter what happens to the local economy.

It is certain that the local ecological awakening will be aided by religion. In fact for the majority of Lucim citizens (about 90%), the Catholic religion plays a central role in shaping their outlook on life. It is the single most important context for handing down cultural traditions and, to a lesser extent, for shaping the key values and convictions of villagers, which they define as a happy family life, good living conditions and peace and quiet and which they see as necessary for stability. Achieving such conditions also constitutes the main direction of the proposed changes in the life situation of Lucim citizens. Thus people would like to better their financial situation by building a new house, buying a car, more fashionable clothing, etc. But these purchases they see as the means to the ends of improving their frame of mind and increasing their prestige in the community. Farmers also desire the modernization of their farms, especially by acquiring new machines. Unfortunately, very few of them associate increases in the standard and quality of life with a more active search for a job, for additional sources of income, or entrepreneurial opportunities. Instead they count, as in the past, on the state for assistance.

Earlier in this paper we described the life ambitions of Lucim citizens as oriented to a "small-scale stabilization," that is where the social institution of family and all family-related values have a special place. Significantly, even though there is great variation in the occupational characteristics of households (as discussed about 65% of Lucim's 150 households are agriculturally-based and about 35%, are households of industrial and service workers) there is little if any difference in the idealized model of the household no matter whether we deal with agricultural or wage-earner households. On average, household size consists of four people though at an average size of 4.4 people farm households are slightly bigger than those of wage-earners. As it is in the whole of Poland, nuclear families are the norm here. Only about 15% of households are extended family households consisting of grandparents and other relatives.

In Lucim households, despite the changes of the transition, one can still observe certain universal ideals closely related to the emotional-expressive, educational, and economic functions of the family. Lucim citizens quite uniformly accept a family model based on strong emotional ties expressed by having children and resonating to common existential goals. Marital love is not considered the strongest feature of family life; more important are those factors that help in sustaining harmony, unity, and efficiency of a family. Children are highly valued and parents often sacrifice their own well-being to promote their children's start into adult life.

Other important features of the model family are good living conditions, an income allowing for an increase in consumption, and good health of family members. Much lower attention is paid to the role and social position of the family within the village community, a phenomenon that can be interpreted as acceptance of the present political economic situation.

The exceptionally important position of the family among the range of processes and phenomena influencing local consciousness in rural Poland is only partly a result of tradition. Far more important is the rapid urbanization of these areas after World War Two. In the traditional rural community (i.e. before 1939) the focus on family was only one of a number of orientations and the universal goals; only rarely seen as an ultimate goal of existence. Family was considered to be a social group, stable and built on tradition, internal organization, where relationships did not depend on feelings and emotions but roles played by its members. It was an institution concentrating all its efforts, on one hand, on fulfilling its members' needs required for physical survival, and on the other hand, on defending basic elements of the entire rural community value system, the system based on the main principle defined as holy, incomprehensible by humans, life- bringing mother-earth (Chalasiéski 1938).

For contemporary citizens of Lucim, family as a social value is much more emotionally charged; it is not any more an institution concentrating its efforts on values important for rural community but rather a tool for fulfillment of own individual goals, needs, and desires. These individualized goals force them to treat family as a haven, a place where one can escape from crises of everyday life such as unemployment, financial problems, lack of social security and optimism for the future. Family is also treated as a place where children are being risen. Children are one of the most important value categories realized in a family life of every Pole.'

Closing our discussion of the local dimensions of the Polish village and farming crisis, let us consider for a moment issues of culture. If we assume that the cultural activity of a person is, on one hand, an important ingredient in their ability to contribute to society, and on the other hand, determines the participation of an individual in an increasingly global cultural community, then Lucim citizens' participation in this process is limited indeed. They mostly passively experience mass culture (TV, papers, radio) which has very little to do with a whole world of experiences for those who are physically removed from it (inhabitants of rural areas). Furthermore, cultural activity today is rarely associated with participation in various activities outside of one's own community (e.g. trips to theaters, exhibitions, amateur cultural activities or selected aspects of folk culture). In recent years such phenomena disappeared from the cultural scene of Lucim as well as other Polish villages and towns.

Possibilities of Rural Development in Poland: An Ecological Perspective

As we have suggested, to resolve the multi-dimensional crisis of the rural areas in Poland requires a new philosophy for their development. It should more widely include cultural values and also take into consideration the preservation of the natural environment (Wieruszewska 1992). The understanding and participation of citizens in these areas are needed if they are to recover the natural ties between themselves and their world. Having this in mind, for the last several years in Torun, work dealing with the search for a paradigm of development of the rural areas has taken place. In those investigations we seek to harmoniously combine the economic rationality and new technological possibilities with the protection of the cultural and natural heritage of villages. This especially means that we must support individual family farming as the foundation of most rural economies. This is needed not only to enable the production of quality products, but also to help sustain the way of life, the rural economy, and the cultural landscape of all such areas. For these reasons, we are opposed to processes which would wholly withdraw farming from marginal areas, or which would excessively concentrate food production on the richest or more accessible farmlands.

This paradigm also seeks to identify possibilities for diversifying farm incomes (Slee 1989). Farmers, and particularly those on small farms who may not be able to make a living from farming alone, should be encouraged and enabled to diversify their income through other activities on or off the farm. This may be in non-food crops such as forestry or woodland management or part-time work of many kinds within the wider local economy. In Lucim, for example, we can imagine farm-based tourism (especially so-called soft tourism) which is seen by many European governments, local authorities, and others as a growth sector in national and local economies. These bodies increasingly look to rural areas as a new tourist destination, and perceive that tourism can bring new economic life and new opportunities into these regions. Tourism is already bringing significant new income into rural areas, creating jobs and encouraging value-added enterprises. It is also prompting action to protect and enhance the heritage of landscape, history, and culture which is a major part of the tourist attraction.

For the harmonious economic, cultural, and ecological development of rural areas, especially in Poland, we also need a modern infrastructure of roads, railways, energy and water supplies. New or modernized facilities of these kinds are needed, and should meet acceptable modern standards while not doing damage to the rural environment. Perhaps the most significant aspect of infrastructure required is that of modern telecommunications, which can assist the revival and strengthening of rural economies and services. They encourage decentralized economic activity and offset the rural handicaps of distance and sparse population. So-called Local Tele-information Centers (Tele-cottages) permit small and medium-sized enterprises in rural areas to gain access to markets, suppliers, and collaborators at any distance and to increase their work efficiency. They help in service provision (through telephonic shopping, electronic libraries, fax-based inquiries). They bring training and education to people where they live.

In our investigations for a new paradigm of development of the rural areas we should also not forget the practice of traditional customs and cultures, which are a major factor in the well-being of rural communities and have high importance to the people, and which also contribute to the cultural richness of Europe. It may be reflected also in the confidence with which rural communities have to tackle their own problems and cooperate with each other in their social organization and adapt their collective systems to modern needs. This vitality may depend, however, upon the stability of the population, with balance between age groups, and a strong kinship structure. In many Polish rural areas, the decline of population and the rapid expansion of mass culture have weakened this vitality, and have led rural people to underestimate their own abilities and to undervalue their traditional resources and culture. In this situation we must seek to stimulate the understanding and involvement of rural people, through animation of local development, appropriate educational system, and training.

We realize that outlining a pro-ecological program for transformation of rural areas in Poland is only a start for series of actions needed to limit the crisis, which economic, social-cultural and local dimensions were described in previous sections of this paper. Steps that follow are connected with persuading inhabitants of rural areas to accept outlined by us ideas and to actively join in their realization.

Lucim's first experiences in implementing the program are quite optimistic. Difficulties of everyday life, fear for the future, visible threats to natural environment are the best arguments supporting the thesis that shaping the future cannot be done by the method of trail and error, without using existing knowledge. Simultaneously, especially in the young generation, the need for experimentation is particularly felt. Since modernization means liquidation of 80% of local family farms, leaving only 20% of the biggest ones, which after enlargement would be able to achieve productivity comparable with this of West European and North American farms, searching for new ways for development seems to be an alternative. For many of Lucim citizens successful implementation of this doctrine means not only loss of employment but also of their "little motherland" where they were born and raised and with which they associate their future. Another consequence of adopting the dogma of modernization is continuing deterioration of the natural environment. Modernization means increased use of artificial pesticides and fertilizers, which will cause further deterioration of natural environment, increase of farming costs, and weaken health of many people. Other negative results should be noted here as well; those are worsening of social-cultural environment by its urbanization, thus destruction of peasant ethos which, in turn, can cause weakening, not only local but also, national identity.

All this leads to the situation that every reasonable proposal of reversing negative trends meets with interest of the majority of rural areas' inhabitants no matter what their financial status or social position. Similar attitudes were also observed in Lucim, where in 1991 we began work on the comprehensive program of its revitalization. Our project thus aims to develop and empirically test a system that uses modern telematic equipment in the process of introducing so-called soft tourism to rural areas. The spread of this style of vacationing will enable recreation in the open, provide conditions which maximize the advantages of leisure and reduce the disadvantages of mass-tourism. At the same time it will ensure the improvement of the economic situation of the inhabitants of rural areas (additional profits, for example from taking in lodgers, producing, processing and selling ecological foodstuffs) and render a service to holiday-makers.

It will also ensure improvement in the natural village environment (by eliminating conventional methods of intensive agriculture); make the protection of traditional landscapes more effective and lead to a restoration of traditional village architecture (such as old residential and communal buildings) there by providing guest accommodations of high cultural standard. A key element of the proposed system will be the Local Tele-Information Center (Telecottage), situated within the rural area being developed as a potential recreational center and as a place of information dissemination for potential visitors. We are planning to equip each telecottage with satellite communication, telefax and electronic mail systems connecting it with all potential tourist facilities and making it possible, if necessary, for tourist suppliers and consumers to directly contact the telecottage and through it, the outside world.'

References

Balcerowicz, L. 1993. "Wies, rolnictwo, rynek" (Village,Agriculture,Market), *Gazeta Wyborcza* 17-18.04.1993.

____ 1994. Laboratorium historii, (The Laboratory of History) in: *WPROST*, Nr 21, pp. 66-67.

Chalasiénski, J. 1938. *Mlode pokolenie chlopow.* (The Young Generation of Peasants).

Kolodko, G. 1991. *Transition from Socialism and Stabilisation Policies: The Polish Experience*, Seminar Paper, International Monetary Fund.

O'Cinneide, M. and Cuddy, M. 1992. *Perspectives on Rural Development in Advanced Economics* (Center for Development in Studies Social Sciences Research Center University College Galwey).

Slee, B. 1989 . *Alternative Farm Enterprises: A Guide to Alternative Sources of Income for the Farmer.* Farming Press

Szot, E. 1993. "Kredyty - najwazniejsze narzedzie polityki rolnej," (Credits - the Main Tool of Agricultural Policy) . *Rzeczpospolita - Ekonomia i rynek*, 19.02.1993.

Vonderach, G. ed. 1990. *Beitrage aus der neueren europaischen Landsoziologie.* Bamberg: Wissenchaftliche Verlagsesellschaft.

Wieruszewska, M. ed. 1992. *Renewal of the Rural Areas - Between Myth and Hope.* Warsaw: Institute of Agricultural and Village Development of the Polish Academy of Sciences.

PART TWO

Society Up For Grabs

7

Ferenc Erdei and Antal Vermes: The Struggle for Balance in Rural Hungary

Chris Hann

Erdei Ferenc derek ember, / Megdicserjuk szemtol szembe! /
Magunk kozul ot valasszuk, / Szavat mind megfogadjuk!
Eljen, eljen a Nemzet!

Ferenc Erdei is a decent man, /Let's praise him very openly! /
He is the one we choose among ourselves, / we accept his every word! /
Long live the Nation!

This jingle was recalled in 1993 in the village of Tázlár in south central Hungary by a man who had committed it to memory some forty years earlier, in the darkest years of Stalinism. Ferenc Erdei (1910-1971) had been *the* candidate in the parliamentary constituency of which this village formed a small part. This particular villager, known to me since the mid-1970s, had been the leading force behind the re-establishment of the Smallholders Party in this area at the end of the 1980s.[1] I was left in little doubt that, in his eyes, Erdei represented the despised *ancien regime.*

Antal Vermes is another good friend in the village of the same age. He vouchsafed some quite different information about Erdei. Antal too is, and always has been, emphatically anti-communist. However he holds a degree from what was once known as the Karl Marx University of Economics and has vivid and positive memories of Ferenc Erdei addressing packed lecture theaters in Budapest in the 1960s. The performances of the small, swarthy man with the booming voice were always electrifying. Even more striking was the message of those lectures. In the years immediately following the accomplishment of mass collectivization Erdei, who as the Minister of Agriculture had been responsible for launching Hungary's first collectivization drive in 1949, and who had played a major part in formulating the latest laws governing the operation of the Hungarian equivalent of the *kolkhoz*, now dared to warn his audiences of the dangers inherent in the Soviet model. Specifically, he highlighted the incompatibility of collective farms and vineyards ('*a szolo nem birja a kolkhozt*' --literally 'the grape can't endure the collective farm'), and this was a point of more than academic interest for a young student from an area in which small-scale wine production played a major part in the local economy.

I find Erdei's life and work of considerable interest in attempting to assess recent changes and prospects in the Hungarian countryside. The vicissitudes of his personal career and his posthumous reputation seem to exemplify much that is central to the history of Hungary in the twentieth century. I have no space in this chapter to do full justice to the subject at either level and in any case others are far better qualified to tackle this task.[2] My modest objective is to present in each of the following sections some brief details of Erdei's biography alongside some fragments of life history from the village of Tázlár. I try to show how the ambiguities and ambivalences of Erdei's life can be related to the ideologies and real struggles of millions of people in rural Hungary, some of whom began to experience more 'balance' in their lives in the reformist phase of socialism and have reason to fear new forms of imbalance in the 1990s.

The Pre-Socialist Era

Ferenc Erdei produced the classic accounts of social structure in pre-socialist Hungary.[3] Given his personal background (he was the son of a poor onion-grower who lived near the small market town of Mako in the southern zone of the Great Plain) it is not surprising that he paid particular attention to the position of the peasantry. He became part of a movement of intellectuals which raised public consciousness of social problems in the countryside in the years during and after the Great Depression. But Erdei differed from most of his 'populist' *(nepi)* colleagues not only in his social origins but in the rigor and clarity of his sociological analyses. He recognized that Hungary's development had been distorted, that 'embourgeoisement' (*polgarosodas*) had been frustrated by a social structure which had retained many feudal and even caste-like characteristics. Development sociologists and anthropologists in later periods would refer to such phenomena in terms of dual economies, or the 'articulation' of different modes of production; but the essential insights of such models as later applied to the so-called Third World were clearly prefigured in Erdei's analysis of pre-socialist Hungarian society. Some of Erdei's most important intellectual influences were Marxist, in a period when such literature was not easily available in Hungary and the Communist Party was a banned organization (Erdei 1972: 2) . But, as far as rural social structure is concerned, the picture painted by Erdei is by no means a simple imitation of Lenin's *The Development of Capitalism in Russia.* On the contrary the succession of monographs which culminated in *Hungarian Peasant Society* demonstrates a rich appreciation of distinctively Hungarian conditions.[4]

Erdei's critique was most effective when he discussed those areas of the Great Plain which he knew intimately from childhood and from the regular field trips he made during and after his student days. One such area is the *puszta* zone of sandy soils between the rivers Danube and Tisza where Tázlár is located. Erdei explored this zone in the 1930s and *Running Sands* (1937) was perhaps his first publication of significance, showing his gift for sharp observation and sensitivity to the language as well as his embryonic talents as a theoretician.[5] He found the settlement of Pronayfalva to be "without any nucleus of a village."[6] Its *tanya* dwellers had no historic links to the market towns closest to them. Rather they were products of the pressures which forced many thousands of peasants to leave their homes in the late nineteenth and early twentieth centuries in search of better living conditions on the previously uninhabited sandy soils of the interfluve.[7] Many of the migrants who moved here hailed from Erdei's own home territory of Mako and Szeged. The size of the parcels they were able to buy as capitalist real estate far exceeded the dimensions of what they owned or could expect to inherit from their patrimony in an area of rapidly increasing population. They therefore built their new houses on the *puszta* and the lucky ones, those who bought up pockets of high quality soil, were able to prosper. Others were less successful and found the challenge of adapting to the very different ecological conditions altogether too much for them. The outcome was a settlement which, though hardly a microcosm of the national society, was a very direct product of tendencies at work in the wider society; and in terms of its social structure most of the groups identified by Erdei in his analysis of the national structure can be found here, from Count Ferenc Vigyazo, owner of thousands of hectares of sand and forest which he never so much as visited, to the landless who survived as farm servants or through day laboring on the farms of the wealthy.

Most residents were nowhere near either of these two extremes. They were family farmers with an acreage which on the face of it compared rather favorably with national figures. However this can be attributed to the adverse ecological conditions, since with yields far below those of more fertile regions families here needed comparatively large holdings merely to subsist. Particularly during the Depression years many families sunk deeper into poverty--the poverty that was witnessed by the young Ferenc Erdei. But the families of Antal Vermes and his wife were typical of the large middle peasantry which took shape during this period and, by dint of very hard graft, and without making significant progress towards embourgeoisement, did at least manage to avoid the slide towards the rural proletariat. Antal does not know exactly when his grandfather came to Tázlár, but he thinks it was from Szeged around the turn of the century. He was a Calvinist. According to family tradition they originated in Transylvania. Antal's father was definitely born in Tázlár on the small *tanya* established by the first generation, and according to another family tradition he had some kind of run-in with the communists when fighting flared up at a nearby railway station during the revolution of 1919. The Vermes family's strong anti-communist sentiments may date back to this time. Antal's wife Julia comes from a Catholic middle peasant family established in Tázlár at about the same period, and they are related through their mothers, both descendants of one of the first settler families to arrive here from Szeged in the 1870s.

From Socialist Cataclysm to Reform and Prosperity

For the last twenty-five years of his life Ferenc Erdei was a Very Important Person. The published work from this period is perhaps of less note, but as a politician, university administrator and Secretary of the Hungarian Academy of Sciences he was a household name for anyone growing up in Hungary in the early socialist decades. This is not to say that he was a popular figure. His first major post, as a leader of the National Peasant Party, was to serve as Interior Minister in the first government to be formed after the Red Army 'liberated' the country. When the Communist Party succeeded in effectively eliminating all political rivals a few years later Erdei chose to stay with the powerholders. He was Minister of Agriculture, until 1953 and must bear a major share of the responsibility for the rural policies of the high Stalinist period. He is also held accountable nowadays for his actions in 1956 when he negotiated again with the Russian 'liberators'. From this tragedy he emerged as a close ally of Janos Kadar (though he may also have been in some respects a liability, precisely because of these political circumstances). Without holding further ministerial office, under Kadar he occupied a string of prestigious posts and was undoubtedly an influential figure right down to the time of his death in 1971. Not long before his death he produced a final monograph: called simply *Town and Country* (1971), this is a study of his own Szeged area and represents a return to his roots, and even to the fieldwork methods of his youth.

The manner in which Erdei exercised influence, though it is hard to document, may reveal much about the peculiar hybrid that developed as Kadar's version of socialism from the early 1960s. In his own special field of rural policy, it is well known and documented that Erdei was involved in the formulation of the cooperative laws which governed the *kolkhoz*-type collectives established across most of Hungary by 1961. What is not so well understood (and I do not pretend to understand it fully myself) is the influence he seems to have had in modifying the application of these laws and initiating developments which led to their effective subversion in the 1970s.[8] By this period Hungary had introduced the New Economic Mechanism, and the winds of decentralization had rather specific effects in the agricultural sector. The rural family was once again encouraged to take the initiative as a unit of production, at least in those many activities where it could be shown to have the competitive edge over the collective sector. What developed in practice was a sort of balance, a symbiosis of the large-scale and the small-scale, which in theoretical terms looked more like the 'vertical integration' of A.V. Chayanov than the Leninist-Stalinist models implemented in the USSR.[9] And indeed, with Erdei spending much of his time during this period at the Agricultural University at Godollo working out the optimal combinations of private and collective, of small-scale and large-scale enterprise, the comparison with Chayanov may not be too far-fetched. By now Erdei was prepared to acknowledge the errors of the 1940s and 1950s, but he always defended the decisions to pursue collectivization. It was justified, he argued, because the full unfolding of the scientific-technical revolution found agriculture in the countries which had undergone socialist transformation by the beginning of the 1960s already organized on a large scale. The example of Poland and Yugoslavia shows that the large-scale modernization of agriculture is no easier if left to a later period, and indeed it may become more difficult (S. Erdei 1972: 7-8).

But what was it like to be a villager in Tázlár during these years? I have little data on the 1940s, and the impact of the 1945 Land Reform measures was probably smaller than elsewhere because the number of very large estates was low. The first cooperative farm, the *Red Csepel*, was founded with external support in 1949 (see Hann 1983). The early 1950s witnessed the most serious attacks on the alleged *kulaks*, or rich peasants. The father of Antal Vermes was labelled such, though his farm of twenty-eight *hold* had to support ten persons at this time.[10] He spent much of the next few years in jail, but when he came out he was not allowed to join the cooperative which was using his own confiscated lands, nor was he able to find a job in any nearby factories. Eventually he was assisted by the Calvinist Church, and through cutting fodder for the church he was able to get access to their flour at a time when the ordinary cooperative farmers were going hungry. Some of those farmers were commanded to grow cotton, an absurdity given the ecological conditions of Tázlár, but a good illustration of the damage done to the economy during these years of 'politics in command'.

The Vermes family experienced more misfortune after 1956. Antal's elder brother and a friend served with the National Guards (*Nemzet Orseg*) that Fall. Among other activities they burned communist propaganda and patrolled the center of the village with rifles. According to Antal they probably saved the life of at least one Communist Party secretary, when he was physically threatened by some over-exuberant drunken youths. But after the revolution had been defeated a band of Kadar's *pufajkasok* ('greycoats'--special forces named after their distinctive uniform) toured the villages of the area enquiring about who had served with the National Guardsmen a few months previously and seeking revenge. Antal's brother suffered a burst spleen, never recovered fully, and died a painful death two years later.

Things began to change slowly for the better in the 1960s. Antal's father was now reluctantly dragooned into a cooperative, along with virtually every other local farmer. They were still not terribly successful in their early years, but at least here they allowed their members to preserve a high degree of autonomy (most families spent very little time engaged in collective sector activities, but continued to maintain their previous pattern of small-scale mixed farming; see Hann 1980, 1993a, for more detail concerning the 'specialist cooperatives' of this region). Settlement policies continued to feature a high degree of coercion as the state attempted to concentrate the population in the village center and refused to give permission for the modernization of tanyas. Yet these initially hard-line policies were increasingly softened during implementation. By the end of the 1960s *tanya* electrification schemes were being introduced, and the children of kulaks who had been definitively barred from further education in the 1950s now found the gates of the country's best universities open to them. Antal went up to the Economics University in 1963. His future wife Julia went to teacher training college a few years later, whereas her elder sister, in spite of being a consistently excellent student, had been prohibited from such a career ten years earlier.

For a few years after their marriage Antal worked as an accountant at a cooperative farm some hours distance from Tázlár, but by the mid-1970s when I first met him he had become chief accountant of the recently unified Peace Specialist Cooperative in his native village. Julia had a job at the village primary school, and they were renting a house in the center whilst beginning to prepare for their own housebuilding. They worked hard during these years: apart from their full-time jobs there were two young children to be looked after, and also pigs and poultry, not to mention work in the family vineyards when required. The first year of my fieldwork was one of crisis in the leadership of the cooperative, and for a short period Antal served as the sole chief executive. He was then edged out as a result of the machinations of the external authorities (for full details see Hann 1980). For a further year he was employed at a state enterprise in a nearby town, but he never settled down at all in this position. Soon he found himself branded 'politically unreliable', and for the last fifteen years this university graduate has not worked outside his family farm. He has built this up to thirteen hold, including two and a half hold of vines, most of which represents recent investment. Antal has long had his own tractor to assist him even in this, the most labor intensive branch of production. He has also had his own car throughout this period, and his two-storeyed house is among the best equipped in the village. Like millions of other small producers he feels he made a contribution to the nation's prosperity in these years. His professional career may have been sabotaged because he refused to conform and never concealed his opposition to the Communist Party; but he was able to prosper by following an alternative strategy, one identified by Erdei as that of the specialized 'farmer', because, with 'economics in command', the older themes in socialist ideology were increasingly downplayed in the later Kadar period.

The Post-Socialist Era

As a tumultuous century in Tázlár draws to a close many people are nowadays looking back over the times I have outlined so schematically above. Evaluations differ, of course. Let us stick to the family of Antal Vermes and bring his story up to date. By 1993 his daughter has made him a grandfather and his son is completing his university education in history and theology. Throughout his career as a private farmer Antal has retained his membership of the Peace Cooperative and some of his land is rented from the cooperative. He has attended meetings regularly, frequently in order to criticize the leadership, which however has been far more stable in the 1980s than at any previous time. Antal has not actually made much use of cooperative services, and has generally preferred to use other channels for marketing his produce, though for many other villagers the cooperative has been indispensable.

In 1989 Antal was one of a small group of some twenty persons which relaunched the Independent Smallholders' Party in the village. They agitated successfully to have their emblem replace that of the now virtually defunct Communist Party in the offices of the local council. In the national elections of Spring 1990 the voters of Tázlár and most of the surrounding region returned a Smallholder deputy to parliament. However in the local elections held in the Fall personalities seemed more important than political parties. The contest for mayor was won by the ex-communist Executive Secretary (VB Titkar) from the previous administration, and most of the other council members had been members before (see Hann 1992). Antal was one of the few newcomers, and he used this new stage to put forward the same demands that he was already trying to articulate through the cooperative. Basically, he supported the Smallholders' national policy calling for as full a return to the land ownership structure of 1947 as possible. He urged the abolition of the cooperative and the distribution of all its lands to the members in accordance with the above principle.

These goals were repeatedly frustrated in the next few years, during which the smallholders in Tázlár showed that were no more cohesive than their party was at the national level. Antal himself no longer has anything to do with the organization, which has only a nominal existence in the village today. (In the meantime his wife Julia has become the leading organizer of the Christian Democratic People's Party, the party which Antal himself expects to be supporting at the next elections.)

The post-1989 transformation can be traced in three major steps, which have been implemented in Tázlár in successive years. First, in Summer 1990 all members of the cooperative were given 'property tickets' (*vagyonjegy*) amounting to the total value of the non-land assets. Although the principle of one member one vote has been retained these tickets are now very unevenly distributed. The amount received by members depended upon a complex formula intended to assess their contribution to the cooperative's performance over the preceding twelve years. The formula is a major bone of contention for Antal Vermes because it gives greater weight to the salaries earned by cooperative employees and leaders and to the value of produce sold by members through the cooperative than to the value of the resources originally contributed by founding members. He himself has come out poorly from it, particularly in comparison with senior cooperative leaders who do not even belong to local families at all. Very few of these tickets were converted to other forms of wealth in the years which followed. They could be sold outside the cooperative only if no other members or the cooperative itself is willing to take them. To my knowledge no such sales have taken place, and these tickets have been used only in the purchase of hardware and other goods from cooperative sell-offs. They are perhaps better viewed as shares, since they have actually paid a small dividend in the first years of this scheme's operation.

Second the government has introduced a series of Compensation Laws which falls considerably short of ensuring that villagers regain possession of their family plots. Instead the laws provide for the issuing of vouchers to those whose claims are approved. The vouchers can be used to bid for land through auction, but they can also be used to acquire non-agricultural assets, they can be commuted into a pension and social security benefits, and they can be sold freely for cash.[11] The implementation of these laws has been inevitably slow and bureaucratically cumbersome. Acquiring the necessary documentation to establish that one's family owned land or other assets more than forty years earlier is a daunting task for most rural people. Nowhere has the implementation of this national law been more fraught with tension than in the areas of specialist cooperatives, where there have been many changes in land use since 1947, and not just conversions from the private sector to the collective but from one individual farmer to another. Even Antal is hard pressed to adjudicate in cases where, for example, a farmer has had some land confiscated by a cooperative or state farm, but on the land he has been offered in compensation (perhaps of better quality) he has planted and tended vines for two or three decades: should he now have to hand such a vineyard back to the heirs of the original owner, who might be city dwellers with no interest in the land at all except to make a fast buck out of it if possible? The local smallholders have sometimes modified their fundamentalist stance in the face of cases like this, but in general they have remained intransigent.

Third, in 1993 the cooperative initiated steps to redistribute its lands among the members. The currency for this exercise is Gold Crowns, the historic measure of quality which also guides the allocation procedure under the Compensation

Laws. In this instance the allocation is subject to the same restrictions on transfer as the property shares distributed two years earlier. The formula used to guide the distribution is essentially the same, but many farmers have a much stronger sense of injustice. Many families, including that of Antal Vermes, established vineyards privately as their principal form of capital accumulation in the boom period of the 1970s. Generally they did so on land that they regarded as fully their own, though in many cases legally it had already become part of the cooperative's holdings. Now, with cooperative land available for redistribution, the members are entitled to claim it back according to its value in Gold Crowns. Their allocation depends in part, thanks to the above-noted formula, on the value their land had when they entered the cooperative; but if they want to buy back vineyards they must do so at the much higher rate the land commands in this form. Antal prefers to highlight cases such as this, which affect him personally, and which he and most other villagers see as a clear iniquity, rather than more problematic cases where two or more persons can lay claim to the same patch of land.

Equally clear in the eyes of the Smallholders was the right of local farmers, generally members of established middle peasant families, to claim back soils of exceptional quality on the edge of the village which had been taken into the collective sector amid great controversy in the mid-1970s. When the cooperative leadership was slow to release these lands rumors spread that they were being held back for allocation to some of the organization's few remaining full-time workers. This possibility provoked Antal (who has a small stake in these fields himself) to organize a petition, which was followed up by a peaceful reclaiming of the land at stake through direct action by the forty farmers concerned. Two years later they are still waiting for their legal title to be confirmed, but the cooperative has made it clear that it has no wish to fight the case.

In these examples Antal is not simply an embittered individual. He has emerged as a spokesman for a distinct group of farmers, mostly rather inarticulate and confused by the recent changes, rather older than Antal himself, and almost without exception coming from the ranks of the former middle peasantry. These people see the non-local leaders of the cooperative and the employees, who tend to come from families that were of significantly lower status in the past, as forming an alliance against them, together out to deprive the rightful owners of the Tázlár soil of the inheritance which is due to them.[12] In this context the Smallholders fear is that the cooperative leaders will start buying up shares and Gold Crowns from other members to add to the substantial allocation they already have. They will then hive off for their own use the most attractive and profitable of the cooperative's assets, including profitable small factories as well as forest land that can be quickly plundered for financial gain (similar patterns were being widely noted elsewhere in rural Hungary in the media in 1993).

There is also a deep clash here between alternative models of the economy and how it should be managed. In this respect the world view of Antal Vermes (perhaps like that of Ferenc Erdei) is a curious amalgam of the peasant values he imbibed in childhood on the Great Plain and the Marxist political economy he picked up later during his student years. Both strands emphasize the importance of hard work (production), and are skeptical of ideologies which proclaim that pure markets and competition can solve the country's economic problems. The ex-communist 'Green Barons' are perceived somewhat paradoxically to stand for the new market economy and to be scheming to make a quick buck for themselves out of the collapse of the socialist structures, while ignoring the longer term interests of agricultural production and the national economy. Antal tends to see a conspiracy between these local enemies and the government, whose failure to support the agricultural sector he deplores as a ploy to facilitate the consolidation of power and ownership rights by the new elites. He further believes that the country's 'open market' policy is merely an invitation to the farmers of other countries to dump their surplus on the Hungarian market. Instead of kowtowing to international financial institutions he would prefer the government to pursue protectionist policies, and also to repudiate the debt built up in the socialist period.

Thus behind this individual and his family and their local conflicts lie some issues of much wider significance. There also lie some very deep human emotions, but not nearly as much economic rationality as those who drafted the Compensation Laws had hoped. Some villagers, generally those in the eldest age cohorts, will do almost anything to get back the land with which their family is historically identified. It doesn't matter if it consists of nothing but running sands, it doesn't matter that there is no-one left in the family to work the land, it doesn't matter if the tax bill turns out to be more than the land might possibly fetch if rented out. What matters is that a historic injustice is remedied, and the sweat expended by the ancestors in converting these inhospitable lands to cultivation is not betrayed again.[13] This sort of feeling is what seems to motivate Antal himself. He is not very anxious to build up the size of his farm, but he is quite determined to regain the plots associated with his own family, as well as some others which formerly belonged to the family of his wife. When I suggested that if he succeeded he would have parcels so scattered as to make his farm far less efficient than it is at present he insisted that this was not relevant at all. Of course he has no illusions about being able to pass on the farm as a going concern to his children, neither of whom has any interest in farming. Even in other families where the children have not obtained qualifications leading them to pursue other careers outside the village there is very little enthusiasm for private farming among the younger generation. Certainly those who became prosperous in the age of reformist socialism, those for whom embourgeoisement finally became a reality thanks to well-integrated small-scale agriculture, do not now see farming and land as a sensible investment.

The cooperative survives, in spite of the depressed agricultural markets and the complete withdrawal of all the subsidies which had previously sustained cooperatives in regions like this, which had to cope with adverse ecological conditions. Since 1992 it has not engaged in any agricultural production, and many of its services were privatized in the 1980s (Hann 1993a). It makes most of its money from sideline activities which create jobs in small factories for the large pool of available female labor. However profitable these remain for the time being it is hard to see how these can support a relatively large administrative apparatus indefinitely. But most people seem to feel that the cooperative has to survive, not just to mop up the large areas of land that are simply unwanted by individuals, but to provide marketing outlets, and also some basic welfare services which no-one else is willing to take on. Recent general meetings have demonstrated that the leaders still have the confidence of the mass of the members, even if the guerilla warfare between Antal and the cooperative leaders continues unabated (Hann 1993b).

And what has happened to Ferenc Erdei? His theoretical legacy is looted by later generations of social scientists, not all of whom acknowledge their debts.[14] Of greater significance here is that post-communist Hungary does not seem to know quite what to do with him. He is not exactly an un-person. In his home town of Mako (where he is buried fairly inconspicuously alongside other family graves) his study is a major exhibit at the municipal museum. A minor street bears his name--nothing prominent in the center. In Budapest there is nothing at all. People cannot yet forget what happened in the 1950s, and Erdei is still too firmly identified with so much of what went wrong, particularly in agricultural policy. But there is another side to his legacy, as I have tried to show in this chapter. Erdei was a humanist in the truest sense, a man who probably understood the conditions of the twentieth century Hungarian peasantry better than anyone else. He worked consistently to improve those conditions, and in the last years of his life, by the discreet and informal techniques that were the most effective instruments of Kadar's brand of socialism, he achieved very considerable successes. These successes have not been widely recognized, even by many who have been among the beneficiaries. There is certainly a danger that the positive elements in the Erdei legacy will be squandered in the 1990s, as the swing of the political pendulum threatens to push the whole rural sector into another cataclysm. But in the survival of the Peace Cooperative in Tázlár (however attenuated its form), and in the reluctance of the majority of villagers to go all the way with Smallholder ideologists such as Antal Vermes, I see some signs of hope for the maintenance of balance, and perhaps even the attainment of a better balance in the future.

Notes

Antal Vermes is a pseudonym for a villager I have known since 1976. However, the data for this chapter were mostly collected in short annual fieldtrips in the period 1990-1993. An earlier version was read at a seminar at the London School of Economics in November 1993. I am also grateful for comments and advice to Mihaly Sarkany, Nigel Swain, and Katalin Kovacs.

1. This party had been the single largest party in the country in the 1940s, before being squeezed off the political stage following the infamous communist 'salami tactics'. For details of the reemergence of this party and its precipitous disintegration a few years later see Swain 1993a. In Tázlár the same informant who remembered the election jingle about Ferenc Erdei could also supply one for this party: *Ha Magyar vagy, nem szavazhatsz masra, / Csak a Fuggetlen Kisgazda Partra!* ('If you are a Hungarian you cannot vote for anyone else, / Only the Independent Smallholders' Party!')

2. See Kulcsar 1988 for a full and very positive evaluation of Erdei's work. The Budapest sociologist Tibor Huszar has also published valuable analyses, particularly of Erdei's formative years; for the most recent see Huszar 1991. Huszar has also edited a selection of Erdei's writings in English translation, to which he has added a concluding chapter that focuses on Erdei's contributions to Hungarian sociology: see Huszar 1988. A useful outline sketch of Erdei's life is provided by his brother Sandor Erdei (1972).

3. Published at the rate of one per year: *Hungarian Town* (1939), *Hungarian Village* (1940), *Hungarian Peasant Society* (1941), *Hungarian Tanyas* (1942). There is also an important manuscript from this period dealing with the structure of Hungarian society in the inter-war period which was not published during Erdei's lifetime; it can be found in Kulcsar 1980, and in English translation in Huszar 1988, pp. 7-93. I am grateful to Laszlo Peter (personal communication) for pointing out to me Erdei's great debt in this work to the historian Istvan Hajnal.

4. See Swain 1992 for an English-language presentation of this, perhaps the best synthetic work in Erdei's *oeuvre*. Fragments can also be read in English translation in Huszar 1988, pp. 155-208.

5. In their commitment to writing that would constitute good literature as well as good sociology/sociography (on this distinction in the Hungarian context see Hann 1987) Erdei and some of his contemporaries offer interesting parallels to the recent literary turn in some so-called post-modern Western social science, including social anthropology.

6. Erdei 1957 {1937}: 174. Tázlár was called officially Pronayfalva between 1906 and 1947, when the name was changed back to Tázlár. The reasons for the change are obscure, but Baron Pronay was apparently a nobleman from whom the earlier settlers hoped for some patronage. There is no evidence of his ever even visiting the community, let alone favoring it with aristocratic largesse, and there have been no serious suggestions in recent years that the village should revert to the pre-1947 name. This pattern of dispersed settlement was rather different from the pattern which concerned Erdei most throughout his life, and which he believed to be more characteristic of the Great Plain. This was the pattern not of village networks but of market towns surrounded by a large hinterland of scattered farms or *tanyas*. Erdei argued consistently that distorted capitalist development had unhinged the proper social links between town and countryside: these needed to be restored for rural poverty and other problems to be overcome.

7. The assumption that these migrations were forced upon peasants may be a serious oversimplification, one that fitted well with Erdei's political standpoint. Research in progress by Dr. Antal Juhasz of the Ethnography Department of the University of Szeged suggests that some migrants may have been motivated as much by 'pull' factors as 'push'. See Juhasz 1990.

8. Szelenyi (1988:151) notes that Erdei had a close personal relationship with Kadar in the 1960s. Personal contacts in Budapest have suggested to me that the most important channel in ensuring that the agricultural sector benefitted from the 'reformist' spirit was the Economics Minister Lajos Feher, with whom Erdei also had very close relations. I have also heard suggestions that he was personally responsible for allowing experimental forms of cooperative to flourish in those regions of the Great Plain where small-scale vineyards were historically significant. According to these views Erdei had understood the economic rationale for the 'specialist cooperatives' since serving as a parliamentary deputy for this region in the 1950s, and his understanding of the deeper human issues went back much further still.

9. The definitive account of Hungarian agriculture in this period is Swain 1985. On symbiosis see also Hann 1980; on Chayanov see Shanin 1987.

10. One *hold* is rather less than one and a half acres, and is officially equal to 0.57 hectares; however villagers' statements of the size of farms in the past do not necessarily correspond to precise cadastral measures.

11. For a full discussion of the Compensation Laws see Swain 1994a.

12. This corresponds to the broader conflict identified elsewhere in the Hungarian countryside by Swain and others, between traditionalist Smallholders on the one hand and the 'Green Barons' (i.e. the former socialist managers of the cooperatives and state farms) and their alleged allies on the other. See Swain 1994b for an interesting argument about some unintended consequences of this conflict.

13. It should not be assumed that everyone is motivated by factors of this kind. I suspect that, in the self-help operation described above to regain possession of the lands on the outskirts of the village, some people went along not so much out of loyalty to their parents and grandparents as from an unwillingness to see the land be taken over by others who had no right to it - ie. standard 'dog in the manger' psychology.

14. For example a recent detailed study of the place of small farmers in Hungarian society pays more attention to French social theory and international rural sociology than to Erdei (Kovach 1988). The fullest use made of Erdei in English accounts of Hungarian society is that made by Szelenyi and his associates (1988). Szelenyi, though generous in his recognition of Erdei's creative contributions in the pre-socialist era, postulates a sharp divide between this early Erdei and the Erdei who sold out to marxist ideology after 1945. On my reading there is no such ideological break and Szelenyi's documentation of the success of the rural population in pursuing 'socialist embourgeoisement' provides the best confirmation of the continuity in Erdei's priorities throughout his career.

References

Erdei, Ferenc. 1957. (1937) *Futohomok; a Duna-Tiszakoze*, (Running Sand; the Danube-Tisza interfluve), Budapest: Gondolat Kiado.

Erdei, Sandor. 1972. *Erdei Ferenc eletrajza*, (Biography of Ferenc Erdei), (A makoi Muzeumi Barati Kor Ertesitoje, ed. Ferenc Toth), Mako, Manuscript.

Hann, C. M. 1980. *Tázlár: A village in Hungary*, Cambridge, Cambridge University Press.

____. 1983. "Progress toward collectivized agriculture in Tázlár, 1949-78', *In* Marida Hollos and Bela C. Maday (eds.), *New Hungarian Peasants: an East Central European Experience with Collectivization*, East European Monographs No. CXXXIV; Brooklyn College Studies on Society in Change No.26, New York, Brooklyn College Press.

____. 1987. 'The politics of anthropology in socialist Eastern Europe', in Anthony Jackson (ed.), *Anthropology at Home*, (ASA Monographs No. 25), London, Tavistock Publications.

____. 1992. 'Market Principle, Market-Place and the Transition in Eastern Europe', *In* Roy Dilley, ed, *Contesting Markets: Analyses of Ideology, Discourse and Practice.* Edinburgh, Edinburgh University Press.

____. 1993a. 'Property Relations in the New Eastern Europe: The case of Specialist Cooperatives in Hungary', *In* Hermine G. De Soto and David G. Anderson, eds. *The Curtain Rises: Rethinking Culture, Ideology, and the State in Eastern Europe*, Atlantic Highlands, NJ:Humanities Press.

____. 1993b. 'From Comrades to Lawyers: Continuity and Change in Local Political Culture in Rural Hungary', *Anthropological Journal on European Cultures*, 2 (1):75-104.

Huszar, Tibor ed. 1988. *Ferenc Erdei Selected Writings*, Budapest, Akademiai.

____. 1991. *Parhuzamok es keresztezodesek: Erdei Ferenc, Bibo Istvan es a Marciusi Front*, (Parallels and Intersections; Ferenc Erdei, Istvan Bibo and the March Front), (A Makoi Muzeum Fuzetei 68), Mako.

Juhasz, Antal, ed. 1990. *Migracio es telepules a Duna-Tisza kozen*, (Migration and Settlement on the Danube- Tisza interfluve), Szeged.

Kovach, Imre. 1988. *Termelok es Vallalkozok: Mezogazdasagi Kistermelok a Magyar Tarsadalomban.* (Producers and Entrepreneurs; agricultural small Producers in Hungarian society), Budapest: Tarsadalomtudomanyi Intezet (Social Science Institute of the Central Committee of the Hungarian Socialist Workers ' Party).

Kulcsar, Kalman, ed. 1980. *Erdei Ferenc a Magyar Tarsadalomrol.* (Ferenc Erdei on Hungarian Society). Budapest, Akademiai Kiado.

Shanin, Teodor. 1987 "Introduction", *In* A V. Chayanov, *The Theory of Peasant Economy*, Madison, University of Wisconsin Press.

Swain, Nigel. 1985. *Collective Farms Which Work?* Cambridge, Cambridge University Press.

____. 1992. *A Presentation of Ferenc Erdei's Hungarian Peasant Society*, Center for Central and East European Studies, University Of Liverpool.

____. 1994a. '*The Legislative Framework for Agricultural Transition in Hungary*, Center for Central and East European Studies, University of Liverpool.

____. 1994b. '*Political Parties and Agriculture In Hungary*, Center for Central and East European Studies, University of Liverpool.

Szelenyi, Ivan et al . 1988. *Socialist Entrepreneurs: Embourgeoisement in Rural Hungary*. Cambridge: Polity Press.

8

Changing Conflicts and Their Resolution in Polish Communities Today

Jacek Kurczewski

Attention to conflicts is present throughout the history of social sciences though opinions on the social consequences of conflict vary. An influential minority holds, however, that conflicts have positive social effects that outweigh all of their other disruptive and disintegrative effects. This position is explicitly assumed by Polish experts who advise local communities . For instance, Grazyna Gesicka writes:

> Appropriately "played" conflicts may have even positive influence on development of a group. A conflict situation in itself is not dangerous. It becomes dangerous...only when it is accompanied by lack of integrative capacity. It is possible to change conflict from zero-sum game into "integrative bargain", that is, situation in which parties define together the common interests zone (Gesicka 1993:22).

Most recently, Hirschman (1994) argued that democratic market society lives on the "steady diet of conflicts" that it learns to manage, in contrast to Communist society that suppresses overt expression of conflicts but ends up in stagnation. However, these "peaceful contradictions," as Hirschman calls them in a knowing reference to Marxist distinctions, are conflicts centered around divisible issues, the so-called "more-or-less conflicts." They stand in marked opposition to "either-or" conflicts around non-divisible issues, and which may not be handled so easily or effectively. Nonetheless, Hirschman's distinction between the nature and treatment of social conflict in communist and capitalist society is a suggestive one and calls into question how social conflict itself changes in a single society as it changes from communist to capitalist. This chapter then is an attempt to compare local social conflicts in Polish communities as they were in the old days and as they are today in a country undergoing vast and rapid socio-economic and political change.

With this purpose in mind I decided to re-study the nature of social conflict in a number of communities that I had considered some years past. Thus, in early July 1993 I visited the small, prosperous village of Sadowne where twenty years earlier I analyzed the operation of its Social Conciliatory Commission. This organization was formed to help local authorities deal with everyday neighborhood conflicts. Because of its success at this, the Sadowne Commission was advertised as a showcase by its advocates in the Communist umbrella organization, the Front of National Unity. More than showcase Sadowne, at that time I also looked at the operation of the Commissions in two small Mazovian towns nicknamed Wagram and Lotow (Kurczewski and Frieske 1978). From this study I became interested in dispute settlement patterns more generally and continued such research in the late 1970s in two other small towns, Lesko and Olesno in Silesia, administrative centers of rural regions in Poland, and compared them to similar processes in Warsaw (Kurczewski 1982, 1993b).

In the late 1970s there was marginal social scientific interest in everyday disputes. Macrostructural conflicts generated by the political domination of the communist Party-State over an atomized society was devoid of channels of popular expression and people had few instruments to defend their own interests. Consequently, examining everyday disputes was considered a narrow, even futile, topic of inquiry.

With Poland transformed I returned to Sadowne and those other towns to again consider questions of local conflict and their relationship to society and local politics. I had little idea whether the Social Conciliatory Commissions still existed. In fact, I was rather skeptical about their fate if other organizational transformations in Poland were any guide. After all, in Poland today there is no Front of National Unity, and the Communist Party, now re-named the Social Democracy Party, is only one of the important opposition parties in a pluralistic parliamentary democracy. Further, there are no longer communist satellite organizations like the Circles of Country Housewives, Voluntary Reserves of Civic Militia, and Clubs of Country Press Readers that were used by the socialist state to organize life in the Polish countryside and compete with Roman Catholic parish life.

Though I expected little when I returned in Sadowne, to my surprise three gentlemen gossiping in the sun opposite the closed local government office acknowledged that the Social Conciliatory Commission was still active. It would soon have its thirtieth anniversary, now somehow managing without the official support of the Party and its Front of National Unity. Given the continuity of this organization in the face of such extraordinary change in Poland I was motivated to consider how it has responded to the changes in social life ushered in by the transformation and how, in fact, local conflicts themself have changed in this period.

Disputes in the Shadow of Communism

In order to gain a sense of the nature of conflict in transitional Poland we need to provide a bit of context by looking at disputes in the socialist years. Until the mid-1970s Poland was administratively divided in large *voivodships* (provinces) and further into counties (sing. *powiat*) whose seat held all local authority including the courts. After this centuries-old division was abolished in favor of a larger number of small counties, local politics became less threatening to the central party-state authorities in Warsaw. However, the administration of justice also changed so that the jurisdiction of local courts was greatly restricted. Because of these administrative changes, in my early examination of rural conflicts, along with Sadowne I also selected two rural small towns of Lesko and Olesno for a number reasons. Most important was the extent of disputes found in each.

Lesko was previously a county seat that, in the 1960s, had one of the highest rates of civil disputes for such a jurisdiction. The second locality, Olesno, was also a county seat, though with one of the lowest rates of civil disputes among rural counties and restricted numbers of criminal personal accusation cases as well.[1] At the same time, the counties were similar as both were in areas of former overt ethnic strife. Though I wanted to see if this played a role in local conflict, random interviews in the towns suggested this was not the case. Instead, small town inhabitants reported a number of other sources of conflict in the 1970 surveys, as indicated in Table 8.1. Along with sources of conflict, we also looked at types of community dispute settlement in the late 1970s (Table 8.2).

Though not the proximate cause of conflict, local disputes in communist Poland were, in some ways, intensified by the early history of the state along with its social policies. For example, though people dismissed problems of national minorities as of the past, this was actually not the case in Olesno which was a strong pocket of German Silesians who registered as Poles after the War. With communism's advent, however, and the influx of the resettled Polish population from poorer eastern areas that Poland had to surrender to the Soviet Union following the 1939 invasion and later Yalta agreements, this group sought to distinguish themselves by emphasizing their German-ness. Though this created tensions in the local community such problems were never discussed openly during communist rule, as official policy eliminated references to the German minority in Polish territory. Consequently, when I lived in Olesno (which was named Rosenberg before 1945) I soon learned about the division of the town into "newcomers" and "autochthones." The latter included those who registered and were accepted as ethnic Poles from the Polish minority that inhabited German Silesia before the war. Better off homes (where German was spoken) were filled with West German goods and had Mercedeses parked in front.

Table 8.1 Causes and Frequency of Disputes in Three Polish Towns in the Late 1970s

Dispute Type	Warsaw, 1977/78 n=334	Olesno, 1977 n=229	Lesko, 1978 n=211
Reputation	14	15	16
Bodily injury	5	9	7
Dispute in Neighborhood	14	10	13
Land/Borders	4	7	8
Leases	2	4	6
Debt	11	14	10
Sales of Goods and Services	12	10	10
With Civic Administration	12	9	10
Labor-related	14	11	16
Other	12	11	4

Table 8.2 Principles of Dispute Settlement in the Late 1970s

Type of Action	Warsaw %	Olesno %	Lesko %
Surrendering One's Claims	31	31	28
Informal Compromise	33	27	33
Official Satisfaction of Claims	31	41	34
a. Via Court Action	(3)	(7)	(3)
No Data	5	1	5

Lesko was also a border town, located in southeast Poland and, like Olesno, located in a region of mixed ethnicity. It was a Polish outpost in an area predominantly occupied by a Ukrainian Uniate population who, with Soviet and then German tolerance, bloodied the Poles during World War Two thus revenging twenty years of Polish rule. After the war the Ukrainian insurgence continued until forced resettlement and ethnic "cleansing" of the area. With democratization the former (Ukrainian) inhabitants re-emerged and demanded compensation for property lost in the-so-called "Wisla" resettlement action of late 1940s. The nearby border city of Przemysl where tens of thousands of Poles were forcefully resettled after 1945 from neighboring Soviet Ukraine was contested more vigorously by Ukrainian nationalists, and thus was an incessant place of conflicts, especially over church property. Church ownership had changed from the Roman to the Greek Catholic rite and back again. Both rites are under the Pontiff in Rome and this stressed the delicate position of the Church which in Poland normally is not directly involved in conflicts but instead may serve as a mediator or go-between in them. The intervention of the Pope himself was necessary to force the defiant Polish nationalists defending an order located in a former Uniate church to agree to a compromise exchange of churches. But one must consider that this ethnic cleavage was in post-War Poland, after German Nazi extermination of Jews, and thus represented a very unusual situation which caused both localities to differ from the average.

Changing Conflicts in Transitional Poland

With the end of the socialist state in 1989 and the implementation of democratic, market-based systems, the transformations in Polish political economy and society has been extraordinary. Conflicts too have changed appreciably. In particular, where before citizens were reticent to challenge many state decisions and local authorities, today, in fact, such phenomena are rife. This is especially seen in one case recently discussed in the Polish press which is only exemplary because of its commonplace character.

A City's Mayor Versus Its Unemployed

On August 4, 1993 an article entitled "Wheel-barrow from Praszka" (Kucharski 1993) appeared in Poland's most popular newspaper, *Gazeta Wyborcza*. According to the article, after a three day protest a crowd of one hundred people carried away Wlodzimierz Skoczek, Mayor of Praszka, a town in the Czestochowa voivodship, on a wheel-barrow after he refused to resign his office.[2] Before that action a group of unemployed workers and farmers from "Self-defence" (the militant farmers' union) occupied the community's office from morning until afternoon. The action itself was organized by the seven member Praszka Unemployed Committee along with one Antoni Arndt, the candidate of the Czestochowa Self-Defence chapter in the coming parliamentary elections.

The national leader of Self-Defence, Andrzej Lepper, known for his frequent conflicts with the police, was quoted in the article as saying that "Praszka is a commune with the largest percentage of unemployed in the country and its mayor is not doing anything to help them." According to the newspaper, however, Mayor Skoczek had opposed the removal of the voivodship employment office from Praszka to Olesno and struggled for inclusion of his commune on the priority list for unemployed workers developed by the Council of Minister's Office. Skoczek, himself a candidate for senate on behalf of the ruling Democratic Union, was quoted as saying that "Self-Defence (was to blame as they) persuaded people to go on a rent strike due to the employment situation." Furthermore, the Mayor said that if people felt he was doing a bad job representing them they had legal means to recall him. Nonetheless, despite his protests and counter-claims, the crowd would have none of it. Though the mayor is also handicapped he was taken by force by the people and carried away on the wheel-barrow (Skwiecinski 1993).

On the second day of the confrontation the Deputy Minister of Labor, Helena Goralska, arrived in Praszka. Supporting the mayor, according to press, she pointed to Antoni Arndt, the Self-Defence militant and also among the unemployed, and said that he should be ashamed that "one so young and in good health as yourself is on the dole." Later, however, during a meeting of the local government, three hundred people arrived at the government office shouting at the Deputy Minister that they did not have the wherewithal to survive. As the paper noted, there is some truth to their complaints since, out of 8,000 inhabitants of Praszka, more than 2,000 are unemployed, of whom only 438 receive unemployment benefits. Praszka is in the straits it is since it was a typical one factory town that fell victim to the dismantling of the communist bloc and the loss of Eastern markets for its industrial output (Waszkielewicz 1993). [3]

However, despite the structural reasons behind the circumstances of its unemployed, Praszka's workers were nonetheless outraged. Thus, another of Praszka's Self-Defence leaders, Boguslaw Przybyl, who established "Solidarity" here in 1980 said:

> As we are unrepresented by the city council and mayor, as we were unrepresented by parliament, so we are unrepresented by the government that sold us out to the foreign capital. These matters affect the whole country. When we are done here we will go to Belweder (the official residence of the Polish President) but now we have our problems to settle.

On the third day of the Praszka affair matters came to a head. After the protesting workers repeated their demands that the mayor resign and their request was rejected, it was then that Skoczek was taken by force in sight of the news cameraman invited by the Self-Defence people.[4] Subsequently, three people were arrested by police. However, though the locals complained about this, their actions were characterized as fair by the Prime Minister, Hanna Suchocka. Earlier she had considered the forced removal of the mayor as scandalous and suggested that an inquiry into the actions instigated by the Self-Defence was needed.

In response to the Praszka protest a local government session to deal with the workers' complaints was held on August 4, 1993, though clearly it was a late reaction to the unrest. Hubert Ksiezarczyk, head of the Employment Office in Olesno, came and explained that 68 percent of the fund for the prevention of unemployment is spent on Praszka. He said the town is considered a special case as employment in the local factory that exported mainly to the USSR declined from 4,500 to 1,500. In the Olesno region, of 4,700 unemployed, 2,100 are from Praszka. The unemployment fund helped retrain 300 people in Praszka and the money left allowed another 104 persons to be employed in public works until the end of the year. But nobody at the meeting would listen to this. The Deputy Minister who participated, was verbally attacked so she left the office with the help of the police. Later the mayor and fourteen councilmen resigned from their offices. Still, according to police reports cited in *Gazeta Wyborcza* a candidate for local office in the coming elections and two other Praszka people were accused of assaulting the mayor.

After a few days hiatus on Monday, August 9, the protesters again occupied the local government offices.[5] Due to the provocative tactics of Self-Defence, Praszka was in the headlines for much of early August 1993, a fact which may have influenced the autumn elections. First the protesters demanded that the town be officially recognized as a region under severe unemployment, and that unemployment benefits for 1,500 unemployed be prolonged. They also demanded amnesty for the riot participants and for the local and voivodship police chiefs who were investigated by the national police for their passivity in the face of the rioters. Finally they requested that a commission be sent to Praszka to investigate communal finances.

To sum up the meaning of the events in this small town conflict, we see the state compromising itself in a very short period of time. In the first stage the mayor was carried away on the wheel-barrow in face of police passivity. The second stage saw the disruption of the local council session by an aggressive crowd. Third, and possibly the worst compromise in some sense, was the televised intervention by the Deputy Minister of Internal Affairs, who said that the state will not put a policeman behind each mayor, consequently local authorities should act in such a way so as to not cause threatening conflicts. If today state authorities will allow the occupation of the town government in Praszka, the next stage of compromise would make it difficult for state to maintain any sort of hold on power (Skwiecinski 1993) .

We shall see later that the acute social problems of Praszka, a local community that depended almost totally on one firm, also exist at the individual level in form of court cases brought in by the local Housing Cooperative. This organization functioned for housing investment, ownership and management in the last decades of the Communism. They now are involved in litigation with an increasing number of tenants unable to pay their increasing fees. Apart from "POLMO," the company whose dominance and fall is behind the local drama, Praszka also has a public agriculture service firm, a local government housing firm, and an agricultural cooperative as well as 482 private business people registered.

Coming back to our case, let me note that though the first set a precedent, it was followed in two days by another of similar character. Also, while the second case was another example of a local small town mayor carried away on a wheel-barrow, unlike the first case it was not the unemployed who were dissatisfied, but the local small merchants with a decision concerning location of a new market place. Thus, we can suggest that these two cases are not so idiosyncratic but represent a wider process characteristic of the new Poland.

When I visited Praszka in October 1993, the dust of the protest was slowly settling. The town and its surrounding villages were run by Mr. Zygmunt Chmielewski, who was nominated as Commissar by the Government until the next local government elections. In his office I met Mr. Skoczek, the former Mayor, who points to the political character of the dispute. When I asked him about local unemployment he pointed out that in the commune's 1993 budget of twenty-two billion *zlotys* (one US dollar equal almost to 20,000 *zlotys*) the social benefits for the needy was about 1.6 billion *zlotys*, three times more than the previous year's. Commissar Chmielewski led me to the local Polish Organization of Unemployed, where poor people queue for instructions on how to get jobs and money. In contrast to the official explanations offered above, Mr. Arndt, the elected president of the unemployed organization's Praszka chapter, claims his organization has great local support. However, the official number I can get is that of 180 persons who were present at election of the board. Mr. Arndt rejects a political interpretation of the conflict and points out that people in need were in fact left with little support and in great need. To show the lack of concern for the unemployed, Mr. Arndt suggested that out of the twenty-two billion *zloty* 1993 commune budget the government assigned 1.5 billion for construction of a sport hall, a luxury item in town of 9,000 inhabitants and 1,800 unemployed on August 31st. So, like in a gestalt-type puzzle, a similar amount of funds is pointed to by each of the opponents as evidence for their counter-claims.

The conflict in Praszka in a sense is unusual as there are few communities in Poland where extreme acts and props like wheel-barrows are used and where democratically elected local authorities are attacked and forced to resign their office. In most other communities conflicts are acted out in a much quieter way, without resorting to the use of police. On the other hand, the Praszka conflict is in some ways characteristic of the new democracy. The activists of Self-Defence are repeating the patterns of popular protest that were used against the totalitarian power of the Communists. It is difficult to forget that this type of behavior was similar to those used not long ago by the same people who nowadays represent official law and order. The difference, however, is that today the authorities have been freely elected. It's not that these officials are now unresponsive to the needs of their constituents, but rather that Polish society learned the success of collective action which it will readily use even if the institutional means of vindicating rights are available.

Conflicts in County Courts Today

The Praszka affair illustrates one kind of developing conflict in transitional Poland; that which emerges from the common experience of many individuals, i.e. unemployment. Other conflicts are more a result of inter-personal social relations. However these too have changed in response to the wider social and political economic changes characterizing Poland today. For example, considering both the Wegrow and Olesno judicial districts (Wegrow is the location of Sadowne where the idea of the neighborhood dispute commission originated and Olesno the district in which Praszka is located) we can get a sense of general dispute patterns in the contemporary period (see also Kurczewski 1982,1993b) which are summarized in Tables 8.3 and 8.4 below.

Most interesting in Table 8.3 and 8.4 is that the frequency of private accusation cases has slowly decreased. Slander (art. 181), defamation (art. 182), libel (art. 178), and minor bodily injury (art. 156) characterize most of the cases. The explanation for this is readily apparent; money. According to Polish law, it is up to the wronged person to file an accusation and pay initial court fees if he

Table 8.3 Private Accusation Cases in Wegrow Judicial District, 1989-1993

Year	1989	1990	1991	1992	1993[a]
Civil Cases	345	214	152	111	44

[a] Figures for 1993 refer to period till August 4,1993.[6]

Table 8.4 Private Accusation Cases In Olesno Judicial District, 1989-1993

Year	1989	1990	1991	1992	1993[a]
Total cases	111	53	33	29	12
Olesno area	10	12	2	6	2
Praszka Area	21	---	2	---	---

[a] Figures for 1993 include cases ended before August 15, 1993.[7]

or she is to seek redress. However, there have been drastic increase in such fees in recent years making individuals less prone to file such claims. Thus, it is no accident that the decrease in personal accusation cases is larger in Praszka, a much poorer area than Olesno.

In contrast to the dramatically decreasing number of private accusation cases, civil disputes in general are on the rise after an initial decline in 1990. These disputes are not homogeneous, especially as to the kinds of individuals and parties involved. As might be expected in a new market economy, increases are above all in the number of suits brought by corporations against private persons. In fact, this reflects the basic social problems these local communities suffer. Out of 357 cases of this kind we see either agricultural cooperatives suing farmers for non-performance of labor or other agricultural services (176 cases from 1989 to 1992) or housing cooperatives suing tenants for non-payment of rent (1989--mid-1993: twenty-three cases in Olesno and 140 cases in Praszka). Again, we see how in Praszka social problems were aggravated and the number of conflicts intensified due to the increase in unemployment. As it increases, in fact, the Labor Office appears more often in court records suing recipients for their failure to re-pay investment credits (eighteen cases). The situation is clear. More and more people do not have the means to pay their tenancy fees in town housing or to pay for services provided to their farms. The cases brought by individual plaintiffs against corporate defendants are basically concerned with two of the latter, a local travel agency (five cases) and local administration (six cases) and concern the claim to order the administration to express the intent of continuation of lease of an immobile property.

Table 8.5 Civil Disputes in Olesno Judicial District 1989-1993

Case type	1989	1990	1991	1992	1993
Both Private	40	50	46	45	32
Firm Sues Private	45	45	72	104	91
Private Sues Firm	1	2	---	3	6
Both Corporate	162	58	52	78	71
Total Civil Cases[a]	248	155	170	230	200

[a] Cases registered until August 15, 1993.[8]

As Table 8.5 illustrates it seems that disputes that involve private individuals, housing and property claims are second in importance after monetary claims. Also, the table suggests that the frequency of disputes between individuals seem to remain at the same level throughout the whole transformation.

Village Conflicts Today

I returned to Sadowne, the seat of the first Social Conciliatory Committee, (and seemingly the last one in the country as I was unable to find evidence of another anywhere I went) in September,1993. Located in northeast Poland,

Sadowne is the administrative capital of a commune composed of twenty three villages with a total 7,200 inhabitants.[10] The central village is also the seat of an educational complex that includes the local high school. As a commercial center its court hears only those conflicts that have not been settled at the strictly local level, or those that arise in the town itself. As we shall see these conflicts reflect the predominantly farming character of the area where, according to the 1988 agricultural census, there were 1,518 farms with an average size of 6.5 hectares. The only industry produced ceramic bricks. It is interesting to note, in comparison with Praszka, 321 unemployed were registered in Sadowne in August 1993. The local mayor commented wryly on this situation when he was referred by a friend to have his car repaired by someone whom he later discovered was registered as unemployed.

Following local tradition the local Social Conciliatory Committee that survived the change of political system was composed of local white collar workers and lower level officials such as a post office clerk, bank manager, commune secretary, librarian, and a former administrative officer. The mayor when reminded of the existence of the Committee, wondered whether it was wise to leave the staff of the Committee unchanged, as these are not necessarily the people with local authority and influence. When I asked about the conciliatory activities in Olesno, its mayor, who before was a practicing private attorney said that it might have been a good institution, but no longer existed. In any case there were few individuals in town who could serve as a neutral authority on such a body. Conflicts are registered in a book kept by the ladies who run the Social Conciliatory Committee, among them one who is also the full-time clerk at Sadowne Commune. The following list summarizes the cases that the Committee heard in the last four and half years.

1. Case 1989/1: Details unknown. One of the parties to the dispute felt that the Committee should not review this case so it was referred to another body.
2. Case 1989/2: A road and a bridge were demolished. The dispute ended with agreement that the individual responsible will repair the damages and have the right to use them in the future.
3. Case 1989/3: A mother deeded a farm to her son in exchange for personal maintenance. The inheritance transaction was not recorded in the notary's office and the son no longer wanted to maintain her. The son did not appear at the session, so the case was referred to the Court.
4. Case 1989/4: One neighbor accused another of stealing chickens that were attracted by the neighbor's feed. This was the latest in a series of disputes between two families that has lasted for generations. No agreement was achieved and the case was referred to the Court in Wegrow.
5. Case 1989/5: Horses and cows feed on someone else's ground. The owner of the livestock agreed to keep them under control in the future.

6. Case 1989/6: An old lady complained that a neighbor's two young daughters stole potatoes from her and soiled common living areas. Co-resident agreed to control her daughters.
7. Case 1990/1: One individual without previous notification and agreement, put up a fence on another's property. The communal building inspector issued a decision to tear the fence down. Thus, in this case official authority had already settled the dispute. However, we do not know how far it applied to the conflict between the two neighbors.
8. Case 1990/2: A farmer put up an electric cattle monitor in such a place that it prevented his neighbor from farming the ground on the border. The situation remains unchanged despite repeated admonitions. At the Committee's session the monitor owner agreed to turn off the monitor when his neighbors were actively farming.

No cases were recorded for 1991, but three appear under 1992.

9. Case 1992/1: Two farmers jointly purchased some expensive farming equipment. They did not pay up the whole shares and had not dissolved the joint venture they had formed despite the initial arrangement. Before the Committee agreement was reached that repayment for the one's share will be effected in a given time.
10. Case 1992/2: A man and woman living together were in dispute. She requested that he begin to pay his share of household expenses. The case ended with agreement that he will transfer part of his pension in presence of the Commune's Secretary for household upkeep.
11. Case 1993/1 :Two neighbors quarrelled as to the border between their lots. One prevented the other from putting up a fence. The case ended in agreement on delimiting the lots in the presence of the *soltys* (head of the village).
12. Case 1993/2: One inhabitant forbade the passage of another on a road that is legally recorded in town documents and cultivated the border for his personal use. At a meeting with the Committee both agreed that the right of passage will be re-established and the second party shall stop cursing the neighbor and his family.
13. Case 1993/3: Parties to Case 1992/1 reappeared before the Committee indispute over payment of overdue tenancy fees equal to 700 U.S. dollars. The committee found it impossible to discover the facts of the case. They decided that fees in value of seventy-five dollars will be paid and no further claims shall be put forward.
14. Case 1993/4: Parties came asking for assistance in delimiting the boundary of their lots. Though this was done, their disagreement continued. It was agreed that the land surveyors will make a further delimitation. Subsequently the dispute continued with a new item on the agenda, namely who is going to pay for the services of surveyors.

Thus, in three and one half years the local conciliatory agency dealt with eleven cases of interpersonal conflict, mostly between neighbors quarrelling over property borders. Out of these disputes, at least temporary agreement was achieved in six. In sum we see that conflicts arise mainly out of material considerations and are thus similar to those from earlier periods (Kurczewski and Frieske 1978). It can be suggested that in communities like Sadowne where most inhabitants are dependent on private agriculture, there is a permanency to the kinds of conflicts that occur. Even in the 1970s I was told that the same parties often appeared with different conflicts before the Committee. The regularity of conflict, then, indicates the permanence of social relations but may also serve as a warning to those who believe that conflicts in general can be eradicated with the help of special techniques, training and education. The repetitiveness of conflicts may also explain how the Conciliatory Committee can continue to function, though long forgotten by local authorities.

That these kinds of conflict are prevalent in this kind of agricultural community is also easy to see. The density of population, general low standard of living, the small scale of agriculture that is subsistence oriented are all factors which increase the value of every small tract of land or service. Contested borders seen regularly from one's window can easily become a major burden in one's life. As it often leads to crime, it is obvious that the conflict is even a more normal aspect of social life than the crime itself. But it does not mean that local conflicts in Sadowne are limited to those largely dyadic ones involving parties of equal social status. Two cases that involve local power may illustrate better the social life of Polish countryside today.

The Case of the Temperance Priest

In 1993 Parliament amended the law on the prevention of alcoholism and drunkenness giving local governments the power to decide on the number of liquor licenses to be available to local vendors in shops, restaurants, and bars. In Sadowne at the time there were two liquor stores but a local priest claimed that the Commune council intended to increase the number to nine. However, the mayor said that only one was actually added and that this was necessary in order to enable competition and break the monopoly held by the Communal Co-op[9] which was also selling ersatz liquor to local customers.

The mayor gave me access to a considerable amount of official correspondence between the police, the prosecutor's office, and the mayor concerning local moonshine factories in the area. However, the priest's description of the local liquor distribution was altogether different. He thought that local politicians were interested in making access to liquor easier. The mayor, who sympathized politically with the Christian Democrats said that the priest's action was a breach of the constitutional principle of separation of state and church. The priest came to the meeting of the Commune's Council and presented his position. He also sent a letter to his bishop urging him to condemn the council members. It is interesting to note that this conflict was between a priest who in his temperance campaign apparently was not supported by his parishioners, and the local politicians who, though far from willing a conflict with the church, justified their actions by interest of the vast majority.

The Case of the Unwanted Electric Current Transmission

Another case seems typical if not universal throughout Poland today. The mayor told me about a petition signed by a dozen or more inhabitants who protested the decision to place an electric transmission pole locally. It is widely believed that to live near electric transmission centers of any sort is dangerous. Early on under the Communist governments it was easy for the administration to decide where to place such equipment. Resistance was not institutionalized and was easily repressed by the police. By the 1970s it was more difficult if a community was organized, and nowadays it is almost impossible to overcome community resistance. Symbolizing this issue is a fallen national public radio transmission pole north of Warsaw. Despite several attempts to persuade the local people to have it replaced, reinstalling the pole is impossible as the community doesn't wish to have it placed there.

Back in Sadowne, as soon as its mayor issued the localization decision it was contested. He quickly changed his mind and decided to place the pole elsewhere, but this decision had a similar effect. The opinion of the local public health monitoring agency is always sought in such cases, and after the petition appeared that agency said there were some legitimate grounds to the resistance. Citizens also have recourse to appeal to the voivodship court since it has power to void the decision of local government. Since many issues of this kind end up at the voivodship level, even unanimous support by the local council does not mean the mayor's decision would stand.

Now, both these conflicts are relatively small, but they illustrate how politics has changed in the post-communist transition. Thus the mayor of Sadowne today must respond to the general interest of the local community whether that may be the desire for access to cheaper liquor of better quality, or the conflicting demand for public health and better telecommunications. Though local officials also had to mediate between their community and the party-state in the past, they never were confronted with the same demand nor with the diversity of issues as they are in democratic Poland.

Local Conflicts in Small Towns Today

Unlike his counterpart in Sadowne the mayor of Olesno is not concerned about access to liquor. In this town with its strong German traditions, beer drinking is part of local culture and not something on the margins of social life. In Olesno, then, it is not surprising to learn that despite a much larger increase in the number of liquor licenses there was not a word of protest from the local clergy. As to the ethnic conflicts that were common in the late 1970s, I could find neither a Pole or German who claimed such inter-ethnic conflict here and now. Informal links with Germany were maintained by the families who lived here before 1945, whether of German or Polish identity. The division of the community into "autochtones" and "newcomers" was always acknowledged and in principle was even kept in mind also by the Communists when they distributed the nomenklatura posts. It does not mean that there are no local conflicts here though. One in particular is suggestive of the essence of transitional society.

The Case of the Closed Nursery

The public network of nurseries, kindergartens and other educational services is an element of the Communist welfare-state that many in Poland sorely miss. This is especially so today since the number of people in need has increased. From my survey a picture of society emerges that shows it more and more divided into two large groups in so far as the desire for state services is concerned. The first are those who have great concern for the welfare of their children and very much desire continuation of state-supported educational services. The second group are those who, due to their lack of skills and education, feel estranged and alienated from the new, and to them unintelligible and unpredictable, market economy. Given their general alienation they are much less concerned about access to such state services. In response to the latter group and the general economic downturn, the mayor of Olesno, well-known for his left-wing sympathies, decided to close the communal nursery arguing that it was too costly and there were too few children enrolled. This decision was passed by the commune's council in March 1993. As could be expected, however, it was quickly protested by the concerned parents. In their petition they explained that it is unnatural to expect all the children at such an early age to be present on any one day in the nursery and argued twenty-three children actually use the nursery instead of the nine the council cited. The protesting parents also said that the Council's decision was made without due process as the Council refused to hear their complaint. They even compared some members of the Council to "twelve angry men". The protesting parents then raised another social aspect by referring to the new law restricting abortions. "Won't the threat of loss of their jobs cause Olesno women to buy abortion-inducing and anti-conception pills instead of aspirin or other headache remedies?" they asked, playing the religious card. Subsequently the Czestochowa voivod annulled the decision to close the nursery as contrary to law. However, the Mayor appealed that decision to the Administrative Court and won. As to the concerned parents, they established a co-op that helped settle the issue. Now what they pay does not equal the costs of the former nursery since there are no administrative costs..

Local Conflicts in Transition: A Summary

Though Olesno is close to Praszka, in Summer 1993 the two towns seemingly stood at opposite poles regarding the development of their social problems and conflicts. In the first place the two towns differed in the extent to which formal channels of conflict resolution were utilized. The turmoil in Praszka grew as the unemployed organized themselves and ultimately led to the dissolution of local government and direct intervention of the central authorities. In contrast, in Olesno, the lot of the mothers who lost access to kindergarten was decided at the local level by democratic practice. But despite these differences the two are structurally of the same type. In both Olesno and Praszka groups that enjoyed state social services (e.g. free nursery, secure jobs) suddenly lost them. Consequently the state in the person of local authorities, though under the new law locally elected, nonetheless became the opposition in each conflict. As previous social rights were now deemed privileges, the underprivileged expressed their discontent and then organized themselves to formally oppose local government. In this way, such conflicts transformed local life and even spawned new political actors.

We don't know yet what the future of these interest groups will be. However, there are some groups such as the Movement for Defence of Women's Rights and Interests in Olesno, created by local educated women, that are successful in advising the poor and may very well extend their reach to the national stage. Meanwhile the movement of unemployed in Praszka, though pressured by formal government agencies, was also strengthened by its encapsulation within a nation-wide movement. This further led to the development of a self-conscious group of activists of whom some plan to use the movement as a springboard into professional politics. Meanwhile at the level of the public knowledge of these conflicts, Praszka and Olesno differ only as to the relative size and resulting influence of the conflict on social life. While not all the inhabitants of Olesno know of the closed nursery, the unemployed of Praszka occupy the front pages of the national press and the lead story on the TV news. In Sadowne, the most rural of the townships under comparison, the level of conflict is also limited to the local community.

Such conflicts have potentially great significance for national level political processes. Though 1989 marked the beginning of the construction of the rule of law in Poland, the achievements of parliamentary legislation are permanently critiqued in the press and public opinion (Kurczewski 1993d). Few people realize that the constitutional principle of a "democratic state of law" is fulfilled not only through the existence of supreme tribunals that issue judgements on the constitutionality of legislation or the constitutional liability of politicians but also in the local conflicts of the kind described above. Paradoxically, then, as such conflicts manifest throughout Poland, democratic practice will be strengthened. In this regard it is interesting to note that what is particularly remarkable in almost all cases we have discussed was that proper legal channels were used by the parties to the conflict. Though the results were not always satisfactory for those involved, the legalization of the dispute, making it public and official, is a precious outcome of the changes in Poland over the last four years.

But even this picture may be distorted due to the peculiarity of the stage that the process of change is passing through at the moment. Certainly there is a continuation of conflicts between individuals, the only ones made public under communism . Now, however, previously individualized conflicts with authorities are carried over into new forms and, as such, not only become public, but are also collectivized in a way. Thus they restructure the social world of the locality and nation and create new actors who link personal claims with group politics. Furthermore conflicts today suggest that since 1989 the government has been taken more seriously by Poles. Thousands of city councils are now active in the process at an intensity equal to the national parliament. Localities now have new political actors and old ones with new political identities as well. In a solemn hall of the ancient royal city of Cracow, for example, one president of the council was successfully voted out of office after a dozen failed attempts. This illustrates the heat of the political struggle that goes on at the local commune level. To understand those debates one need develop an anthropology of local interests to clarify them.

In any case, we have certainly come a long way since the communist period. Then, for example, knowledge of social conflict was suppressed to such a degree that the weekly *Polityka* declined in the 1970s to publish an article by me and Prof. Jadwiga Staniszkis. In that article we pleaded for recognition of conflicts so these could be 'peacefully settled.' As benign as this was the article was still not published as we used the words "social conflict" in its title. Despite the refusal to acknowledge the fact of social conflict, we must make note of two more points. First, some conflicts were deliberately instigated by Party authorities in order to achieve political goals. Thus, for instance, in 1968 the conflict over reforming and liberalizing communism was changed into an anti-Semitic purge aimed at diverting people's attention from supporting students and intellectuals. Similarly, in 1966 the authorities mobilized Party activists to wreak havoc at the festivities celebrating a millennium of Christianity in Poland which were organized by the Catholic Church under Cardinal Stefan Wyszynski. Second, individual conflicts were allowed to emerge at the institutional level in form of civil or private accusation disputes before the court, despite the disgust of more orthodox Marxist scholars and politicians, who considered it unworthy of the apparatus of the socialist state to be involved with such mundane matters. Out of these critiques then came ideas to suppress private accusation procedures, to raise the costs of judicial proceedings, or to supplement the court with less serious conciliation by the reliable citizens in the neighborhood. Whatever the aspirations, the reality was that in Communist Poland conflicts were privatized at the individual level. The Party--and this seems to be a common feature of the totalitarian regimes--suppressed expression of conflicts at the collective level and channeled it into the mass of individual conflicts. Conflicts at the collective level were only those that were organized on the initiative of the ruling elite itself. Finally, the individualization of conflicts by no means meant that conflicts between individual citizen and the state, whether as administration or as the almost universal employer (agriculture excepted), were allowed to develop freely into an uncontrolled dispute. On the contrary, these were often suppressed with help of the discretionary power of the administration itself and diverted out of the court as much as possible. Such practices continued even after the judicial review of administrative decisions, though on procedural matters only, was restituted at the beginning of 1980.

The "steady diet of conflicts" continues today in courts and in community neighborhoods, as the number of cases dealt with by local conciliatory bodies attest. And though most conflicts continue to be characterized as property disputes between individuals, more and more individuals enter into conflict with authorities. As this develops we expect the next stage to be characterized by organized disputes between interest groups and local administrations. In this process communal actions like writing petitions, setting up committees and organizing protests become routine and party politics becomes intertwined with local issues, conflicts and actions. Local conflicts like that in Praszka which make national headlines allow some politicians to gain over others but also enable local people to feel that national level politics takes account of their actions and problems, and in this way helps overcome the alienation of the political class.

As democratic Poland has instituted the constitutionality of local self-government, local conflicts may enliven local politics as well so long as they are opened up to the expression of public interest and require politicians to be publically accountable. Still, the key question remains whether conflicts will primarily be of a zero-sum game or not.. If the former, the chance is that they may undermine the functioning of democracy in the country as a whole. Even here, our cases suggest some possible developments. Even the Praszka conflict, in which the unemployed challenged the constitutional order, and which resulted in the breakdown of local democracy and the intervention of the central government representative, holds out something positive. After all, the political goal of the unemployed was to involve by all means available the central government in the local issue that was beyond the local means to be settled. Subsequently, in recognition of local needs, the government facilitated an increase in locally available job positions and sent additional emergency aid as well. Conflict thus produced political awareness on the part of central government and helped to calm the moods. It may sound ironic, but in fact it is rather prophetic that the down-sized Praszka factory recently recorded an up swing in production.

Notes

1. On the private accusation procedure and its role in everyday disputes see Fuszara (1987, 1989) where she presented the detailed study in Warsaw and two rural districts on how this procedure which according to Polish criminal procedure mostly applicable in case of libel, slander or a minor bodily injury and which accounted for about one fourth of cases reported to police was used to get compensation out of the court and to defend one's moral value in social context. In these cases the public prosecution is absent and the victim of the crime is the private prosecutor before the court that renders the verdict and may punish the offender with fine or short-time imprisonment.

2. A note on wheel-barrows is necessary. In Poland their use is part of a well-established ritual of degradation. I first heard of this in 1956 when rebellious workers put communist factory directors or Party apparatchiki on wheel-barrows and crowds shouted obscenities as they were carried away. Furthermore, the meaning of the ritual is intensified as wheel-barrows are symbols of working people. A person ritually degraded in such a way could not hope to govern any longer, even if the powers-that-be still supported them.

3. Transition to market economy was marked by sudden appearance of unemployment that is still on increase. At the end of 1989 the percentage of registered unemployed in active labor force was 0.3, in 1990 6.1, in 1991 11.1, in 1992 13.6 and at the end of 1993 15.7.

4. In response to questions about why the press was present one of the Self-Defence leaders humorously said in defense of his cause that "a bit of demagoguery always helps.".

5. Occupation of government offices was a practice begun by protesting farmers in 1980. Why farmers preferred this strategy is obvious. Workers strike by occupying their factories. Polish farmers own their farms, so halting or limiting their production would only harm themselves. Consequently they take over the premises of local or central authorities to focus attention on their cause.

6. Data for this table was collected by M. Iwanska.

7. Data for this table was collected by I. Krzesak.

8. Data for this table were collected by I. Krzesak.

9. The co-op was a commercial organization that, under Communist rule, held the monopoly on liquor sales in the countryside and which provided the infrastructure to the so-called "green nomenklatura."

10. After the 1975 administrative reform the country was divided in several thousand communes, of rural, urban or even metropolitan character, each with its own local government. After 1989 local government comprised an elected Council that appoints the Board of the Commune with its head whom we translate here as Mayor.

References

Fuszara, Malgorzata 1987. "Negotiating rights and duties in private accusation cases settlement" *In* J. Kurczewski, Ed., *Niedzica Castle Papers on Rights and Duties*, Warsaw: IPSIR UW

____ 1989. *Everyday Conflicts and Holiday Justice*. Warsaw: IPSIR UW.

Gesicka, Grazyna 1993. *Local Committees*. Warsaw: Development Fund.

Hirschman, Albert O. 1994 "Social Conflicts as Pillars of Democratic Market Society", *Political Theory* 22(2): 203-218.

Kucharski, Tomasz 1993. "Wheel-barrow from Praszka," *Gazeta Wyborcza*, August 4, 1993.

Kurczewski, Jacek 1982. *Dispute and Courts*, Warsaw: IPSIR University of Warsaw.

____ 1993a. "Charm of the Pears at Willow Trees," *Res Publica Nova*, October.

____ 1993b. *The Resurrection of Rights in Poland.* Oxford: The Clarendon Press.

____ 1993c . "Sad and Frustrated," *Polityka*, September 17, 1993.

____1993d. Democracy Under the Rule of Law: A Short Review of Polish Experience. Warsaw: Sociology of Custom and Law, University of Warsaw

Kurczewski, Jacek and K. Frieske 1978. "The Social Conciliatory Commissions in Poland." *In* M. Cappelletti and J. Weisner, Eds, *Access to Justice, Vol II, Promising Institutions, part I.* Aaphenaandenrijhn/ Milano, Sijthof/Giuffre 1978.

Skwiecinski, Piotr 1993. "Compromise," *Zycie Warszawy*, August 9, 1993.

Waszkielewicz, Bernadetta 1993. "Unemployed Tempest in Praszka," *Rzeczpospolita*, August 5, 1993.

9

Uneasy Accommodation: Ethnicity and Politics in Rural Bulgaria

Daniel Bates

Throughout Eastern Europe, the regions of the former U.S.S.R., and the Balkans one issue dominates political discussion: the specter of politicized ethnicity. The bloody aftermath of the dissolution of Yugoslavia gives a special poignancy to this for the Moslem minorities of Bulgaria. Is internecine strife inevitable; can local and national political structures peacefully accommodate ethnic and cultural diversity? "We are as much part of Bulgaria as anyone else, and our culture and language must be respected," a Turkish member of Parliament told me. "We are not guest workers here and we won't live like guest workers." A Bulgarian business person from the same region expressed an oft-repeated opinion of the new prominence of Turkish and Moslem minorities, "The Turks think they are *bey* (master) once more; no Bulgarian should ever have to live under Turkish rule again." Although there is profound skepticism among many of Bulgaria's Turks that they will be allowed to live normal lives, openly practicing their religion and expressing their cultural heritage following years of forced assimilation, in the northeastern region of Bulgaria, one of the two main areas of Turkish-speaking population concentration, Turkish is once more heard in cafes and marketplaces. More important, it is heard in the local corridors of power, as recently elected officials deal with their newly enfranchised constituents. At the same time, this has to be seen as an uneasy accommodation given Bulgaria's history of anti-Turkish nationalism. Legally or otherwise over 100,000 Turks left the country for Turkey in 1992 (HÖH 1993, No.29:1-2).

Even so, the case of Bulgaria is clearly instructive, perhaps even hopeful. The largely Turkish-supported political party, the Movement for Rights and Freedoms (MRF), has emerged as a strong voice for Turkish cultural interests and at the same time has become a largely constructive force in Bulgaria's new democracy. The empowerment of an ethnic political party might seem to confirm the fears of many that with the fall of socialism centrifugal forces of ethnicity and regionalism will take hold. Indeed, Bulgarian nationalists miss few opportunities to denounce the MRF as a threat to national integrity, even as a "fifth column" for a renewed Turkish incursion into Europe (see Konstantinov 1992:76). In fact, the MRF is centrist in terms of social and economic policy, and entirely pragmatic in tactics, and has become pivotal to Bulgaria's transition to multi-party politics and a market-based economy; the present and previous post-Communist governments achieved power only with MRF support. While the MRF is committed to the promotion of perceived Turkish and Moslem interests, accusations by nationalists that it promotes Islamic militancy are very wide of the mark. Nothing could be farther from the Movement's stated policy and, indeed, would be politically self-defeating. The party explicitly presents itself as part of a, probably idealized, European tradition of recognizing minority rights; one of its slogans is to "Make Bulgaria the Switzerland of the Balkans." As a largely rural-based party, the MRF takes positions, such as favoring price control of essential services like water, fuel, and transport, and commodity price platforms and control for wheat, tobacco, and other crops, which reflect rural interests in general. In this the Movement finds itself uneasily aligned with the Bulgarian Socialist Party (BSP), the renamed and, arguably, reformed Bulgarian Communist Party (Glenny 1990; Creed 1991, 1992).

This discussion, focusing primarily on the Turkish population in the region of Shumen in northeastern Bulgaria, will attempt to provide an understanding of aspects of Turkish minority political organization at the local level, the factors giving rise to the rapid mobilization of a politicized minority, and possible consequences for the region and for the country as a whole.

Background

Despite frequent nationalist outbursts in the press and Parliament, and despite the often highly nationalistic posturing of the BSP (Tomova and Bogoev 1992, Brown 1989) and a number of right-wing neo-fascist parties, Bulgaria is experiencing one of the most peaceful transitions of any of the countries of Eastern Europe. The legitimizing and empowerment, under law, of religious and national minorities has so far engendered a political environment in which major economic and social issues can be addressed. It also has helped to draw into the mainstream a major, hitherto alienated, segment of the population. Should this process halt, or worse, reverse, and should minority out-migration continue, Bulgaria is likely to face a serious labor shortage in agriculture and construction.

While the movement to private enterprise and a market economy in the face of massive economic problems, due mainly to loss of traditional trading partners and of inexpensive oil, is far from easy, Bulgaria has stabilized its currency, reduced inflation, and undertaken one of the most stringent austerity programs in Eastern Europe (Glenny 1993:260). Although many Bulgarians are disturbed by the new assertiveness of the Islamic minorities (Tomova and Bogoev 1992), the MRF has helped preserve the center in national politics. Even if the BSP could form a government without MRF support, it would lack legitimacy given that it reflects only 30% of the national vote. The alternative, represented by what is left of the Union of Democratic Forces (UDF), is an unwieldy amalgam of splinter groups with a hazy anti-communist ideology and without a coherent policy other than rapid privatization. The present government is the second democratically elected coalition government in which the MRF is a not-so-silent partner. By recognizing the legitimacy of the MRF, two governments (and the Constitutional Court) have accepted the legitimacy of parties organized on ethnic lines, in spite of Article 11 of the 1991 constitution, which forbids political organizations based on ethnic, racial, or confessional principles. The implications of this for future political stability are significant given the demography of the country. The December 4, 1992 census, as unofficially reported in the press, put the national population at 8,473,000, with self-designated Bulgarians constituting 85.8% of the total, Turks 9.7%, and Gypsies 3.4%, the remaining 1.1% being Armenians and Jews (Tomova and Bogoev 1992: 2-3; HÖH, 1993, No.13:3; Insider, 1993, No.3:37). [1]

The area in which the research presented here was carried out, Shumen district of Varna Province, is soon to be reorganized to become one of Bulgaria's 13 new provinces (*oblast)*, and is part of a larger region of the northeast where Turkish speakers and other Moslem populations have been long established. The bulk of the Turkish-speaking population throughout Bulgaria is rural dwelling. Shumen and the northeast in general differ from the other main area of Turkish concentration in the southwest, the Rhodops, in being relatively prosperous. Although the city of Shumen (population ca.105,000) is a major industrial center and while smaller manufacturing concerns are to be found throughout rural areas, the region is heavily agricultural. At the time of this study in 1991-92, Shumen consisted of ten municipalities, 110 villages, with the Turkish-speaking population concentrated in eighty-two villages. Moslem communities are distinguishable from Christian by the presence of mosques or churches, or by the dress of the women, and homes are generally of solid masonry construction, each surrounded by well-tended fenced gardens. The region saw a great deal of infrastructure investment during the forty-five years of Communist rule, and everywhere communities are electrified, usually have piped water, paved streets, and in the larger villages, impressive, even over-built public buildings such as schools, day-care centers, movie houses, administrative offices, etc.. Most rural homes, too, are of post-1955 construction and as a consequence usually do not have the adjacent sheds or barns for livestock and crop storage that were part of pre-collectivized household production.

The 1991 Elections

The October 1991 elections provide a point of entry for a discussion of ethnic politics and politicized ethnicity. Bulgaria's second nationwide balloting since 1989 was notable in Shumen for several reasons. First, the large-scale demonstrations and protests by Turks in May 1989 in this district had set in motion the events which can be directly linked to the subsequent collapse of communism in Bulgaria (Petkov and Fotev 1990). A local Turkish intellectual made the somewhat exaggerated claim that "If it had not been for the uprisings of the Turks, Bulgaria would be a second Cuba today." Second, in the period since 1990 the hitherto invisible Turkish minority of the province organized itself politically, becoming part of a disciplined national political movement. Third, despite provocations and often strident nationalist opposition, as well as a local political elite eager to preserve its influence, the elections went off without serious incident. The vast majority of citizens, of all ethnic groups, took their responsibilities seriously. Over twenty parties locally, and forty nationally, contended for 250 seats in parliament as well as for mayorships (*kmet)* and other local offices. However, the key parties in the Shumen area and, as it transpired, nationally, were the MRF, the BSP, and the UDF.[2]

The MRF: The Political Culture of Exclusion

Even though the MRF presents itself as a party promoting human rights, it effectively promotes a political culture rooted in community identity; in fact, it can be said that the MRF has undertaken a self-conscious effort at creating a Turkish communal identity that spans considerable regional variation and which, to some degree, embraces non-Turkish Moslems. In what Konstatinov terms a "we/they minority type of discourse" the MRF stresses the shared experience of collective Moslem suffering at the hands of the majority (Konstantinov 1992:77). This is not to be confused with nationalism, separatism, or irredentism (which are repudiated by all MRF leaders). It is the assertion of cultural identity rooted in shared language and/or religion, within a multi-ethnic state. The MRF is frequently accused by political opponents of using intimidation to maintain the unity of the party and to prevent Turkish candidates from running on other slates or as independents. This is generally unfounded; what non-minority political observers find hard to account for is the near complete lack of interest among Turkish-speaking Bulgarians in ethnically Bulgarian dominated parties, even liberal ones such as the UDF. Threats and intimidation are simply not needed given the deeply rooted alienation of minorities as a result of the policy of forced assimilation (see Georgeoff 1981; Eminov 1986, 1989; Konstantinov 1992).

Speeches, articles in the MRF newspaper, and discussion groups frequently focus on the need to maintain unity in the face of external threats to identity and religion, reference to oppression in the past, and a recollection of Turkish cultural accomplishments. In 1990, Turkish theater and folklore groups were formed in Shumen and in many villages. Quite literally, they had to invent their repertory, drawing more often on Anatolian sources than local Rumeli (Western Turkish) ones. Literary and cultural circles were founded to promote Turkish language and culture and to fight assimilation. Like the MRF, the national Association for Turkish Language and Culture, founded in Shumen as a teachers' organization, has demanded compulsory language training in Turkish for ethnic Turks in the national school system. By support for village folklore groups, Turkish literary and arts groups, language training and some religious activity, such as religious instruction and the rebuilding of mosques and pilgrimage sites (such as the *tekke* of Demir Baba in the northeast), the MRF promotes a sense of political community. One apparent problem with this idiom of politics is that it is hard to maintain appeal to Moslem Gypsies and Pomaks;[3] also, it clearly threatens the often expressed objective of the MRF leadership to become a truly national party.

One of the MRF's first accomplishments in Shumen was to reopen the Nuuvab School for the training of religious leaders. To achieve this it had to work with the national Moslem religious hierarchy which was still in the hands of Zhivkov appointees. Founded in 1922, the school was, prior to the socialist era, a bastion of religious conservatism and against the secular reforms then underway in the Republic of Turkey (Şimşir 1988). Arabic script was used in the school until 1945, long after it was dropped in Turkey. Nevertheless, the Nuuvab School was a major educational facility for the Moslem community, with many of its graduates going on to earn university degrees in secular subjects. Thus, the institution had great significance throughout Moslem Bulgaria. Simply reclaiming the physical facilities from the Shumen authorities in 1990 was a major achievement, and one accomplished in the face of nationalist opposition. For the first two years, teachers had to take turns sleeping in the main building to prevent vandalism. In 1991 the newly reopened school accepted some 60 male and 25 female students selected from Moslem communities all over Bulgaria. While instruction was primarily in Bulgarian (indeed, some fifteen Pomak students knew no other language) it offered, in addition to religious instruction, a mandatory curriculum in Turkish language, history, and literature.

Unlike comparable Islamic institutions in Turkey, male and female students socialize easily, faculty, administrators, and students do not wear Islamic garb (other than in prayer or in courses dealing directly with religious practice), and generally the students participate in activities, such as plays, dances, going to coffee shops and discos, which are frowned upon if not forbidden in strict Islamic institutions. Currently the institution seems to promote a sense of Islam as a cultural heritage and thus defines the boundary of the larger community which was earlier targeted for forced assimilation. The program of forced assimilation, which aimed at creating a monolithic Slavic Bulgarian cultural identity, in practice struck directly at virtually all outward symbols of the Islamic faith: Islamic names were outlawed, plaques and inscriptions in Arabic script obliterated, tombstones defaced, Islamic dress and rites relating to circumcision, burial, and marriage restricted or banned (see Eminov 1983, 1986, 1989; and Karpat ed. 1990). Consequently, one of the demands of Moslem protesters, even prior to the formation of the MRF, was for religious freedom. However, given the nature of Islam in Bulgaria and in contrast to Turkey either in the nationalist period early in the century or today, there is little inherent conflict between religious and secular vehicles for shaping community identity. This may, of course, change as Islamic institutions shake off the legacy of the socialist era. The principal of the newly reopened school was trained as a history teacher rather than a religious scholar and the first vice-principal, an individual who strongly subscribes to Ataturk's principles of secularism, was also for a period regional president of the MRF. Since the pre-1989 religious establishment is tainted by close collaboration with the Zhivkov regime, the younger, secular-educated MRF presently has considerable influence in shaping the resurgence in religious interest among Moslems. In Shumen, as in other districts, the local MRF organization coordinated mass picketing of the regional *mufti's* offices and ultimately secured the appointment of a replacement agreeable to them as well as to the regional congregation. The *mufti's* office controls the appointments of local *imams* (clergy responsible for leading the prayers and delivering Friday sermons), the administration of mosques, the appointment of religious teachers, the acceptance of students to religious schools, and the management of religious properties.

As endowments are being returned to religious institutions, there is considerable property at stake. Prior to 1944, few Moslems attended public schools and most Moslem education was supported by endowments in the form of land and other income-producing property. There is a general revival of religious interest in Bulgaria but there is also little doubt that this is vastly greater among Moslems; mosques are being built throughout the Moslem regions, most villages have started up schools to instruct children in the Koran, and several hundred students have been sent abroad to study in Islamic institutions. The MRF encourages community members to use its organization as a route to the local bureaucracy. For example, local MRF organizations offer assistance to those preparing land or property claims and take an active role in re-establishing village cooperatives, about which more will be said later. Its political mode might be described as "disciplined consensus." Every effort is made to minimalize factional differences, to keep the Movement from splintering as electoral success brings new responsibilities and new opportunities for individual advancement at the perceived expense of others. Those individuals who do not support the Movement are often referred to as "uninformed," "victimized," or "bought." This last reference is to those who stray from MRF positions, who establish (as has happened in several instances) local organizations rivaling the

MRF, or, as happened in the study region, those in largely Bulgarian villages who have taken firewood or cooking oil from BSP organizers.

Virtually all formal political activity among ethnic Turks is expressed within the MRF. In the Shumen region every Turkish village has an MRF office or "club." The district is divided into nine organizational areas, each with two coordinators who work with village representatives. Most activity among the Moslem populations in the region leading up to the elections was coordinated by the Shumen office of the MRF. Campaigning as we generally understand it was not part of the MRF's preparations for the election. Education, guidance, and counselling are more accurate terms. Speaking almost exclusively in Turkish to Turkish audiences, representatives and candidates attempted to communicate the importance of unity for the community, described efforts planned to initiate Turkish language instruction, and finally, showed people how to recognize the MRF ballot. Direct confrontation or debate with representatives of different parties were avoided.

The BSP: Nationalism and Rural Politics

The major support of the BSP also lies in the rural areas, of which Shumen is entirely typical. In 1992, for the first time in over two decades, agricultural production overtook that of heavy industry, in spite of a net decline in agricultural sectors. While this is not surprising given the near stagnation in heavy industry and mining, it is an indication that, to the extent that it keeps in touch with its rural constituency, this party will continue to play a major role in Bulgarian political life. The Shumen BSP operates out of a modern four-story building, whose red flag flying at a jaunty angle from the roof and red posters and banners leave no doubt as to the party's tactics of drawing on recollections of a better past. As with the MRF and the UDF, its headquarters contain a restaurant and social club for members, but it was the only party locally to have a working photocopying machine and printing establishment. Under the Zhivkov regime, the regional Party organization had great autonomy and was the apex of an obvious system of patronage (Creed 1992; Glenny 1993) which, to a lesser degree, is still maintained by the BSP. Although it has lost control of much of the Turkish-dominated countryside, its municipal officials are (or were) indefatigable in issuing urban business permits, leasing public buildings to private entrepreneurs, and entering into private contracts to rebuild or manage formerly city-run businesses. In spite of strongly expressed nationalist or anti-Turkish views, the BSP-controlled city government has not hesitated to enter into commercial agreements with Turkish investors and entrepreneurs.

It is useful to look locally to understand the BSP's high level of support. The BSP is widely acknowledged to be the best organized, most disciplined, and best funded of the twenty-three parties represented in the region. It may well have the most able candidates, given that it dominated the economic and political scene for nearly sixty years without any non-Turkish opposition. In Shumen at least it is hard to find educated, trained individuals who were not in some manner involved with the Communist Party. Despite the much noted reforms of 1989 and 1990, the local BSP promotes what some call "nostalgia politics," thinly disguised appeals to a cossetted and secure totalitarian past. Its local strength is considerable and in the 1991 elections it far outstripped the opposition with thirty-five percent of the votes. The BSP candidate won the Shumen mayoral elections (after a run-off) and the party dominates the city council. Most ethnic Bulgarian BSP supporters interviewed were quick to disassociate themselves from Marxism and the Zhivkov era Communist Party, but were vague about what they actually want that distinguishes them from other parties. All noted a commitment to "democracy" and a "free market." Turkish BSP supporters were predictably few in numbers. The only local Turkish BSP mayor was a pragmatist who thought that he could do more for his village as part of the BSP regional organization, but that he might shift to the MRF in the future. While the local BSP leadership clearly represents entrenched interests, the elderly and the unskilled support it as a consequence of economic reform.

At the local level, fear of the future sums up the atmosphere in which the BSP recruits. Through 1991 and 1992 flurries of rumors circulated to the effect that pensions would be terminated, that public health care would be privatized, that free schooling and child care would be abolished. Between December 1989, when the Communists lost their political monopoly, and December 1993 prices have soared over 400% and unemployment has risen to over twenty percent. Among ethnic Turks, unemployment is perceived to be higher. The troubled transition to private land ownership has left many bewildered; most lack equipment and facilities to farm efficiently as private owners but the new cooperatives have yet to take root effectively (see Creed, this volume).

Coercion and threats are also not entirely absent from the local scene, which makes the calm of the 1991 election and its peaceful aftermath the more striking. The districts of Shumen and Razgrad are loci of intense nationalist activity, undoubtedly in proportion to the size of the Turkish minority. Prior to the 1990 Constitutional Assembly elections, the MRF offices in Shumen were destroyed by a bomb; in nearby Razgrad in January 1990 the ultra-nationalist Worker's Nationalist Movement, led by the number three candidate on the BSP parliamentary list, proclaimed a purely Bulgarian "republic"; demonstrations against Turkish language instruction in schools were widespread, and local publications wrote of the threat of "Turkish oppression." In a number of district villages divided along ethnic lines or where the Bulgarian population is a slim majority, nationalism was expressed in slogans like "no Bulgarian should be governed by a Turk." In one village, according to MRF activists, BSP activists threatened reprisals if MRF ballots were used. In another community, prior to a run-off for mayor between the BSP-supported "independent" candidate and the

MRF candidate, the local MRF party leader alleged he was taken by force, and threatened with death should he call out MRF supporters. It is an article of faith among MRF leaders that foreign ultra-nationalists from the Netherlands and other West European countries with large Turkish immigrant populations have made sizeable cash contributions to local anti-Turkish groups. MRF members allege that much BSP support comes from individuals motivated by fear of legal reprisals for their role in the forced assimilation programs of the 1980s.

The BSP does have some support among Moslem minorities. It is difficult to evaluate its extent, but regional voting patterns suggests that it is less than three percent. This includes those who owe their positions to local patronage, former community leaders under the Communists who moved comfortably into the new BSP, and from predominantly Bulgarian villages where the BSP dominates and who simply want to get along with their neighbors. The *mufti* of Shumen, the officially recognized leader of the local Moslem community, owed his job to government patronage and appeared on local television stating, I was told, that Moslems need not fear the BSP; that the racial policies of the old Bulgarian Communist Party were the fault of Soviet influence. Other religious leaders, including Genchev, the Grand *Mufti* until 1992, called for Moslems to vote independently from any party, a remark interpreted as a call for support for the BSP, or at least against the MRF. Still, most of the communist-appointed national Moslem religious hierarchy, institutionalized by treaty at independence in 1878 to administer religious properties and trusts (see Crampton 1990), has now been replaced at MRF insistence.

The UDF: Democracy and the Rural/Urban Divide

In Shumen the 1991 election saw the UDF coalition thoroughly beaten by the BSP, drawing less than fifteen percent of the vote. It had likewise been beaten by the BSP in the 1990 elections. The blue posters of the UDF stressed the end of communism and the primacy of democracy and economic reform, but offered few promises, such as those of the BSP, to reduce unemployment and to distribute land to the landless members of cooperatives. The UDF, reputedly with considerable American support (Glenny1993:175ff; Smollett 1993), mounted a western-style campaign with tables in the main streets manned with volunteers distributing pins, pamphlets, and little flags, selling tape cassettes of catchy songs, and candidates shaking hands with passers-by. In 1991, as the main nation-wide opposition organization, the UDF could succeed only if it could avoid losing its likely supporters to "look alike" off-shoots, and by working with the better disciplined MRF.

Nationally, the MRF has had an ambivalent relationship with the UDF. Generally they shared the anti-communist principles which motivated the organization. However, the MRF leadership had no desire to dilute their minority rights agenda to suit the leadership of the UDF, which strongly opposed both ethnic-based political organizations and laws which would recognize communal rights as opposed to individual rights. The MRF has always demanded, for example, that Turkish students be provided compulsory courses in Turkish language in state schools in order to counter processes of assimilation. Locally, the MRF leadership was wary of too close links with the UDF. They supported UDF candidates where they did not field their own, but were aware of the UDF's frequent inability to recruit qualified individuals and of their limited appeal to rural voters. At the village level, UDF organization was extremely thin. UDF groups and other liberal parties argued that there was no reason for the MRF to field its own candidates; that ethnic rights were already secure. Since the collapse, in January 1993, of the UDF-led government following the withdrawal of MRF support in November 1992 in protest at the government's agricultural policies, the UDF has openly spoken out against the MRF's influence, but has itself largely dissolved into factions.

In 1991 nationally the UDF did well in cities, other than in the Turkish regions, and poorly in the countryside. Quite simply, the non-Turkish opposition has been unable to recruit able rural candidates and to set up local organizations comparable to the entrenched BSP. But the rural appeal of the BSP goes well beyond the current inability of the UDF to recruit strong candidates. As Creed notes, there is a significant division in Bulgarian society between urban and rural sectors, and when rural people are given a choice, "certain ideas and achievements associated with the socialist system and its representatives still held a resonance for them" (Creed 1991:58-59; see also 1993). Chief among these is a strong sense of egalitarianism and an ancillary fear of inequality, as well as the idea that the provision of health care and employment is a basic responsibility of government. The MRF rural membership, however strongly it rejects the nationalism embraced by the BSP, does share these views.

The 1991 Election Results

Early reports on the BBC and on Bulgarian radio and television predicted a crushing defeat for the heirs to the Bulgarian Communist Party, although this seemed improbable from the vantage point of the northeast. In the end, the BSP, almost universally referred to by non-members as "the Communists", only slightly trailed the UDF, thirty-three to thirty-four percent, with the MRF in third place at eight percent. In a heavy turn-out (80% nationwide) the MRF acquired twenty-four seats in Parliament and a considerable and controversial influence in the new government. Of those elected by the MRF to Parliament, four were Pomak, four Bulgarian, and the remainder Turkish. Further, the MRF won the mayorships of 652 villages, twenty-seven municipalities, and placed 1144 individuals on city councils. There are few European examples, and none in recent Bulgarian history, of a party perceived to represent minority ethnic interests holding the balance of power. While this is very much attributable to the leadership skills of the MRF, and while it may be only a transitory phenomenon, it has to be understood in terms of remarkable local-level organization and mobilization of a segment of population previously subjected to a campaign of forced assimilation of a ferocity not seen elsewhere in Europe.

In Shumen the MRF fielded seven candidates for parliament on the district-wide ballot, of whom two received sufficient votes to go to Sofia to take up four-year terms. The two elected to parliament were ethnic Bulgarian MRF members but resident elsewhere. Four other candidates, ethnic Turks, received sufficient votes to win the mayorships of four important municipalities. The remaining candidate, the district MRF president, was not elected. A peculiarity of the election law is that it allows a party to run parliamentary candidates in more than one district and thereby ensure that individuals favored by the party's central organization are elected. Individuals who fall from party favor, however popular, may not appear on party ballots. It would seem that this aspect of the electoral law favors the disciplined BSP and MRF rather than the faction-ridden UDF and the myriad other parties. For example, in this case it facilitated the election of two ethnic Bulgarians, viewed as important by the MRF central organization, over locally more popular Turkish candidates.

The election results in one large village, which has perhaps ten non-Turkish households, are indicative of the MRF's support. Of 306 households, 1,103 people, there were 738 eligible voters, of whom 664 actually voted. The MRF received 503 votes, UDF thirty-six, BSP thirty, and the Agrarian Party twelve. The remaining ten parties, including the "real Communists", the BCP, the Marxist Party, the Business Party, and UDF splinter parties totalled only forty-one votes. (The fact that the discredited BCP received eleven votes was taken as evidence of ballot confusion.) While not monolithic, the MRF is clearly the principal vehicle for political action among ethnic Turks. Pomaks and Moslem Gypsies are another matter.

Turkish Villages and the Future of Ethnic Politics

Village politics are focussed on who occupies the mayor's office, the composition of the council that will assist this individual, and on the composition of the co-op leadership, or those charged with the disbanding village cooperatives, the "TKZS."[4] In many respects these officials are critical to the day-to-day management of the economic transition now underway in Bulgaria, acting as they do to privatize property, attest to certain property claims, dispose of state property, give out commercial licenses, and the like. In this the MRF used its influence with the UDF government to secure appointments to Land

Commissions as well as to transition cooperatives where extant ones were placed in receivership.

The nature of village administrative buildings themselves reflect both the dominance of the Socialist state in local affairs and its investment in community development. The mayor's office in many villages is often as large as that of an American university president, and contains along with the usual emblems of officialdom, an array of telephones and intercoms, a massive wall-system with an over-sized TV set and radio, liquor cabinet, extensive shelving (now largely empty), a conference table for ten to twelve, arm chairs, sofa and coffee table. In addition, depending on the village and its place in the settlement hierarchy, there will be scaled-down versions of the same for assistant mayors, secretaries, cultural officers, managers of water, sewage, roads, etc. With the fall of the Communist regime, this top-down line of authority has changed in some respects. Village institutions now have far more autonomy in most spheres of action, albeit with vastly curtailed resources. At the same time, the broad outlines of decollectivization and the break up of cooperatives are imposed by the central government, with little regard for local conditions and popular sentiment (see Creed, this volume). Thus newly-installed Turkish leaders while having the freedom pursue contacts with foreign firms and to encourage investment in sectors of local choice nevertheless have had to take decisions which have been strongly opposed by many of their constituents.

Almost every predominantly Turkish village has elected Turkish speaking leaders belonging to the MRF. In one township near Shumen comprising fourteen villages, thirteen villages elected MRF leaders and one produced a three-way split, thus forcing a run-off election. In the run-off the MRF unsuccessfully supported the UDF candidate against a BSP candidate. The crucial issues here were land and the continuation of the existing cooperative. The BSP convinced a third of the villagers that the formerly landless members would not be given land rights with the end of the co-op, and that people would lose their pension rights. As this one shows, the village co-ops touch on every aspect of economic life and their future is the focus of great concern, misunderstanding, and conflicting interests. In another village, with a minority population of Pomaks, an MRF headman was elected by a margin of one vote over a BAPM candidate. Here the Pomak minority did not support the MRF candidate, but the race was complicated by the fact that he was the son of a long-time Communist mayor. In short, while personal rivalries and family histories are important (sometimes paramount), and while there are definite differences in political behavior reflecting ethnic cleavages among Moslems, the MRF is still a remarkably cohesive oppositional force. The dynamics which under-scored voting and mobilization can be seen from the settlement system and characteristics of the rural population.

The Turkish population of Shumen is concentrated on the rich farm lands of the plains, stretching west towards the Danube. One municipality, Venets, comprises fourteen villages, all predominantly Turkish, with a total population in 1992 of approximately 10,088. Village sizes range from forty-five households with 170 inhabitants to 720 households and 3,000 inhabitants. Overall, ethnic Bulgarians make up 12%; Moslem, Turkish-speaking Gypsies 15%, Pomaks and Tatars less than two 2%. Since 1985, the most extreme year of the forced assimilation measures, population has declined twenty-three percent from 13,272 to 10,088. Three related demographic factors affect the political equation. First, Bulgaria is experiencing a national decline in population size, a decline in birth rate, and an increase in the percentage of the population of retirement age (fifty-five for females, sixty for males). Second, since the late 1950s there has been a nation-wide pattern of rural to urban migration, most particularly on the part of ethnic Bulgarians. Third, approximately 1,000 households from the sample villages departed *en masse* for Turkey in the summer of 1989. Many more had prepared to leave but were prevented from doing so when the borders with Turkey were closed in August. About half of those who left returned by 1992, but a significant number of them (about 46% of a sample of eighty-nine household heads) now state that they plan to leave once more. Empty homes and unkempt gardens in every village are constant reminders of migration as a result of past oppression, and equally, that it still is an option for ethnic Turks, though not so easily for Bulgarians or Gypsies. Not only has the country-side been left more and more to the minorities, but even as agriculture overtakes industrial production as the chief component of national product, a significant percentage of the rural work-force is profoundly ambivalent about its future in the country.

One of the ways minorities cope with real or perceived social and political exclusion is by their domestic arrangements. Thus the Moslem minorities of Bulgaria not only form endogamous, closed communities, but also tend toward large families. Reliable fertility data are unavailable, but fairly reliable household data are. The average household size for the fourteen villages of this study is 4.05 (2,704 households), while the Bulgarian national average is 2.8. For 115 households of ethnic Turks directly surveyed, the mean household size is 4.4. Locally supplied official data for fifty-three Bulgarian households yield a mean size of 2.1, while ninety-eight Moslem Gypsy households average 5.4. The Bulgarian households are not entirely typical as they include teachers and officials, some of whom are single. But however limited the data, they do confirm the widespread perception that minorities tend to have large households, even if they do not directly confirm sharply higher birth rates. The domestic organization of ethnic Turkish households and neighborhoods shows that primary kin ties are felt vital to security. Following the forced name changes 1984-85, many informants said that they refused to take employment outside areas of Turkish settlement, nor would they allow their children to do so. The Turkish population of the northeast is endogamous. In the fourteen villages I heard of only a few marriages between Pomak and Turkish households, all in one village, and in one household of another village, the wife was Bulgarian. Inter-faith and inter-ethnic group marriage is greatly frowned upon, and although marriage with a Bulgarian Moslem is described as "acceptable from the religious point of view" it is still "undesirable as they are not Turks".[5] In any event, Pomaks, Turks, and Moslem Gypsies do not inter-marry, nor do they marry Bulgarian Christians in any significant numbers. Moreover, marriage, unlike in Anatolian Turkey, is strictly exogamous with regard to known relatives and thus comes to link households throughout the region. Post-marital residence shows a strong tendency for residence in the village of the groom's family, giving a strong sense of long-time family association with particular communities. As a consequence of a preference for patrilocal residence, most married couples live for extended periods with the groom's household. This should not obscure the fact that ties with the wife's family remain strong. During the 1989 exodus, most households attempted to leave in the company of related households, not infrequently the wife's parents or siblings.

Land reform and employment, as noted earlier, are major issues of rural politics, cutting across ethnic and religious lines. There is little or no direct inter-ethnic conflict between Turks and Bulgarians over access to or ownership of land. Since the political repression of the Moslems occurred after land was collectivized, no land other than house lots (which were privately owned) changed hands under duress. At the moment pre-communist expropriations or involuntary sales of formerly widespread Turkish holdings are not being challenged in the courts, as these claims have been settled by inter-government treaties. Since the lands now being privatized were collectivized in the 1950s, it is usually heirs of the original owners who bring claims to the municipal or village Land Commissions established in late 1991 to oversee privatization. Since ethnic Bulgarians have fewer heirs their claims are on average larger than Turkish claims.

Collectivization occurred locally in the summer of 1955, and although some families held out for years, the systematic imposition of high taxes in kind on the holdouts resulted in all land ultimately becoming enrolled in the TKZS. During the initial period, payment to members was largely in kind, later shifting to full cash accounting. In 1977 the fourteen village cooperatives were merged into one large collective administered in Venets--part of national program of agricultural industrialization (APK). At this time all remaining demarcators of property lines and traditional fields were eradicated. The new collective was, informants said, the source of both corruption and mismanagement as well as a source of opportunity. It increased the number of administrators and non-farming workers. It provided the opportunity for many to pursue secondary occupations in the black or grey markets of construction, crafts, and services, often using collective farm equipment and supplies. In early 1990 the APK was dissolved into its original constituent village cooperatives, but according to members, much machinery was disposed of at "fire sale" prices, often to relatives and friends of administrators. The new cooperatives were to be transitory until privatization took place, and in 1992 they were dissolved in order to weed out corruption (the government's line), or to root out former communists from seats of rural influence (the view of local informants; see also Creed, this volume).

Certainly, so-called lustration rules have since accomplished the latter as no former official of the APK or TKZS can serve in the newly-emerging co-ops even though many were democratically elected to do so. Generally, even those administrators who simply took over in 1990 to head the transition were eliminated from co-op office. In 1991 the newly-elected UDF government's objective, too, was to promote private farming, change attitudes about cooperative agriculture, and foster a market in land. These efforts (moderated since 1993) disrupted production, since arable land was not fully planted or was under-utilized as pasture. Still, by late 1993, a number of new, volunteer cooperatives are completing a full cycle of production. The yet unanswered question is how productive and how profitable they are for members, since they lack solid infrastructural support.

At the time of the study, the overwhelming majority of Turkish farmers interviewed (85% of 115), indicated that they wished to continue in some form of cooperative farming. Villages sometimes divided over the issue of continuing one village-wide cooperative or forming numerous small partnerships or co-ops, but the overwhelming sentiment was for some variety of cooperativism. The Turkish population, like the population in general, has a large number of people not interested or unable to undertake private or commercial farming. Many rural households have men employed in off-farm jobs (about 40% of 115 households interviewed), and few households have the requisite equipment or storage facilities. Also it is doubtful if a land market will develop soon, as there are strict restrictions on who can purchase and even if sellers were to emerge, land values under discussion are so high as to preclude a profitable return from such investments at current commodity prices. Even urban dwellers indicate that they intend to hold on to whatever they receive.

One effect of collectivization was to make agricultural property a form of frozen trust to await future disbursement while collectivized, inter- and intra-familial transfers were effectively impossible. Accordingly, the only change has been in the number of potential claimants, and as a consequence most household claims are very small. Most, if not all ethnic Bulgarians and Turks in the region have filed claims on land owned prior to collectivization. Many claims are in dispute, either because of under-reporting at the time of collectivization or because of conflicting claims of heirs. Most local Gypsies were formerly landless and their claims, only recently recognized by law in 1993, are based on their labor contribution to the co-op. This claim on state lands on behalf of landless members of cooperatives was supported by both the MRF and the BSP, reflecting their shared agrarian power bases.

The size of anticipated land claims per household is 2.2 hectares. If one extrapolates simply on the basis of arable land and number of households in the fourteen villages, 2.6 arable hectares per household are available for possible distribution, not counting possible claims from city dwellers or heirs resident abroad. While Bulgarian farmers of all groups have a deserved reputation as excellent horticulturalists, unsubsidized private farming is unlikely to secure European standards of living for most rural dwellers. On the positive side, horticulture offers an important hedge against inflation in food prices during economic transition. Families with access to sizeable garden plots are without doubt better off than those relying solely on salaries.

Another potential issue in a society with strong egalitarian views is inter-village and inter-household variation in wealth. In Venets, villages have .76 hectares to 13.4 hectares of potential land available per household and household claims range from zero to twenty-five hectares. While large farms are unlikely to emerge, there will be a great range of small ones with vastly differing market potential. It is unlikely that many of those who hope to live off land rents or passively participate as land owners in the new co-ops will have sufficient income from these sources. Informal indications are that the newly-formed co-ops, even with drastic reduction in administrative costs, are running in the red. Input expenses, like mechanized tillage, seeds, and fertilizers are soaring while commodity prices are relatively low.

Conclusions

The general thrust of the MRF message is that only through unity can the Turks and Moslems survive in a sea of potentially hostile forces. This is expressed not only in political rhetoric, but in self-conscious cultural revitalization at the local level. This being so, it would be easy to conclude that politicized ethnicity is incompatible with political stability. At the moment, at least, this does not seem to be the case, but major fault lines might emerge in the present accommodation. Nationally, the most obvious threat is the re-emergence of a nationalist majority in Parliament, probably involving the right-wing of the BSP, which would re-institute some variant of an assimilationist policy; for example, curtailing state-supported education in Turkish or state-supported TV and radio programming of minority directed programs. It is, however, unlikely that any elected government would return to the draconian measures of the past, but any actions perceived to threaten Turkish or Moslem freedom of cultural expression will reinforce the often expressed fears of Turks and Moslems that they have no place in Bulgaria. If so, they will likely "vote with their feet", since by now most Turkish-speakers have kin and contacts in Turkey. This heightened sensitivity in the Turkish/Moslem community is understandable given the recent history of oppression. It is why some equate continuing voluntary out-migration to Turkey with "ethnic cleansing". Many are ready to see a malevolent hand still pushing the Turks from their country and their homes.

However, at the national level, the MRF is for the moment contributing to the relatively calm transition, since its leadership is adroit at compromise and tactical alliances, excluding only the most rabid of nationalist political forces. While favoring privatization, the MRF also stresses the rights of the rural landless, and the necessity to maintain social support systems and minimize unemployment. Thus the MRF has worked closely with the main state employees trade unions, something the UDF could not accomplish. Still the threat of a backlash exists, particularly now that the MRF has split with the UDF and its successors. Nationally, MRF policies, apart from its community rights agenda, conform to the mainstream of rural public opinion. Following the 1991 elections for many months major newspapers railed against "ethnic politics" and "the Turkish party"; by 1993 the level of publically expressed concern appeared to be far less. Nevertheless the MRF exercises more influence than the numbers of its constituents would imply, and it may not be able to sustain this influence in the long term.

At the local level, where accommodation has to do with who lives with whom and under what circumstances, the election in Shumen district of Turkish mayors in four important towns and seventy-nine villages brought the debate of the place of Islamic minorities in Bulgaria home with considerable immediacy. In many communities, the election showed ethnic Bulgarians that, like it or not, they lived in an undeniably Turkish political environment; in villages where Turks were a clear minority, most ethnic Bulgarians seemed to cope with this with good humor. Villages more equally divided were scenes of nationalist demonstrations and one tried unsuccessfully to secede from a municipality run by newly-elected Turkish officials. But in a nearby village with a majority Bulgarian population, as a gesture of good-will village officials organized a benefit concert of Turkish music for earthquake victims in Anatolia. In some instances, inter-Turkish or Moslem factional disputes before and after the elections were more visible than those along the Bulgarian-Turkish divide.

An important part of the ethnic equation also depends on how the MRF manages the transition to a free market and democratic politics at the local level and how its constituency comes to view its social and economic future in Bulgaria. The national organization speaks of a future where the party will have a large non-Moslem constituency based on its human rights agenda and social and economic policies, but in practice they necessarily have had to promote a "we/they" idiom for political discourse. Not only does ethnic political discourse have inherent limits to its appeal but also, by promoting a sense of a distinctive Turkish community in Bulgaria, the already profound ambivalence felt by Turkish-speakers as to their place in Bulgarian society is exacerbated. Unlike other segments of Bulgaria's population, they do have a real option. Further out-migration will clearly threaten any form of national political participation on the part of the Turkish community.

Conversations with individuals from all sectors of Bulgarian society suggest that most are extremely sensitive to world opinion and are offended by the public attention occasioned by the policy of forced assimilation. Most, too, seem eager to avoid ethnic strife despite often virulent nationalist expressions of anti-Turkish sentiment. Yugoslavia is a reminder of the costs. For their part, thanks in part to the discipline and visible effectiveness of the MRF, there is little reason for Turks to respond extra-legally to nationalist provocations. The MRF strongly advocates a continued Turkish presence in a multi-cultural Bulgaria and strongly opposed out-migration.

So the Bulgarians and the Turks have an uneasy accommodation, but so does the MRF with its constituency. Having so successfully represented the interests of that constituency up to now, can the organization continue to do so as those interests change in response to wider economic and social developments? The emphasis on clearly defined community rights, for example, may prove increasingly irrelevant as rural communities, Bulgarians and Turks alike, have to deal with the economic realities of the free market. Already local discourse has clearly shifted from issues related to communal identity to economic concerns. Further, different segments of the large Moslem constituency may reasonably diverge or at least come to express different priorities. Many local leaders express dissatisfaction with the national MRF leadership, saying that it is "out of touch"; or "too concerned with private business." Islam, presently a cultural force, could provide an alternative basis for local community leadership, although "fundamentalist" appeals seem non-existent at the moment. The worst-case scenario for all concerned would be a massive out-pouring of disaffected Turkish-speakers to Turkey. This would be disastrous for Bulgaria's long term recovery given its demographic structure, and it need not happen. Just as Turks in Bulgaria are uncertain about their future in their native land, they have doubts about their place in Turkey. As one Shumen MRF leader said, "The best thing would be for the MRF to achieve its goals and become irrelevant."

Notes

I wish to thank the following individuals who assisted me in fieldwork or in preparing this paper: Haşim Akif, Gerald Creed, Ali Eminov, Krustyu Petkov, Resmi Şerif Mustafa, Greg Johnson, Detelina Radoeva, Eleanor Smollett, and in particular Judith Tucker.

1. See also Konstantinov *et al* 1991 and Tomova and Bogoev 1992: 1-15. The latter report puts the numbers of Pomaks (Bulgarian-speaking Moslems), at 268,971 and Gypsies (Christian and Moslem) at 576,927 (see Konstaninov 1991, and Igla et al (1991) for other estimates. The best discussions of the Pomaks are Silverman 1984 and Konstantinov 1992b) but see also Marushiakov et al (1992). The census is interesting, too, because for the first time it notes an absolute decline in Bulgaria's population, a birth-rate below replacement, an average household size of 2.8, and an age structure in which retired individuals out-number those under age 17.

2. The electoral system allocates seats in Parliament according to population, from thirty-one electoral districts. The system has at least two peculiarities that will shape Bulgarian politics and government in the future. First, through proportional representation, it encourages the formation of small parties. Second, because of a requirement that a party poll at least four percent nationwide to send a representative to Parliament , a sizable percentage of the ballots cast do not contribute to the make-up of the chamber. For example, the main faction of the Bulgarian Agrarian Popular Movement, which ran well in some localities and which was widely expected to be of pivotal importance, received only 3.8% of the votes nationally and thus did not enter Parliament at all. The thirty some other parties also failed to qualify. In all about 25% of the votes went to parties that did not meet the 4% test. These votes were assigned to the three parties that did, proportional to their polled strength. Thus the MRF claimed 10% of parliamentary seats.

3. MRF leaders and others often expansively refer to Bulgarian speaking Moslems as "Turks", but never similarly include Turkish-speaking Gypsies. Pomaks themselves are ambivalent. Few migrated to Turkey during the exodus in 1989 and there is little intermarriage with Turkish speakers. Ethnic Bulgarians often assert that the MRF pressures the Pomaks and Muslim Gypsies to consider themselves "Turks"; this is against stated MRF policy. For what it is worth, one Bulgarian news magazine reported that in the 1993 census some Bulgarian-speaking Moslems, under pressure from the MRF to identify themselves as Turks, chose to list themselves as "Chinese" (Insider 1993, No.2, p.38). It seems clear that notions of identity among Pomaks is complex and probably shifting. Many, it is asserted by Turkish-speaking teachers, wish to have their children study Turkish; generally, public school authorities prevent non-Turkish pupils from taking Turkish language courses (in the northeast, at least).

4. In mid-1992, though most of the land allocations had been posted in most villages under the names of the original owners who had contributed it to collectivization, very little had actually been surveyed and handed over (see Creed, this volume). In most cases, villagers simply formed new cooperatives as successors to the defunct collectives. These, in turn, were disallowed soon after the UDF government came to power. The result was confusion and paralysis as competing factions argued variously for one new cooperative versus numerous small ones.

5. This, of course, directly contradicts the idea, forwarded by some Turkish leaders, that "Pomaks are really Turks." Another frequently noted reason for the lack of intermarriage between Pomak and Turkish Moslems is that the Bulgarian Moslems were targeted earlier for forced assimilation and that should inter-marriage occur, children would be unable to bear Moslem names. For whatever reason, the various Moslem communities in Bulgaria have historically been almost as isolated from one another as from the dominant Christian society. By one account, there are only 5,000 mixed marriages in the entire country (Tomova and Bogoev 1992: 8).

References

Brown, J.F. 1989. "Conservatism and Nationalism in the Balkans: Albania, Bulgaria, and Romania." *In* W.E. Griffith, Ed. *Central and Eastern Europe: The Opening Curtain.* Boulder: Westview. pp. 283-313.

Creed, Gerald W. 1991. "Between Economy and Ideology: Local-Level Perspectives on Political and Economic Reform in Bulgaria." *Socialism and Democracy*. Vol. 13, May 1991: 45-65.

____. 1992. *Economic Development Under Socialism: A Bulgarian Village on the Eve of Transition*. Ph.D. Dissertation, CUNY.

____. 1993. "Rural-Urban Opposition in the Bulgarian Political Transition." *Südosteuropa*, 42 (6): 369-382.

Crampton, R. J. 1990. "The Turks in Bulgaria: 1978-1944." *In* Kemal Karpat Ed. *The Turks of Bulgaria: The History, Culture and Political Fate of a Minority*. Istanbul: Isis Press: 43-78.

Eminov, Ali. 1983. "The Education of Turkish Speakersin Bulgaria." *Ethnic Groups*. Vol. 5, pp. 129-150.

____. 1986. "Are Turkish Speakers in Bulgaria of Ethnic Bulgarian Origin?" *Journal of Muslim Minority Affairs*. Vol. VII, No. 2 503-518.

____. 1989. "Are There No Turks in Bulgaria: Writing History by Administrative Fiat." *International Journal of Turkish Studies*. 4: 203-222.

Georgeoff, John. 1981. "Ethnic minorities in the Peoples Republic of Bulgaria." *In*
George Klein and Milan Reban, Eds. *The Politics of Ethnicity in Eastern Europe*. New York: Columbia University Press.

Glenny, Misha. 1993. *The Rebirth of History*. London: Penguin, 2nd ed.

Hak ve Ozgürlükler Hareketleri. 1993. *Hak ve Ozgürlük*. Sofia: Movement for Rights and Freedoms Press.

Igla, Birgit, Yulian Konstantinov, and Gulbrand Alhaug. 1991. " Some Preliminary Comments on the Language and Names of the Gypsies of Zlataritsa (Bulgaria)." *Nordlyd. Tromso University Working Papers on Language and Linguistics*. No. 17: 118- 134.

Karpat, Kemal ed. 1990. *The Turks of Bulgaria: The History, Culture and Political Fate of a Minority*. Istanbul: Isis Press.

Konstantinov, Yulian. 1992. "'Nation-State' and 'Minority' Types of Discourse-Problems of Communication between the Majority and the Islamic Minorities in Contemporary Bulgaria." *Innovation*. 5(3): 75-89.

Konstantinov, Yulian, Gulbrand Alhaug and Birgit Igla. 1991. " Names of the Bulgarian Pomaks". *Nordlyd. Tromso University Working Papers on Language and Linguistics*. No. 17: 8-117.

Konstantinov, Yulian. 1992. "Minority Name Studies in the Balkans: The Pomaks". *Folia Linguistica* XXVI/3-4: 404-433.

Marushiakova, Elena et al, eds. 1993. *The Ethnic Situation in Bulgaria*. (Project on Ethnic Relations 1992) Sofia: Club 90 Publishers.

Petkov, Krustu and Georgi Fotev, eds. 1990. *Ethnic Conflict in Bulgaria: 1989*. Institute of Sociology: Sofia.

Silverman, Carole. 1984. "Pomaks" *In* R. Weeks,Ed. *Muslim Peoples: A World Ethnographic Survey*. Vol. II, 2nd ed., Westport, Conn.: Greenwood Press.

____. 1986. "Bulgarian Gypsies: Adaptation in a Socialist State". *Peripatetic Peoples*. Number 21/22 (Dec. 1986). pp. 51- 62.

____. 1989. "Reconstructing Folklore: Media and Cultural Policy in Eastern Europe". *Communication* Vol. 11, pp. 141-160.

Smollett, Eleanor. 1990. "America the Beautiful: Made in Bulgaria". *Anthropology Today* 9(4): 9-12.

Şimşir, Bilal. 1988. *The Turks of Bulgaria (1878-1985).* London: Rustem and Brother.

Tomova, Ilona and P. Bogoev. 1992. "Minorities in Bulgaria: A Report of the 1991 International Conference on Minorities (Rome)." *The Insider: A Bulgarian Digest Monthly*. Sofia: Iltex :1-15.

Verdery, Katherine. 1983. *Transylvanian Villagers: Three Centuries of Political, Economic , and Ethnic Change*. Berkeley: University of California Press.

10

All Is Possible, Nothing Is Certain: The Horizons of Transition In a Romanian Village

Steven Sampson

Shock Without Therapy

The so-called "transition" in Eastern Europe has usually been discussed in terms of the transition to a market economy (privatization) and to Western style liberal democracy. Using these two categories, we have spent considerable effort to measure how far various Eastern European countries have come on the transition scale. By standard measures, the northern tier of Eastern Europe--Poland, Hungary, the Czech Republic, Slovenia--seems farther along than either the Balkans or the states of the former USSR. Poland, Hungary and the Czech Republic are destined to benefit more from further Western inputs because they are more "on the way" to privatization and more democratic.

This paper deals with Romania, one of those countries where the normative indices of "successful" transition have not appeared. Romania was the last East European country to enter the Council of Europe. It is continually criticized from outside and by the non-government opposition for its slow progress of privatization and for political corruption. Unlike the rest of Eastern Europe (except Serbia) Romania's communists are not trying to stage a comeback; they never left. Ceauşescu's cronies sit in the bureaucracy and in the parliament. Some of his most ardent supporters formed part of the Romanian delegation to the Council of Europe. The president has courted xenophobic nationalists and ex-communists, and in 1994 they have even taken cabinet posts. Unlike the case of other East European dissidents who went from opposition to government posts, most of Romania's former dissidents remain on the political margins. And while Romania's ethnic tensions have not led to a Bosnian situation, conflicts remain frequent between Hungarians, Gypsies and the Romanian majority.

Virtually all change for the better in Romania is attributed to pressure by "the West," be it Brussels, Strasbourg, the World Bank, and other foreign or international actors. Romania risks not so much being exploited by the West but simply ignored. Western foundations, companies and aid programs are gravitating toward those Eastern European countries which can utilize aid provide a stable climate, who can bite the bullet of "structural adjustment," and furnish suitable conditions for Western aid agencies and profits for private companies. By any index, Romania is not high on the list. And this makes the gap between expectations about the transition and its realities that much greater. In the meantime, Romania is now undergoing inflation, stagnation, unemployment, corruption, and corresponding social and ethnic tensions, much the same as other East European countries have experienced. Yet the positive effects are relatively small. To use the cliches of privatization, there is shock but not much therapy.

The Transition and "the Transition"

"We are a society in transition" has become the phrase to explain just about every anomalous phenomena in Romania today. The transition is particularly acute for Romanians who live in rural communities. Romanian villagers don't know much about the workings of the Common Market or the World Bank, but they talk about them. They experience the "society in transition" every day; they see it on television, read about it in the papers (if they can still afford to subscribe to them), they talk with villagers who travel abroad, they discuss their personal economic projects among each other, and they decide on strategies for their children.

While the transition as desired by the West seems to have stopped short in Romania, it would be grossly misleading to conclude that the post-1989 changes in Romania are somehow less profound than elsewhere in Eastern Europe. At the local community level, at the level of people's social interactions and perceptions, Romanians' lives have been transformed profoundly in the last couple of years. Writing of Ceauşescu's Romania a decade ago, M.Shafir (1985) invoked the concept of "simulated change" to describe a Romania which appeared to deviate from the Soviet model but which in fact was more Stalinist than even the USSR. Today we might accuse the regime of Ion Iliescu of simulating marketization and Western style democratic institutions. Romanian political debate is full of accusations that "nothing has happened," that Iliescu's "original democracy" is simply "form without foundation."

At the local level, however, not all the changes are simulated, nor are they intended. The transition in the Romanian countryside is undoubtedly of a quite different sort than simply a trajectory toward democratization and marketization. Moreover, Romanian villages may be changing faster than the national metropolitan institutions. The changes involve the emergence of autonomous households as economic units--the prerequisite for civil society--without the accompanying rise of public life. Villages may thus be experiencing the emergence of the partial civil society.

For anthropologists and social scientists, who have often assumed that innovations diffuse from the center to the provinces, from city to country, and from the powerful to the powerless, we may find it unfamiliar to envision the transition in Eastern Europe occurring faster in so-called "traditional" areas. But we should expect that the transition is also of a different order as well.

This paper will describe certain elements of the transition in Feldioara, a large, urbanized village in southern Transylvania, near the town of Braşov. Feldioara, with about 3,500 people, is a large, well developed village on the main road and rail line north of Braşov. The village once had a Saxon German population of well over 1,500 persons, now down to a few dozens due to emigration to West Germany. Feldioara's continued population growth is due to the arrival of migrants from other regions of Romania who were attracted to the village because of its proximity to nearby industrial employment in the factories of Braşov. The village also has several administrative functions for the immediate area, and is one of the few villages containing its own high school.

Because of its geographic position and the presence of nearby minerals plant, Feldioara had once been on a list of future towns under Ceauşescu's rural planning program, a program which was never implemented (Sampson 1984a). In the mid-1970s I carried out anthropological fieldwork in Feldioara to study the urbanization process, which like so many other aspects of Romanian social life was a combination of unrealistic expectations, bureaucratic distortions, laudable intentions to improve the quality of life, and daily practices of survival under nearly intolerable conditions. Not only was the plan to urbanize the village never fully implemented, the changes that did occur were often unenvisioned or unintentional.

I continued to return to Feldioara for short periods until 1984, when I was deemed persona non grata, and again from 1990. My focus was on how people developed informal mechanisms, to cope with the vagaries of a system which was repressive, irrational and unpredictable. I studied both bureaucracy and corruption, both the official and the second economy, both formal and informal leadership, both official censorship and informal rumors (Sampson 1983, 1989). I even began to speculate about the anthropology of secret police and of collaboration in a society whereby loyalty and betrayal, friendship and duplicity, were so integral to Romanian social life (Sampson 1986, 1990, 1994b).

I will begin by describing some aspects of the present situation, both generally and in the village. I will then proceed backwards and emphasize the pre-transition period. This may seem to be the easy way out: my research back then was longer and more detailed than the kind of research I am doing now. But at a deeper level, I believe that we should view the collapse of socialism as a starting point for helping us understand how socialist societies functioned. To put it more concretely, we first begin to understand how systems work after they have fallen apart. This begs the question as to what it is which has fallen apart and what has been maintained. Our failure to adequately address this question is reflected in our continued use of the word "transition," a usage also perpetuated by East Europeans themselves with various degrees of irony and cynicism. Is there a "transition of the transition"? When does the "transition" end? What comes after? Perhaps a better look at local communities in their total sociopolitical context can help us answer these questions. In the latter part of the paper I will try to provide two examples of household strategies within this transition. Initially, however, I wish to elaborate some operating principles of the Old Order in order to show how they reproduce themselves during the transition period.

All Is Possible, Nothing Is Certain

In retrospect, we might extrapolate the basic social dynamic of Ceauşescu's Romania in terms of some simple operating principles reflected in people's everyday practice. Romania, including village Romania, was a society in which anything could happen, but where nothing was definite. It was a society where all things were possible and nothing was certain. In such situations, people were insecure, and individual abilities--especially the ability to manipulate others and maneuver through the bureaucracy--were at a premium.

Moreover, Romania was a society in which it was normal to a have a wide gap between private thoughts and public action, a phenomena common to much of Eastern Europe (Wedel 1986, Shlapentokh 1989, Milosz 1952). Romania was a society of dissimulation, conspiracy and of drama. People assumed misrepresentation in the public sphere; they operated upon the assumption of hidden motives and unseen forces behind every action. There were no mere coincidences; rather there was always some kind of plot, and in the absence of reliable information (or verification), all plots, even the most outlandish, were plausible. Sincerity was viewed suspiciously. As a society of "drama"--of a frontstage and a backstage--everyone was assumed to be playing roles in public. One's public demeanor said nothing about one's private thoughts, beliefs or alliances. Some observers have called this "social schizophrenia," but this term implies some kind of pathology. Rather, we might see Romania as a "dualistic" society in which the gap between public and private, between acts and motives, between the play-acting self and the real self, was assumed to be the normal state of affairs. This is why it was normal to be in the Romanian Communist Party--the largest per capita in the world in 1989--but why the same party had so few genuine communists and disappeared completely following the December events. This gap between public and private also explains why the dissident--the person who actually said or did what he/she believed, who combined private thought and public action--who was deemed sick or conspiratorial.

The operating principles of "all is possible, nothing is certain," and the normalcy of the gap between public and private behavior did not reproduce themselves in a vacuum. They were clearly a means of adapting to a changing, random, and often brutal social order in which resources were so scarce or access so uncertain that retaining absolute moral or ethical principles or abstract loyalties would be counterproductive. This is in fact the definition of "opportunism" as opposed to "fair play." One may also see elements of "Balkan mentality" or "Orthodox tradition," in which adherence to public ritual is more important than any kind of internal belief. We might see Romanians as experts in the kind of *ketman* described by Czeslaw Milosz (1952), whereby the ability to mask one's beliefs is an admirable talent in the face of despotic authority. Romania has been, and to some extent remains, a society where what James Scott (1984) calls "weapons of the weak" are the only available weapons.

In such a society, there is an intensity to personal relations in which the emotional and the practical are combined. It is an intensity which creates strong bonds of trust and solidarity, as well as tensions and intrigues. Romanian villages are indeed similar to their Polish counterparts in that they are "Villages without Solidarity (Hann 1985)." To use contemporary terminology, Romanian villages are full of "uncivil society."

The persistence of these operating principles is because the key factors which have maintained these principles have been themselves maintained. It is not a matter of some kind of cultural lag from the past. Randomness, caprice, uncertainty, and the need for personal alliances still exist, but for different reasons.

In "transitional" Romania, different tactics are needed to deal with the different kinds of uncertainties and randomness. The daily life of Romanian villagers like those in Feldioara lies in discovering the proper tactics, in a kind of trial and error. For example, in Ceauşescu's time, there was a real enemy, a "them," consisting of Ceauşescu, his family, the regime, the local party cadres, and the secret police. Bureaucratic behavior could be capricious, which meant that one could had to act in such a way so as to foster social connections which were predictable and profitable. Access to material goods was administered via rationing, and via contracting arrangements the bureaucracy could squeeze surplus out of various households. Money was not always crucial, as incomes were low and prices stable. Bureaucratic access counted more than cash. Social or political capital was more important than money.

In the "transitional" society of Romania, "Them" have been replaced by more nebulous market forces which make one's hard earned money disappear with inflation, while others seem to become rich without real "productive" work

(Sampson 1994a). "Them" are a more hazy class of the wealthy or the mafia. Unseen forces of "lack of export," or sudden incongruous decisions by ministries or state companies now cause hundreds of jobs to disappear. Money incomes become more uncertain due to inflation or devaluations. In the meantime, having connections in certain sections of the bureaucracy may mean less as its functions in distributing material goods are eliminated with privatization. The random brutality of the secret police, the *Securitate*, has now been replaced by incessant talk of urban crime or rural burglaries. The CIA or KGB plots which were part of the rumor mill of the Ceauşescu regime have now been replaced by political accusations of plots, scenarios, and hidden plans. Making a career in the Party is now replaced by people being accused of trying to make a career in one of several parties, movements or organizations in Romania, some with the government, some in the opposition (both democratic and nationalist), some with links to foreigners. There continues to be the assumption that public behavior masks private projects. What makes the opposition differ from the supporters of the regime is not conspiratorial thinking, but in their definition of who the conspirators are: the opposition sees plots by "neocommunists," by the *Securitate* or ultranationalist forces opposed to democracy, while supporters of the current regime can blame the Jews, the Hungarians, the Press, or the "West" for Romania's difficulties. (The opposition can of course blame the "West" for being naive about the plots of the neocommunists, etc.). Romania remains a society where there are no real coincidences, no accidents; there are only scenarios and "diversions" (Sampson 1994b).

Scenarios and diversions are part of the political and rhetorical landscape in Romania. At the village level, there are individual projects and social alliances. People interpret others' projects and alliances as full-fledged strategies. But in the "transition" period people are still trying to find their place in an uncertain world, a world where new possibilities appear, and suddenly prove illusory. In such a transitional world, the principles of all things are possible, nothing is certain, take on renewed significance as villagers see that some things are possible for certain people, i.e. those with the talent to maneuver through the system via connections and relations. In focusing on how these operating principles reflect themselves in the village of Feldioara, it will be demonstrated although the transition has maintained these principles, villagers ways of dealing with these conditions is changing. It is changes in these horizons, in their perception of what the world "out there" offers and their place in it, which is at the core of any discussion of the "transition."

To speak in terms of "horizons" is not misplaced in an East European context. After all, when socialism was on the horizon, people joked that the closer one came to it, the more it receded into the distance. The "transition" seems to be that phase in which one horizon replaces another. And under the conditions of economic uncertainty and competition for scarce resources seems to give the "horizon" of prosperity its illusory, uncertain character. That which we call the "transition" is nothing else but the institutionalization of new kinds of uncertainties replacing old ones. It is the uncertainties and randomness of the "economy of shortage," once called "socialism," is replaced by an uncertainty of how to act in a "wild west" capitalism characterized by political manipulation and lack of institutional stability.

Pierre Bourdieu might call this change of horizons a change of "habitus," a re-structuring of the structures. Romanians themselves often lament that "there are no rules anymore," which seems to confirm the emphasis placed by contemporary social theory on the role of practice in structuring cultural behavior. In theoretical terms, we might define transitional situations as those in which practices totally dominate cultural schemata.

Such a concept of transition is not to be thought of an alteration in the villagers' fundamental life values. Villagers in Feldioara, whether pensioned farmers, status-anxious school teachers or MTV watching teenagers, still seek what they sought in Ceauşescu's day: they want reasonable living standards and security for themselves and their offspring. They want dignity and prestige. And they want to see benefit from their investments, whether these investments are fertilizer for their fields or private tutoring for their children. The villagers' attitudes about public institutions (as both a threat to one's personal autonomy and as resources which will be exploited for personal benefit, either by others or by oneself) have changed little. In this sense, there is not much of that sought after "civil society" or "public sphere" which Western experts and aid agencies are seeking. What has changed, however, are the actual means by which people can achieve their goals. In Feldioara, people are trying to determine what kind of horizon is "out there," and they are altering their life strategies accordingly. They are trying to locate themselves in a social field whose signposts for action are unclear. Such lack of clarity--"an age of confusion"--leads to an "anything goes" mentality which villagers experience as a society without limits or as moral decline. Romanian villages are replete with manifestations of "uncivil society." Villagers' lament that things are getting more uncivilized, that people are more unscrupulous, that "we do not have democracy," "there is anarchy," that "there are no rules anymore." Little wonder that there is nostalgia for the kind of order and predictability which the Ceauşescu regime offered. Or more accurately, nostalgia for familiar forms of disorder and uncertainty.

The Global Horizons in Feldioara

In their efforts to locate a horizon, and during the uncertain conditions where this horizon is hazy and receding, individual villagers suddenly find themselves in an unfamiliar social and geographic space. Socially they are rich or poor, or are on their way to becoming richer or poorer. A number of villagers are in fact moving both ways in shorter, more violent cycles of wealth/poverty. People's geographic horizons also change: some villagers will remain in the community; others intend to leave for large towns, and still others seek to leave Romania, either temporarily or permanently. Invariably, the extension of geographic horizons to include "abroad" involves new kinds of interactions with foreigners, Romanians abroad, or returned Romanian citizens, all of whom are seen as potential aides in improving one's life chances, or those of one's children. Like so many anthropologists who have worked in Eastern Europe, I receive letters from close or not-so-close acquaintances asking for small or large favors or simply for information. Some want a job in Denmark, where I live. Others want to know if I can find them a used tractor, or if I know someone who wants to buy icons, or if there is a company which needs medicinal venom from bees. Others simply want an invitation to visit, or to borrow money, or to buy a specific book, or to find some distant acquaintance who they heard lives in Florida, or to send their daughters somewhere as *au pair* girls. Part of the transition is the change in people's potential social network: brokers or resource persons are now farther away and exchanges and alliances now stretch not just from the village to nearby towns, but to other countries in Europe or North America. Bonds of exchange and bonds of trust are changing, especially as involves exchanges of valuable goods, services or money.

The global social field of villagers is not simply a matter of watching Western television and incorporating Western tastes, but of concrete relations with Western individuals or Romanians from abroad who may help them achieve their goals, or even more profoundly, create their horizons, i.e, restructure these goals.

Romanian villagers, like all Romanians and so many other East Europeans, have been obsessed with the West and its cultural manifestations. This obsession may be expressed in quite different forms, ranging from an unmitigated admiration for all aspects of Western pop culture (the Michael Jackson cult of 1992) or a defensive overemphasis on all things Romanian as in the Romanian philosophical "protochronism," or in the more spectacular exorcisms of Michael Jackson's diabolical spirit following the accusations against him. The Western obsession may appear in Romania's formal demand and Romanians informal pleas that the West ought to provide more aid, that the West owes Romania something, or in the paranoid feelings that the West (or foreign countries like Hungary or foreign forces like the Jews) is plotting against Romania. Today, with more foreign influences in Romania, we might be tempted to simply call this Western obsession yet another instance of "globalization (Hannerz 1992)." The role of the "foreign" in Romanian village life pervades people's standards of who they are, who they are not, and what they would like to be. Not global influences but local identities are at stake in determining village horizons. The combination of global horizons and the local operating principles of all things are possible-nothing is certain and mistrust of public behavior, structure the transition in villages like Feldioara. The transition, while not the conventional one, is nevertheless a real one. Paradoxically, it may be more profound out in the village than in the capital. Let us first, however, review the village horizons during the Ceauşescu era.

Feldioara Under the Old Regime: Keeping People in Place

In Eastern Europe, and especially in politically repressive Romania, there existed a contradictory policy on the part of the regime by which Romania was to be an important player on the world stage while individual Romanians would remain isolated from it. Ceauşescu sought to make Romania a key actor in foreign policy, an intermediary between east and west, north and south. In doing so he connected with the world via frequent trips abroad and by inviting foreign dignitaries or selected foreigners to come to Romania when it served the national interest (even American anthropologists; see Sampson and Kideckel 1989).

While Romania and Ceauşescu were playing their global role, ordinary Romanians were prevented from interacting with the world: telephones were tapped, letters to and from abroad opened, and travel abroad nearly impossible. It was actually illegal for Romanians to speak with a foreigner without authorization, or for foreigners to overnight in a Romanian home. More than contact with foreigners, Romanians were also prevented from any non-organized contacts with each other: typewriters were registered, informal associations forbidden, even the bridge clubs were closed since it entailed traveling intellectuals. And laws prohibiting changing residence limited Romanians' possibility to expand their social horizons. The ideal socialist society was that everyone stayed in their place of residence, worked quietly at their job, consumed as little food, electricity, heating as possible, and came together only to celebrate Ceauşescu. The secret police, the *Securitate*, could be anywhere (randomness, uncertainty), even though they successfully promoted the image of being "everywhere."

In villages like Feldioara, villagers could experience the regime in various ways. Ration cards governed purchases at the local store, in which meat was available only a few hours a week. Collective farmers were paid a pittance but could cultivate private plots, but were prevented from selling to city dwellers on the free market. Most villagers commuted by bus to jobs in Braşov, 22 km away, while others worked at the local uranium processing plant or in local administrative, school, health or retail facilities. Officials could easily observe villagers' contacts with the outsiders via letters, central phone calls, and the visitors' foreign cars. Returning villagers, many of them Saxon Germans now living in West Germany, would come back each summer to visit. The American anthropologist and his wife were under constant surveillance, as were my movements in my German registered car.

The village had a collective farm with a largely elderly, feminine work force. Many households had access to the farm, however, because family members were pensioned, or because people took land and worked it independently.

Villagers' social and cultural horizons were governed by working in Braşov and getting education for their children. Where no one was allowed to own land and where houses were inherited, self-built or paid for, extra money was spent investing in family members cultural capital (private tutoring) or buying a car. Investment in a child's education gave status, prestige, and the kinds of new networks a well educated child could acquire in a new job preferably in a nearby town. One could achieve a degree of network security in a system characterized by profound insecurity.

Villagers lived close to Braşov and Romanian law thus prohibited them from moving to the city. Procurement of a residence permit, much like moving from one country to another, was allowed only by marriage or by various corrupt practices. Feldioarans' horizons were thus restricted, and this was only broken by the listening to foreign radio broadcasts, or by the summer visits of Saxon Germans who had emigrated (invariably with their used Mercedes), or by meeting foreign tourists at in nearby Braşov.

This very closure from real life in the West created not just ignorance but also a preoccupation with things Western. The most obvious manifestations were those items of the West which could be acquired on the black market or via the hard currency shops (which only foreigners could enter but whose items were destined for Romanians). These items could be worn, eaten, drunk, smoked or used. (Such an obsession with Western goods should not be considered irrational: in a country where there was no soap, a bar of "Lux" was Western, but also soap). Consumption of these items demonstrated that one had the connections to acquire them--for it was both connections and money that mattered back then--and that one knew how to use one's money for good taste, too. One ought not to underestimate the political content of consuming forbidden fruits, of demonstration of one's disgust with the established order. The crass materialism of the East was as much a political statement as a response to shortage or simple imitation of a foreign lifestyle. This urge to consume was also common in Feldioara: the youth wanted Western cigarettes or cassette players; their parents wanted Western deep freezers or washing machines; car owners wanted Western motor oil and Western spark plugs. The goods in the shops, insofar as they were not consumed, became an alternative currency in Romania, used to bribe officials. Cartons of cigarettes and bottles of whiskey circulated without being consumed.

Feldioara in the Ceauşescu period was a place where the second economy thrived, where bureaucracy and corruption were rampant, where everyone was out for themselves, but where being out for yourself also meant fulfilling obligations for others and asking others for favors. It was a place where rumor, gossip and innuendo thrived. Feldioara was a place of everyday conspiracy, of tension, of fear and of revenge. There was constant talk of tension between or within families, talk of thievery, stealing, mistrust, and fear of betrayal to the police was part of daily life in this village. Where even basic goods became increasingly scarce and where they were distributed either haphazardly or unequally, explanations in terms of conspiracy or privilege became rampant.

Given this social isolation, material shortage, mistrust of and fear of the authorities, the near total collapse of basic functions in Romanian society of the late 1980's (Sampson 1989), led to a corresponding heightening of the value of the informal, friendship links, and to the fortification of the household as unit of defense against a threatening social world. Friendships and alliances had to be continually put to test: through material prestations, via loans, favors, and instrumental use of networks. In a country like Romania, where so much was either illegal or suspect, these social alliances themselves acquired a conspiratorial character, so that social relations also came to involve the keeping of secrets. Claims on loyalty fed fantasies and fears of betrayal. People believed in the value of friends and family; but these values were always being tested to the utmost. People were under pressure from the authorities to fulfill impossible plans; food was scarce, heat was turned off, contraception unavailable, abortion illegal. People also competed with each other ("uncivil society"). The gradual collapse of the Romanian economy meant that getting even basic commodities required connections all of which led to an overheating of social relations. People made compromises with the authorities which entailed real or imagined betrayals. "Everybody made compromises," as one opposition leader has stated, "but some did it for a loaf of bread, and others for to get a nice villa."

The Revolution

Like most villages in Romania, the December 1989 "revolution" (what the Opposition calls "the events of December") came to Feldioara by way of television. During the crucial days around Christmas of 1989, some villagers and Home Guard members were sent to guard some nearby radio towers from saboteurs, but otherwise the revolution went quietly.

Soon after the revolution, the former local party apparatus disbanded, and the major event was the arrival of a truckload of aid from France. Reminiscent of African villages who met the British centuries ago and had to find some villager to become "chief," Feldioarans found a local agricultural technician and a French speaking school teacher to meet the foreigners with their precious cargo, and thus emerged these first villagers to obtain foreign contacts.

And it was foreign contacts, in the context of the Western obsession, that led to the first accusations and gossip about unequal access to new wealth. Not only did the foreigners come with material goods, food, clothing and medical supplies. They also came with channels of access to the outside world. There were the small informal gifts, but there was also the trips: a delegation from Feldioara visited a sister town in France. For most of the local delegation, largely consisting of local teachers and professionals, it was their first trip to the West. Part of the trip had been paid, and the most expensive part, travel and residence in France, was free. It did not go unnoticed in the village that some of these villagers also had children and spouses with them, some of whom ostensibly functioned as interpreters. Regardless of whether the spouses/children/colleagues were qualified (and how does one determine who is qualified to represent a community a few months after the demise of the communist regime), the benefits of the trip remained unclear to most villagers and the members therefore suspect. In short, it was assumed that everyone had some kind of private agenda.

After this trip, other trips followed. The foreigners took a liking to a few young people in the village who they had met or who had acted as interpreters. Throughout Romania similar events occurred, and many young people, especially those who spoke French, English or German, ended up taking trips to the West to visit those they had met. Others became the obvious first recruits for the earliest work or educational exchange programs. Gifts, small monetary payments and other benefits accrued. (I myself helped establish links between Danish school authorities and school authorities in Feldioara and Braşov. The village school ended up receiving some computers, but the Braşov press was intensely critical when the county delegation traveled to Denmark to observe Danish schools).

The immediate post-revolutionary relations brought with them a new kind of "us" and "them." "They" were now those involved in new foreign networks involving access to foreigners, foreign goods, or the chance to earn foreign currency, however little. That several of these individuals had held high posts in the former apparatus did not go lost on some villagers.

In the context of a Romania where Romanian currency and economy simply collapsed when it began to come into contact with Western economic competition, access to Western hard currency came to be the absolute key to economic survival. Like elsewhere in Romania, Feldioarans acquired passports and began to travel. Traveling for villagers meant only in part seeing the world or visiting family members and acquaintances. It meant, rather, business tourism. Through friends and acquaintances in the West, one could live for free, obtain an illegal job, borrow money and buy scarce goods and transport them back to Romania--used cars, electronic goods, clothing. Working in the West to earn cash might mean painting houses in Germany or selling homemade textiles on the streets of Budapest.

The new horizons which opened were prominent when I returned to Feldioara four months after the 1989 events. Villagers spent most of their time telling me about who had traveled where, who had come back with what, and who had not come back at all. Economically speaking, these first few months were a kind of "honeymoon" in Romania. Hyperinflation had not set in, factories had not closed, legal regulations on commerce were nonexistent, and in the consumer shortage economy which prevailed, anyone with anything to sell could make money. For about a year, the empty niches in sale and petty trade and the massive demand for consumer goods generated enormous incomes for some people. This combined with plunder or manipulation of state owned resources, including the collective and state farms to generate additional incomes. Speculation, corruption, and mafia-style organization were most widespread in areas with larger markets and more resources to plunder, i.e., the large cities. Since most villagers either worked in or had families in Braşov, their knowledge of these new income sources was extensive. And since most also had networks there, benefits could be derived, most obviously by selling agricultural produce at free market prices to city dwellers.

The result was an initial satisfaction of pent up consumer tastes--color televisions, cars, trips--together with a subsequent stratification into "have more" and "have less." This stratification only intensified as the collective farm was gradually eliminated and as the Romanian economy began its plummet into hyperinflation, unemployment regulatory free for all and vicious corruption.

Decollectivization and Social Stratification

Feldioara's collective farm had been established early, 1950, and the village also had a state farm unit, IAS. The land was relatively fertile, growing grain and sugar beets for a nearby sugar refining plant (for a more complete description of the collective see Sampson 1984a; for a comparison see Kideckel 1993). In its final years, however, the collective's labor force had declined to a core of agricultural specialists, a larger group of elderly villagers, mostly uneducated women, and periodic migrant or Gypsy laborers used in the summer.

Decollectivization involved several processes, among them the breaking up of the old collective farms, the reconstituting of new associations, some of them as small as a few families, and the giving out of property certificates for the new owners. As in all revolutionary processes, the breaking down of the old system has been easier than the build up of a new one. In particular, "family farms" have proven difficult to operate when families were without labor, capital, or developed retail possibilities. And the arrangements between families have given rise to new forms of social cooperation and conflict, especially in a society where contracts and legal measures are unfamiliar or under suspicion. Let us discuss these transitional forms in turn.

Like so many other state enterprises in Romania, the state farm remained untouched. It continues to specialize in animal husbandry an growing of fodder crops, with its work force salaried like workers. Similarly, the machine tractor station is now a state company which conducts operations of plowing, threshing, etc. for a fee. As before, peasants often need the SMA services at the same time, and speed payments are not uncommon to obtain rapid service or high quality work. Control over machinery and its allocation is primarily what stimulated Feldioarans to purchase their own tractors: From eight in 1990 to nineteen in 1991 to forty-five in 1994.

Two agricultural engineers in the community have established agricultural enterprises containing 470 and 600 hectares, respectively. As no family may have more than ten hectares, the land in these associations has been donated by families who do not have the labor, or time to cultivate their own land. In most cases these are elderly couples whose children are no more at home; in others there are nonagricultural families who have inherited land and now do not want to have anything to do with it.

Families who are full members of the association receive a percentage of the income from the land, typically 30-40%. Families who do nothing but give up land receive somewhat less, 20-25%. Production on the association has definitely increased over the last two years, with wheat at 3,000 kg/hectare, potatoes at 18,000 and sugar beets at 32,000. The head of the smaller association wants more land, and will take from anyone. His biggest problems are poor quality machinery, lack of money, and lack of support from the county administration who saddles the association with a high interest rate and lack of credit. In 1994 there was the additional problem of land tax based on land area rather than quality of the soil. Twenty five percent of his expenses are interest.

The associations were both an obvious transitional solution in 1991 and 1992 and for some peasants the only solution. There were indications that by 1994, however, some peasants were becoming dissatisfied with membership. Several of the smaller associations of families and neighbors collapsed when they could not pay out the promised payments. Their costs of administration and renewal of capital were higher than expected. And with the unclear legal regulations and lack of enforcement, there was the usual amount of corruption.

The elderly, those without capital or labor, have remained in the associations. But most productive peasants have left. Especially the smaller associations of a few families have been riven with conflicts about who owns what, how to allocate work and derive income. The desire for household autonomy has been fulfilled as people buy tractors and horses, the number of horses nearly tripling, from ninety to 225, in 1994. Some villagers have been fortunate enough to have paid off their tractors with the income from the harvests of 1992 and 1993. Several families actually lamented that, "We don't know what to do with our money." In transitional Romania, this can be a problem for the rampant inflation and high interest (80% on loans, 50% in banks) means that keeping money is in effect losing it. In a truly free market economy, the solution might be to acquire more land. But there are regulations against large holdings, and labor is limited. Moreover, larger production would demand more storage facilities or more complex marketing arrangements in the case of, say, milk.

The result of extra money, given the horizons of the newly wealthy peasants, has been to invest in status consumption items: the second car, the bigger tractor, the newest television, the trip abroad, or in the purchase of dollars or gold. The 160 cars and ten jeeps in 1991 have grown to 1,000 cars and twenty jeeps in 1994. Finally, there has been investment in various pyramid schemes such as "Caritas" which, after having made several hundred thousand *Lei* multi-millionaires, finally collapsed in late 1993.

The transition not only created new outside signs of consumption, but had more subtle affects on how villagers view their children. Up to now, an investment in children meant their getting educations to take state employment as specialists or to work as technicians in large industrial enterprises. Needless to say, these sectors are unstable as workplaces and inadequate as to salaries.

What used to be an investment in higher education may now replaced by extreme efforts to get one's children abroad, either working or training. Alternatively, children in households which have land can be kept home because income chances are greater than continuing school. Higher education nor industrial employment do not necessarily generate higher incomes. Villagers now see highly educated engineers from Braşov working the land as farmers on weekends and vacations. Two large factories near Feldioara--a brick factory and sugar beet refinery--are also closing down so that its workers are now becoming farmers or leaving the area altogether. The question is whether this is simply downward or horizontal mobility. In income terms, farmers may be prospering, and it remains to be seen whether the prosperity of farming for some villagers will overshadow the status which education has had in Romania.

What is beyond doubt, however, is that non-farming villagers' horizons have been fundamentally transformed by the simple experience of seeing traditional workplaces and established institutional channels of mobility close down. The social mobility once provided by the Communist Party, whose "social corps" controlled the economy and distribution, is certainly not replaced by the small number political posts in post-Ceauşescu Romania.

New Status Hierarchies

Seen from the outside, the village has changed little in the two decades I have known it: the main road remains largely unasphalted, there is the usual amount of mud and gravel on the side roads, those on the margin of the village still have no telephones, people heat with wood. The pharmacy, butcher, bookstore, hardware store, post office, bank, and local school and gymnasium are as they were. The bakery remains modest bread is now trucked in at a lower price. There are several more kiosks and three cafes. All these shops now have somewhat more goods, of more stable supply.

The real changes, however, are behind the high walls of the individual houses. Each courtyard has a car, or two. Several dozen have tractors or a jeep. Many have built new barns. In the kitchens there are new devices. The living rooms have the obligatory German or Japanese television set. And there are dozens of homemade parabolic antennas.

A few years ago, local functionaries and professionals--the doctors, teachers, engineers--held important positions informally and in the party apparatus. These were positions which combined responsibility and obligations. As is the case for local elites, many found it difficult to balance these formal and informal functions, and the increasing control by the regime created tensions which remain to be fully understood and described (Sampson 1983, 1984a, 1984c).

In the transitional community, however, these local functionaries are among the most dissatisfied groups. First, they are dissatisfied politically, as most side with the oppositional forces which never gained power in Romania, nor even in local elections. Second, they are dissatisfied economically, as they see the peasants or some local skilled workers becoming millionaires and their relative status dropping. Their own state salaries are stagnant and their possibility to make money via private enterprise is more complicated. The local doctor, dentist and pharmacist, for example, were in the process of establishing some kind of partially private practice. But they often did not have the kind of equipment or medicine which urban doctors could have, and therefore not the same clientele.

The school teachers and other state employees had only to bite the bullet. Their supplementary income only came from taking land for cultivation; what several have done. In one instance, a school teacher formed an association with her two brothers and sister. The brothers operate the local road maintenance facility and the sister is also a teacher. The four households together hold about 40 hectares, but it is the older brother who does most of the fulltime agricultural work. The school teacher and her husband, a doctor, purchased a tractor. All the brothers and sister use it to cultivate the land. The family members hold periodic meetings, and she in fact is quite satisfied to have the family acting as a kind of firm. Informal relations of exchange have continued: the children of her brother come to her house for French lessons and German and piano lessons. She and her husband do little work on the land, but they purchase gasoline and let their courtyard be used for storage. She keeps all the accounts and balances for the firm, but as yet there have been no arguments or serious discussions.

The teacher is aware of how many other such associations, some found upon families, others via neighbors, have collapsed. A former activist in local cultural affairs, she also had the talents to ameliorate potential conflicts. Under the new conditions, however, she must find the way of combining kinship relations--always tense--with exchanges of economic resources in a quasi corporate way. The task is not easy, and perhaps this is what the transition is about: learning to combine old arrangements: kinship and exchange, in frameworks which are uncertain. Such arrangements leave much room for personal initiative and difference: all things are possible if there is enough flexibility and initiative. But it is not without its price. The family members all derive income from several sources, and status from different ones. Being a French teacher gives status but no money; agriculture gives money but no status.

It appears, however, that whereas the peasants seem to be able to become more autonomous units, the functionaries may be forced to have to collaborate more with each other. It is this kind of creativity, a creativity wrought with tensions, which is the testing ground of "transitional" society. How do families go from status to contract ties? To what extent do formal firms succeed precisely because of informal means? How does one calculate a balance between piano lessons (cultural capital) and tractor use (application of capital)? It is these kinds of mechanisms which characterize the transition in Feldioara.

Some Conclusions

In situations where the frameworks for human action are being restructured, and where these restructurations are poorly understood by the actors, the operating principle of "all things are possible, nothing is certain" takes on crucial importance. People in transitional Romania are constantly testing their limits and expanding their horizons. In the geographic world where the West takes on significance, and in the social world where one's status relative to others suddenly rises or falls, people must expend considerable efforts to locate their place in as changing world.

It is in these individual, everyday practices of trying to locate oneself, to plot one's horizons, that the transition is having its effect. Invoking phrases like "privatization," "democratic institutions" and "civil society," may be useful as rhetorical devices, and may even be effective code words for East Europeans making connections with the West. But these cliches tell us little about the transition going on in real communities, in the way people evaluate social relations, and in the way new practices arise in a world which is both uncertain and full of open horizons.

In this sense, the "transition" in Romania is a permanent state of affairs.

References

Hann, C. M. 1985. *A Village without Solidarity*. New Haven: Yale University Press.

Hannerz, Ulf. 1992. *Cultural Complexity*. New York: Columbia.

Kideckel, David A. 1993. *The Solitude of Collectivism: Romanian Villagers to the Revolution and Beyond*. Ithaca: Cornell University Press.

Milosz, Czeslaw, 1952 (1981). *The Captive Mind*. New York: Vintage.

Sampson, Steven. 1983. Bureaucracy and Corruption as Anthropological Problems: A Case Study from Romania. *Folk* (Copenhagen) 25:63-97.

____.1984a. *National Integration through Socialist Planning: An Anthropological Study of a Romanian New Town.* Boulder: East European Monographs.

____.1984b. Rumors in Socialist Romania. *Survey* (Winter) 28:142-64.

____.1984c. Elites and mobilization in Romanian villages. *Sociologia Ruralis* 24:29-51.

____.1986. The Informal Sector in Eastern Europe. *Telos* no. 66, pp. 44-66.

____.1987. The Second Economies of the Soviet Union and Eastern Europe. *Annals, American Academy of Social and Political Sciences*, September, pp. 120-136.

____.1988. May You Live Only by Your Salary: The Second Economy of Eastern Europe. *Social Justice* 12: 145-67. special. issue on Informal Economy.

____.1989. Romania: House of Cards. *Telos* no. 79, pp. 217-224.

____.1991. Is there an Anthropology of Socialism? *Anthropology Today*. Spring. pp. 34-38.

____.1990. Towards an Anthropology of Collaboration in Eastern Europe. *Culture and History* (Copenhagen), nr. 8, pp. 107-118.

____.1994a. Money without Culture. Culture without Money: Eastern Europe's Nouveaux Riches. *Anthropological Journal of European Cultures*. Special issue on the transition, Vol. 2(2), pp. 1-21.

____.1994b. Dissimulation, Diversions, Conspiracies (in Romanian). In *Revista "22,"* Group for Social Dialogue. Bucharest, April .

Sampson, Steven and David A. Kideckel. 1989. Anthropologists Going Into the Cold: Research in the Age of Mutually Assured Destruction. *In* Paul Turner and David Pitt, Eds. *Anthropology of War and Peace*. Hadley, Mass.: Bergin and Garvey, pp. 160-173.

Scott, James. 1984. *Weapons of the Weak*. New Haven: Yale University Press.

Shafir, Michael. 1985. *Romania: Politics, Economics, Society*. London: Frances Pinter.

Shlapentokh, Vladimir. 1990. *Public and Private Life of Soviet People*. Ann Arbor: University of Michigan Press.

Wedel, Janine. 1986. *The Private Poland: An Anthropologist's Look at Everyday Life*. New York: Facts on File.

PART THREE

Debates over Meaning and Identities

11

Decollectivization to Poverty and Beyond: Women in Rural East Germany Before and After Unification

Hermine G. De Soto and Christel Panzig

In March 1993, an East German feminist politician and member of parliament representing the *Linke Liste* called upon the German *Bundestag* to debate the deteriorating situation of East German rural women after unification. In her speech, "Perspectives for Women in Rural Communities in the New Federal States," Ms. Bläss called upon the *Bundestag*:

> Dear President! Ladies and Gentlemen! It took the federal government eight months to answer my request for this debate regarding rural women in East Germany. My research results about the situation of rural women are very disappointing. Leading East German agrarian female experts whom I consulted on the present state of the East German rural economy were dismayed and outraged about the ignorance and the lack of knowledge in Bonn about the concrete situation of rural women in East Germany.

Ms. Bläss concluded:

> ...in the rural economy of the new East German states, employment for women can only succeed in the long term if politicians consider in their programs more than before that the overwhelming majority of female employees in East Germany do not work in the model called the family farm, as it is known in West Germany, but the small number of women still employed after unification work in the transformed collectives (i.e., in market oriented cooperatives or the new *Kapitalgesellschaften*) [similar to agribusinesses]. This means that the

government's policy and support for the thirty hectare family farm has to be modified for East Germany. Additionally, most of the newly emerging independent farmers have less than thirty hectares of land. Thus, I demand that the agrarian politicians and the government help to secure for the long term rural employment for women by supporting equally all agricultural property rights and forms presently still in existence in rural East Germany.[1]

Introduction

Since the collapse of the socialist rational redistributive economies (Szélenyi 1988), many rural people of eastern Europe have become ambivalent about the politics of decollectivization (i.e., the process by which there is a "break-up of large-scale farms, organized either as cooperatives or state enterprises, into individually operated farms and their creation as autonomous production units independent of the government" [Pryor 1991:4]). Recent anthropological studies from Romania (Kideckel 1993:62-75), Siberia (Anderson 1993:76-98), and Hungary (Hann 1993:99-119) indicate that "at the same time that Romanian peasants fight to preserve the principle of egalitarian pay and labor control, Siberian hunters lobby for appropriate types of guaranteed education and employment and Hungarian farmers defend the freedom from taxation that their collective gives them (Anderson and De Soto 1993:xi)." Comparable data from opinion polls taken in 1990 convey that less than five percent of rural east Germans were inclined to take the steps into private farming, while in the former Czechoslovakia less than ten percent were ready for the family farm. Similarly, less than thirty percent of the rural population in Bulgaria and Hungary were eager to start private farming (Pryor 1991:23).

However, in spite of such reluctance by the rural population to zealously enter the privatization process, the restructuring of rural eastern Europe is on its way. Anthropologists have studied how capitalist relations of production have affected precapitalist relations, and how in turn these processes developed and changed women's lives (Moore 1988:73-127). Yet, within feminist anthropological literature up to now, no study has ethnographically examined how capitalist relations of production affect rural women who were engaged formerly in socialist relations of production, such as in the German Democratic Republic of Germany (GDR). What we can learn from the "articulation" literature for the anthropology of women in East Germany is that capitalist transformations developed notably unevenly, and that women have been both extremely vulnerable during these transitions and affected differently by these profound structural changes.

In this paper, we examine how these radical changes have unfolded in the countryside of eastern Germany. Particularly, we examine how the economic, social, and cultural reorganization affect rural women's lives, work, and status in society, and how women respond to these unprecedented sociocultural transformations. Since the present processes are, in part, related to the post-World War Two period, our analysis begins with this particular east German history. Additionally, although our research was primarily undertaken in the previous district of Brandenburg,[2] we also draw on our preliminary work and meetings with women from other rural districts of the former GDR.[3]

Rural Women in Eastern Germany After World War Two

The rural developments in eastern Germany leading to collectivization began after World War Two, when East Germany became the *Sowjetische besetzte* zone or Soviet occupied zone. In this period after World War Two, women in eastern Germany experienced a transformation from an agricultural mode based on private ownership principles to a system that was primarily based on social and collective ownership. In contrast to the capitalist mode, the collective mode was built upon a distinct hierarchy of forms of property ownership, similar to the one described by Caroline Humphrey for Siberia (1983) and Christopher Hann (1993) for eastern Europe:

> ...at the top was property that belonged to the state and was worked by wage-labor employees in the manner of the Soviet *sovkhoz*. In second place stood a cooperative form of property (cf. the Soviet *kolkhoz*) according to which the farm was said to belong to its members collectively, though as time went by, working conditions in the collective sectors of such farms came to resemble those of the state farms. Private farming, including the so-called household plot element within collective farms, came at the bottom of the hierarchy....(Hann 1993:108).

During the subsequent Russian inspired land reform, initially 8000 landed proprietors with more than 100 hectares and 4000 rural estate owners with fewer than 100 hectares were expropriated without compensation (Wüpper 1993:14). The 2.1 million hectares of land resulting from the reform was distributed to 119,000 former agricultural workers, 83,000 refugees from the former eastern provinces, and 113,000 pre-World War Two small-scale impoverished East German peasant farmers (Wüpper 1993:14).

These reforms took place during a time when various communities were still coming to terms with the aftermath of World War Two. Among war-torn communities, devastated environments, migrating populations, and chaotic destruction of previous village organizations, perhaps worse than anything else was the significant loss of male residents caused by the devastating wars of the Hitler regime. Thus, the population in the immediate post World War Two period in east Germany comprised three million more women than men.

Because of the geographical fact that Brandenburg borders Berlin--and that the severest battles of World War Two were fought around that capital[4]--many villages, fields, tools, and cattle in Brandenburg were among the enormous casualties of the war. Numerous women in rural districts during this time began to remove debris left behind from the war. However, it was not only these *Trümmerfrauen* who had initiated self-help groups in the small towns of Brandenburg. There were also myriad peasant women and former female workers from pre-World War Two estates who began to cultivate the war torn fields for daily survival.

The influx of thousands of war-displaced Germans, arriving in Brandenburg from former eastern provinces, greatly overburdened the village women in Brandenburg. Frau Liese B., a peasant woman from the village of "E", remembered that "...the resettlers who continuously flowed into our village suffered much worse than us. Weeks on end, twenty and often twenty-five people walked into the village. Most of them were women, children or old people. They had lost everything. When we saw their sufferings, we women wanted to help them."

Part of the Soviet land reform in the district of Brandenburg was intended to create peasant farms for land distribution to the well over 761,000 displaced persons. In most of the newly established peasant households women were heads of households. The peasant women received a few cattle, tools, machines, seeds, and horses through a lottery method. Most often women from different households shared with each other the former estate kitchen for cooking, while estate rooms became lodging facilities for the families, and the estate barns were used for sheltering farm animals and for storing tools. During this time, the village women of Brandenburg began again to re-create the social organization and culture of daily life in the small communities. Older women today recall how, in these chaotic post-war times, they reinvented and reorganized harvest rituals, harvest feasts, and life cycle rituals (e.g. baptisms, birthdays, initiation rituals, village dances, and funerals) and how, through these active engagements and exalted responsibilities, their self-confidence grew in the community .

Yet, despite the women's efforts, initiatives, and energetic participation in constructing and reinventing community and culture--and regardless of their growing status in the village and their predominance in the population--as time passed traditional gender roles were silently reproduced in the countryside. Although most women cultivators after the war received new titles and land shares as "heads of households" and took over most of the work on the new farms, the women were nevertheless excluded from official politics and from important decision making processes in the communities. No woman head of household was admitted into the powerful land reform committees, and neither political party (i.e., the Communist Party [KPD] or the Social Democratic Party [SPD, that later became SED--the *Sozialistische Einheitspartei*]) were ready to break with traditional gender roles, even though the SED platform supported equality for women. Rather, during this period, women became publicly recognized as *die Helferin des Mannes* or "help for men," and the "natural" and highest role envisioned for women was as *zeitweiliger Ersatz* or "temporary substitute" for men in the village.

Only more research can help to explain whether or not women in the countryside in Brandenburg resisted these gendered roles. Our preliminary hypothesis suggests that only a few women succeeded in becoming local politicians (e.g., mayors or county representatives), and it appears that the few women in these public offices performed and reproduced their political roles within the dominant male status quo of the time. On the other hand, in the aftermath of World War Two, the majority of rural women were exhaustively engaged in spending their energy and efforts in first aid for the old, the disabled, the refugees, the resettlers, and the village-sponsored welfare programs, *Rettet die Kinder*, or "Save the Children."

Collectivization

Whereas the first phase after World War Two was marked by Soviet-led comprehensive land reform (i.e., village reorganization, and construction of peasant farms through expropriation of vast private agricultural estates), with the beginning of the 1950s, brought the vast rural experiment of collectivization. To an extent, collectivization was forced by East German leaders who thought the average twenty hectare farm not profitable. In a manner similar to the Russian system in the former GDR the most highly regarded property form was the state owned farm called *Staatseigene Betrieb*, while the second ranked cooperative farm was known as the *landwirtschaftliche Produktionsgenossenschaft* (or LPG). The LPG was the predominant form of farm with the majority of East German women previously employed in such collectives. Like the Soviet Siberian *Buryat kolkhozy* studied by Humphrey (1983), East German LPGs had similar forms of organization. For example, the Siberian charter asserts that "A collective farm is a cooperative organization of peasants voluntarily associated for the purpose of the common conducting of large-scale socialist agricultural production on the basis of socialized means of production and collective labor (quoted in Humphrey 1983:75)." Likewise, the East German charter declared "that the agricultural cooperatives are voluntarily formed associations of female and male peasants, gardeners and other citizens who joined together in a common socialist production process and for a continued embetterment of food supplies and raw material for industry (LPG Gesetz, DDR, VI A 3, p.1, Paragraph 1, Nr. 1)." The East German master statute for cooperatives was introduced in 1959.

In Brandenburg the official collectivization drive began in 1952. In retrospect we can see a pattern emerging during the initial phase of collectivization in this district. This pattern suggests that those female peasants whose farms to stabilized after the immediate postwar period, and who were on their way to becoming middle peasants (see Wolf 1966), began to resist the collectivization programs. Another strata, female owners from the former landed estates, also joined the resistance against collectivization. As the East German state endorsed the socialized and collectivized property ownership of the means of production in agriculture individually owned farms lost economic and social support. Those who were unable to reproduce themselves who were unwilling to give up independence, or who refused to serve as agricultural workers into the new socialist production institutions to relocate, most often into the Federal Republic of Germany.[5] The majority of women from the new small-size peasant farms entered the LPG. Most of these peasant women were either war widows or wives of soldiers missing in action. By joining the LPG many hoped that cooperative work would not only ease the burden of workloads but eventually lead to more security and better standard of living for their families.

The collective organization of work, hitherto unknown to the rural population, radically restructured the social and cultural spheres of everyday life for village women. This restructuring caused innumerable deprivations for women in everyday life, including the "unfavorable conditions" of work on the LPG. This was partly due to the redirection of women's labor power into the meat production branch of the LPGs to forestall a decline in meat production and resulting food storage. Many rural women were moved into the unmechanized brigades of calf and piglet breeding in hopes the increase in labor in meat production would help reduce the growing scarcity. As a rationale for the political, economic, and gender policies of the socialist "rational redistributive economy (Konrad and Szélenyi 1979)" was an ideology that regarded women, as possessing "natural" abilities as caretakers, and thus predestined to take over this "extremely-responsible party contract." Thus livestock production in the GDR evolved into a predominately gender-specific female branch, division which lasted until the GDR fell apart in 1989.

Almost 60% of the women employed in livestock production worked under labor intensive conditions and without any significant modern technological support, a work pattern also reported by Humphrey (1983) and Bridger (1987) from Siberia and other regions of the former U.S.S.R. For example, Humphrey (1983) observed that :

> there are clear correlations between the division of labor and specialization by age and sex. Of the eighty-one people in mechanized work in the Selenga Karl Marx farm in 1965..., seventy-eight were men, while only three were women.... In livestock production, on the other hand, the majority of workers were women (60-70%) and most were middle-aged (1983:229).

Bridger's (1987) study on women's roles in rural development in the former Soviet Union also found gendered work in the collectivized agricultural sector in which:

> it would appear that the long established forms of occupational segregation in agriculture, notably in arable and livestock farming, have been modified by a new division of labor; one in which men operate and service machinery whilst women predominate in manual work using only simple hand tools (1987:221).

From a comparative perspective, we suggest that similar processes developed in Brandenburg, and that women disappeared from the collectives to the extent that manual labor was replaced by mechanized labor. As women recall, "men sat on the machinery," *(Männer sassen auf den Maschinen)*. And only when there was a "shortage of male labor" as in 1968 when new harvest combines were introduced, were women called upon to operate "the modern technology" (*Frauen auf die moderne Technik)*. On the other hand, as soon as male labor was secure in the harvest technology, the image of rural women was formulated with slogans, proclaiming "modern technology was hazardous for the fragile female organism."

The structural changes since World War Two in East Germany affected rural women profoundly differently from their counterparts engaged in simple commodity production[6] on small family farms in West Germany. Despite their unequal but changing work status, women in the LPGs and state-owned farms, who worked as operators of tractors and other agricultural machines, acquired valuable knowledge about running the new technology. Moreover, numerous women, although overburdened with their work as mothers, housewives, and collective workers, took advantage of state adult education programs and completed degrees in skilled agricultural professions. As a result, by 1971, 57% were highly skilled employees in the East German rural economy.

It was also at this time that state planners began to initiate large-scale agrarian modernization policies. Between 1970 and 1980, plant and animal production were separated into distinct collectives. With the new specialization in production, families who previously worked on the same farm, though often in different brigades, were separated to work in dissimilar collectives, located in diverse villages. Now women needed more time for travel, which reduced that available for child care and household duties. Though this segregation of family labor often resulted in internal conflicts within families, more family frustration was fostered by the principle of socialist competition among the collectives. Socialist competition in the GDR was based on regulations similar to those in Siberia (Humphrey 1983) and functioned as a:

> political-ideological mechanism for manipulating the economy. It plays on, and accentuates, regional and sectional divisions. What matters is that the community is divided in this way, and that the divisions are used to create specific obligations for individual people.... The economic production teams, as well as farms, become social groups to the extent that their members are collectively involved in effort, decision and in the sharing out of proceeds (1983:170).

The new specialized, mechanized farms, on the average, consisted of more than 1,000 hectares of arable land or of 1,000 animals. As in previous phases of rural change, women were able to adapt to the modernized and industrialized collective relations of production. During this last reorganization of the rural economy (before unification), many women again began to formally reeducate themselves, mainly in computer technology and engineering, to enter the industrialized collectives. In 1988, a year before the collapse of the GDR, more than ninety percent of rural women held diplomas for skilled agrarian professions. Almost 74% of them were specialized technicians, while 6.4% had graduated as *Meisterin* or "master craftswomen." Furthermore, 7% of the women in 1988 were graduates from agricultural colleges, while three percent were trained agricultural experts with advanced graduate degrees from universities. Yet, in spite of their training, hardly any women held leading management positions in the collectives. Our data show that only one woman became a chairwoman of a collective in Brandenburg. Most women interviewed did not perceive their job relations as unjust. They said their working conditions since 1952 had significantly improved and that over the years they had identified both objectively and subjectively with their collectives.

In contrast to West German villages, which exhibit a loosely structured community social organization (i.e., school, church, mayor's office, voluntary associations such as *Vereine* or clubs etc.), and which transmit a sense of community identity through local rituals and remembered traditions, in rural East Germany economic and cultural identity was closely connected to and predominantly constructed by one's collective. Over the years, for many women, the collectives became a multifunctional social and cultural center. These centers enculturated and socialized the young, secured jobs and college and university placements for women, organized workshops, served food in communal kitchens, provided welfare services for senior citizens and pupils, and organized leisure activities such as folklore events, dances, ceramic classes, and horseback riding. Moreover, the collectives managed and constructed rural cultural centers, restaurants, stores, clinics, housing, and sewage systems. They financed most village projects because of the GDR state's "planned" failure to support infrastructural development in the communities. As Brandenburg women told us, they became attached to "their brigades and collectives" which provided them with "their own income, health care, a regulated work day on the farm, annual vacation and a guaranteed pension." By 1989, these social benefits were perceived as "natural" facts of life, and nobody could imagine they could be lost.

Rural Women After the Collapse of the GDR

For East Germany, unification and the transition into the market economy was more complicated than anticipated. Not only did privatization of land run into diverse obstacles, but the reappearance of formerly disowned farmers and estate owners and their new claims for property are currently causing unforeseen conflicts.

After unification, the immediate aim of the federal government was to privatize the former collectively administrated arable lands and forests. This was to be accomplished through the ideological promotion of the family farm as a model for East Germans. Similar to the government-founded company, the *Treuhand*, that controls and sells former collectively held industrial property, a daughter-company of Treuhand was established, the BVVG, or *Bodenverwertung und verwaltung* to oversee and to privatize 1.5 million hectares of land and 770,000 hectares of forests (Wüpper 1993).

The BVVG began to appropriate and control that part of LPG lands that were not recorded as owned by the individual collective farmers. It's goal as determined by government was to market this land after 1995. Many LPGs were severely affected by this, and with this significant loss of land they were forced first to reduce labor and second to declare bankruptcy. The remaining LPGs were transformed most often into limited companies (GmbHs, *Gemeinschaft mit begrenzter Haftung*) or agrarian coorperatives (*Agrargenossenschaften*).

During this initial phase of land privatization, the most significant labor cuts occurred in livestock production, with the result that thousands of women were laid off. Altogether over half the agrarian labor force became unemployed. The people who were laid off after leaving the LPG usually received the relatively small pieces of land they had brought with them into the collectives. While many of these unemployed would have preferred to start a family farm, many had to lease their land to the GmbH because they did not have capital to start up again, or because they lacked the necessary knowledge and experience for market-oriented, simple commodity production.

The GmbHs currently try to survive with the former collective farmer's leased land, and by entering into an annual rent contract with the BVVG for the previously communally owned land of the LPG. However, after 1995 the highest bidder will be able to purchase the former LPG land.

This process of privatization has produced a politics of land and class favoritism complicated by who can or cannot reclaim or be compensated for former collective lands. The peasant farmers who received land after World War Two under the Soviet land reform are today legally prevented from claiming compensation in land or money. The justification is that during forced collectivization, a huge number of these peasant farmers with their land entered the collectives, or they moved to West Germany. During the industrialization process in the former GDR, large amounts of land were again redistributed by the socialist state to various LPGs or state-owned farms for usufruct farming.

The land of those farmers who left East Germany in the early 1950s was taken over by the GDR state and incorporated into LPGs. If this land was sold after the collapse of the wall, then these previous owners are legally prevented from reclaiming their land. Those farmers who left East Germany during the phase of forced collectivization are legally prevented from reclaiming land, since the GDR state redistributed this land to LPGs. After the collapse of the wall, some of this land was sold and "legally and correctly bought" and thus after unification cannot be reclaimed from the owner. Also, according to the unification contract, the formerly disowned and landed gentry are excluded legally from claiming old ownership rights.

Yet this influential lobby group has refused to acknowledge the contract and instead demands a release of all land. The Kohl government's policy regarding this group, and enforced through the BVVG, asserts that they not only will obtain first preference for contracting land, but in addition this land can be bought back in 1995 by these contract farmers. Moreover, these large-scale farmers are entitled to receive state subsidies and they can use the financial compensation they received from the state for their former property to purchase (in 1995) the property which they contracted from the BVVG (Wüpper 1993). This policy is presently being contested by many managers of the GmbHs and by potential private farmers (Wupper 1993).

Most of the "old" estate owners who, after World War Two, left to live in West Germany, will receive long term contracts from the BVVG for former LPG land, not one-year contracts like those of the GmbH. GmbH managers thus fear that their already economically vulnerable GmbHs will be unable to yield the necessary profit to pay rent to those villagers whose land they now cultivate. The currently surviving GmbHs also try to lease some of their previously held collective land from the BVVG so that they might be able to qualify for bank loans. However, this action becomes an obstacle when the GmbH is in debt from the former socialist economy (Wüpper 1993).

Although the returning "original" owners are presently only able to receive compensation (*Lastenausgleich*) in money, not land, this rule is being contested by those farmers who are most often currently living in West Germany. On the other hand, East German villagers who are financially constrained or discriminated against by the BVVG strategies to receive contracts for starting farms are enraged over these demands,[7] and they demand in turn that the emerging rural gentry in East Germany should give up all claims to the acquired land contracts.

As we mentioned above, numerous LPGs did not survive the initial phase of decollectivization, and those which reproduced themselves under the new politics and relations of production were significantly reduced in size and labor. Between late 1989 and mid-1992, 180,000 rural women and 120,000 men lost their jobs. Since then there has been a continuous rise of unemployment in rural Germany. Numerous women were thus sent into early retirement or *Vorruhestand.* Women who previously worked in animal production, agricultural administration, or social welfare were the first ones to be laid off, but equally hard hit were the academically trained female experts. Today women are often reminded "to take more seriously the care of family and child care duties," an expression which is in line with present employment developments, and which indicates that less qualified men receive preference for available jobs.

Many single rural women from Brandenburg now complain about the rising cost of rent, electricity, gas, heat, and taxes, expenses which currently add to their growing poverty. In the past, under the socialist "economy of shortage" (Verdery 1991) where partial self-provisioning significantly raised one's standard of living, these women were able to earn extra income from the former socialist household plots and stockeeping. Today, the high prices of seed, fodder, water, and electricity work against house plot farming, and less expensive products from West Germany and the European market further make such farming obsolete.

Young women and men, lacking immediate alternatives for employment, have begun to migrate to West Germany. Thus it is currently not unusual to find small communities in Brandenburg whose residents are predominately senior citizens and unemployed women in their forties with their small children. Today one hears again that "men need jobs because they have to feed the family," and that "work in agriculture is too much for women," yet recent surveys suggest that 97% of women from both rural and urban environments consider work a very important need in life for women in all age groups (Fremerey and Kupferschmied 1991).[8]

Decollectivization not only is accompanied by severe economic hardships for the individual, but has also affected people's identities. With the breakdown of the LPG's sociocultural functions, expectations are rising that women should voluntarily provide welfare services for children and senior citizens who now lack resources for nursing homes or *Altersheime*. With few other social institutions to replace the LPG's function of transmitting public culture, many people will now experience village life within an economic and cultural vacuum.

As is well understood from anthropological studies on women and rural transformation, "women who are isolated from strong support networks may find themselves more dependent on men and more subject to male authority within the household (Moore 1988:61)." With the breakdown of the collectives, women lost their previous meeting and discussion places and, in their present isolation, many refuse out of shame to talk with their former colleagues from the collectives. Not only is it true that both men and women suffer under radical processes of capitalist transformation, as Deere and Léon de Léal (1981) suggested, but we must also emphasize that women, in rural east Germany have been hit by unemployment more than men, and also fear men's increased alcoholism and violence directed predominately at their wives.

Statements from four East German rural women representatives reflect on the present and future developments of village life in the new states. The representative from Brandenburg expressed that:

> much got lost in the villages. Many women lost their previous communication networks and the feeling of belonging in the former collectives. Now they long for common experiences. The world became enlarged. But can this enlarged world replace the loss of a home?" The woman from Saxony emphasized that "rural women are the social consciousness of the villages. Presently they most of all need help for reeducation and reschooling for new employment. Work for most women means more than to earn money," while the leading woman representative from Thüringen concluded that "it is good if women join together again and feel strong, so that they will have a strong voice in the village, in the state representation and in the federal representation. Only then will there be a breakthrough in achieving a constitutionally guaranteed equality for women.

Finally, the representative from Mecklenburg-Vorpommern asserted,

> Even though the agricultural association is engaged in developing new projects for unemployed women in the villages, the bottom line is that this is no more than a drop on to the hot stone. Members of the association should be alert and should not let themselves be pushed against the wall. Only if political concepts are developed can we realize our demands. The association has to participate in the making of politics (*Politik machen*).

Beyond Decollectivization

Perhaps more than men, rural women in Brandenburg have remained skeptical about the government's political and ideological focus on the family farm for post-unification East Germany. Though this may in part be related to their vague understandings about family farming passed on from oral history, their expressed skepticism is also based fear of the competition within the European Community which east German agriculture was thrown overnight. For women, individual risk taking and economic responsibility in such uncertain times has been a real concern. Although the new hierarchy of property rights has politically shifted in favor of the family farm, many women are aware that most former collective farmers who risked private farming were part-time farmers in 1992.

The remaining small number of full-time farmers, in order to not lose out to competition with European community farmers and East German GmbHs, desperately try to rent land either from private persons, the church, the BVVG, or former LPG farmers. In their struggle to survive, these full-time farmers the risk of ostracism from their neighbors if they try too aggressively to rent land from the BVVG. Villagers fear that such behavior, if successful, will worsen the already high rate of unemployment by helping to speed up the ruin of the GmbH. These farmers often have to mortgage their house and land to buy a tractor or other farming equipment. They perceive the state policy of delayed land sale as dangerous because they fear that the former estate owners will come back and claim most of the valued arable land.[9]

Women's ambivalence has further grown as they compare the family farm to issues of social security, regular working hours, economic risk factors, vacation, and old age pension. However, in spite of these reservations, some women in Brandenburg have opted for the family farm. When asked why they entered family farming, they replied "What else is left, our LPG is gone. There is no chance for other employment and unemployment is too great--we have no other choices." Although they might not be typical for other regions in East Germany, such answers, nevertheless, seem to diverge from the government's posture "that the former East German collective farmers are now free to choose the family farm."

Conclusion

Even as we write this article, a large number of women in rural Brandenburg still suffer from loss of status, loss of hope for future employment and education, and from the disintegration from public life. On the positive side, rural women leaders have actively begun policies to retain unemployed women. These leaders underscore that only such actions will help women again identify with their villages and build ecologically oriented, environmentally safe lives. These leaders want for women to direct their activities into village tourism and small-scale production sale and of local crafts and foodstuffs. To turn these visions into reality, the women have called on local, state, and federal governments for support, demanding that the transformed GmbHs require equal employment quotas for women and men.

As we have suggested, after World War Two, East German rural women made important contributions to rebuilding a sense of community and relations of production in the countryside, though under distinctly different and largely unfavorable structural and historical conditions. Today once more women are at a historical crossroad, most signs of course point to directions recognized by Christopher Hann (1993:116):

> To judge from the most influential elite spokespersons and the declarations of policymakers, it would seem that the revolutions throughout Eastern Europe are concerned with the protection of bourgeois private property against all other forms of property rights. But one hears less of this sort of thing at the grass roots....

However, we also hear for the first time in German history, feminist politicians', albeit in the minority, who demand as mentioned above:

> that the agrarian politicians and the government help to secure for the long term rural employment for women by supporting all agricultural property rights and forms presently still in existence in rural East Germany (Bläss 1993).

It remains to be seen if these feminist voices will be heard in "the struggle for balance in turbulent times" in rural East Germany.

Notes

Hermine De Soto would like to thank the National Council for Soviet and East European Research for its funding her ethnographic field research during 1991 and 1992 in east Germany. She is also grateful to the generous institutional support of the Women's Studies Program and the Women's Studies Research Center of the University of Wisconsin-Madison, and to Cyrena Pondrom for her continuous encouragement. Both authors take this opportunity to express their sincerest gratitude to all women who were a part of the research project in east Germany during very difficult post-revolutionary times.

1. The entire 1993 debate is available in document #12/2360, 12/3910: Deutscher Bundestag, 12. Wahlperiode. 149. Sitzung, Bonn, 25 March 1993. Additional information on rural women and politics is available in Bläss, 1993, which excerpts from Ms. Bläss's speech translated from German into English by Hermine De Soto. She thanks Ms. Bläss for her help and time. An additional Bundestag debate about the dismal rural situation in the new federal states was held later in 1993 between the secretary of agriculture, Mr. Jochen Borchert, and an east German agricultural expert, Dr. Fritz Schumann. The complete information is available in #14945, Deutscher Bundestag, 12 Wahlperiode, 137.Sitzung, 9 September 1993.

2. Up to 1952 the GDR was organized into *Länder* (states). After the 1952 administrative reform the *Länder* became districts with particular cities chosen as *Bezirksstädte* (district capitals), each with its own district council. Under this reform, the GDR was organized into fifteen districts with capitals at: Rostock, Frankfurt/Oder, Potsdam, Cottbus, Magdeburg, Halle, Gera, Suhl, Erfurt, Dresden, Leipzig, former Karl-Marx Stadt now Chemnitz, and Berlin-Ost. Since unification, a new administrative reform has been under way in which the west German *Ländermodell* is being introduced. The GDR districts and capitals have been replaced with new *Länder*, and new *Länderhauptstädte*. The federal *Länder* or states are: Mecklenburg-Vorpommern, Sachsen-Anhalt, Berlin (east and west), Brandenburg, Thüringen, and Sachsen. With this change, people respond differently. Currently, the older generation still remembers the pre-1952 state organization, and the younger generation suffers from a lack of identification with the re-formed social organization. At present, a conflict is developing in regard to the reconstruction of the smallest local administrative unit, i.e. the *Kreis* (county), with which people often identify. It is on this level also that major local disagreements arise because drawing new administrative boundaries also shifts and reorganizes new county boundaries.

3. During De Soto's fieldwork in February 1992 rural women from all five new states met in east Berlin to discuss *Frauenarmut im Osten Deutschlands*, and exchange experiences about the worsening rural situation. Some meetings and workshops were organized by Dr. Christel Panzig, with De Soto an invited participant and observer. According to our background research, there are presently no anthropological studies on rural women during the transition in east Germany. Recently, two sociologically and quantitatively oriented studies began to systematically outline emerging rural patterns and

female unemployment in regions of Rostock and in Sachsen-Anhalt. These studies can be found in Elke Schmidt's *Landfrauen in Sachsen-Anhalt, Ministerium für Ernährung, Landwirtschaft und Forsten des Landes Sachsen-Anhalt*, Magdeburg, December 1992, pp. 3-71; and in Eberhard Ackermann and Otto Seifert *Umbruch ländlicher Arbeitsmärkte und Frauenbeschäftigung* in *Utopie Kreativ*, Nr. 6, 1993, pp. 28-35.

4. Before World War Two, Berlin was the capital of the united Germany. After World War Two, with Germany's division into two states (i.e., the western part became the Federal Republic of Germany [FRG or in German BRD], while the eastern part became the German Democratic Republic of Germany [GDR or DDR]), the former capital was also divided. East Berlin became the capital of the GDR, and consisted of eleven urban districts or *Kieze*: Friedrichshain, Köpenick, Hellersdorf, Hohenschönhausen, Lichtenberg, Mahrzahn, Mitte, Pankow, Prenzlauerberg, Treptow, and Weissensee. West Berlin lost its status to Bonn as the capital of the FRG. After German unification in October 1990, east and west Berlin were again chosen to become the capital of Germany. Today, the city of Berlin is organized into twenty-three *Bezirke* or districts, the eleven (mentioned above) from the former east German capital and twelve from west Berlin: Charlottenburg, Kreuzberg, Neukölln, Reinickendorf, Spandau, Schöneberg, Steglitz, Tempelhof, Tiergarten, Wedding, Wilmersdorf, and Zehlendorf. A detailed urban anthropological examination on the initial process of uniting east and west Berlin is forthcoming in H. De Soto, "The Urban Revolution: Experiences before and after the Collapse of the Berlin Wall."

5. Because the Berlin wall was not yet erected during this time, it was still relatively easy to undertake such onerous moves to west Germany.

6. For further information on the development of simple commodity producers in the FRG, see De Soto and Pahari (forthcoming 1994), and De Soto (1989).

7. This fear is not unfounded: the waiting-list for forest sales already has 38 applicants, most from west Germany, the rest other countries. Since the highest bidder will receive the land, east Germans are likely to lose out in the competition because of lack of funds.

8. Funk (1993) suggests that diverse women in post-communist societies prefer to stay at home and to enjoy "family pleasures". Our research on rural women reveals a different pattern. While it is true that many women currently pass possible jobs over to their husbands, they do that not to gain missed family pleasures, but because, "*Männer wollen die Hausarbeit nicht machen*" "men do not do the housework." Additionally, women say, "if men are unemployed and stay in the house, they might be drunk when we come home from work."

9. So far over 200,000 applications for land restitution and claims have been made, and well over 500,000 hectares of land still must be returned (Wüpper 1993:7).

References

Ackermann, Eberhard, and Otto Seifert. 1993 " Umbruch ländlicher Arbeitsmärkte und Frauenbeschäftigung." *Utopie Kreativ* 6:28-35.

Anderson, David G. 1993. "Civil Society in Siberia: The Institutional Legacy of the Soviet State. *In* Hermine G. De Soto and David G. Anderson, eds. *The Curtain*

Rises: Rethinking Culture, Ideology, and the State in Eastern Europe.Pp.76-9. Atlantic Highlands, N.J.: Humanities Press.

Anderson, David G., and Hermine G. De Soto. 1993. "Introduction." *In* Hermine G. De Soto and David G. Anderson, eds. *The Curtain Rises; Rethinking Culture, Ideology, and the State in Eastern Europe*. pp. ix-xvii. Atlantic Highlands, N.J.: Humanities Press.

Anonymous. 1993. "Bauern brauchen lang-fristige Pacht." *Neue Zeit* 23:9, 4 September.

Bläss, Petra. 1993. "Landfrauen Ost--Stiefkinder der Bonner Politik." *Weibblick* 13:6-10.

Bridger, Susan. 1987. *Women in the Soviet Countryside*. Cambridge: Cambridge University Press.

Bundestagdokument. 1993a. *Perspektiven für Frauen im ländlichen Raum in den 1993 neuen Bundesländern*. Nr. 12833 12. Wahlperiode, 149. Sitzung, Bonn 25 März.

Bundestagdokument. 1993b. *Lage der Frauen in den neuen Bundesländern*. Nr. 4262 12. 1993 Wahlperiode, Bonn, 2 April.

Bundestagdokument. 1993c. *Haushaltsdebatte Landwirtschaft*. Nr. 12833 12. 1993 Wahlperiode, 173. Sitzung, Bonn, 9 September.

Deere, Carmen Diana and Magdalena Léon de Léal. 1981. "Peasant production, proletarianization, and the sexual division of labor in the Andes." *Signs* 7(2):338-360.

De Soto, Hermine G. 1989. *The Delayed Transformation: Experiences of Everyday Life in a Village in the Black Forest*. Ph.D. dissertation., Department of Anthropology, University of Wisconsin, Madison.

Fremerey, Ulrike, and Peter Kupferschmied. 1991. "Dokumentation": *Frauen in den neuen Bundesländern im Prozess der deutschen Einigung*. Bonn: Pressereferat,

Funk, Nanette. 1993. *Gender Politics and Post-Communism*. New York: Routledge.

Hann, C.M. 1993. "Property Relations in the New Eastern Europe": The Case of Specialist Cooperatives in Hungary. *In* Hermine G. De Soto and David Anderson, eds. *The Curtain Rises: Rethinking Culture, Ideology, and the State in Eastern Europe*. Pp. 99-119. Atlantic Highlands, N.J.: Humanities Press.

Humphrey, Caroline. 1983. *Karl Marx Collective*. Cambridge: Cambridge University Press.

Kideckel, David A. 1993. "Once Again, the Land: Decollectivization and Social Conflict in Rural Romania." *In* Hermine G. De Soto and David G. Anderson, eds. *The Curtain Rises: Rethinking Culture, Ideology, and the State in Eastern Europe*. pp. 62-75. Atlantic Highlands, N.J.: Humanities Press.

Konräd, George, and Ivan Szelényi. 1979. *The Intellectuals on the Road to Class Power*. New York: Harcourt, Brace, Jovanovich.

Moore, Henrietta L. 1988. *Feminism and Anthropology*. Minneapolis: University of Minnesota Press.

Musterstatut der Landwirtschaftlichen Produktionsgenossenschaft (LPG). 1959. Typ III. *DDR Gesetz Dokument* VI A, 3.

Pryor, Frederic L. 1991. "When is Collectivization Reversible?" *Studies in Comparative Communism*, Vol. XXIV, Nr. 7 March:3-34.

Schmidt, Elke. 1992. *Landfrauen in Sachsen-Anhalt*. Ministerium für Ernährung, Landwirtschaft und Forsten des Landes Sachsen-Anhalt, pp. 3-71. Magdeburg.

Szelényi, Ivan. 1988. *Socialist Entrepreneurs Embourgeoisement in Rural Hungary*. Madison, Wi.: University of Wisconsin Press.

Verdery, Katherine. 1991. *Ethnic relations, the "economy of shortage," and the transition in Eastern Europe*. ASA Conference, University of Cambridge, U.K., 9-12 April.

Wolf, Eric R. 1966. *Peasants*. Englewood Cliffs, NJ: Prentice-Hall.

Wüpper, Thomas. 1993. "Agrarwirtschaft in Ostdeutschland, I, II, III, IV." *Frankfurter Rundschau*, 8-11 August, pp. 4, 8, 12, 7.

12

Roma of Shuto Orizari, Macedonia: Class, Politics, and Community

Carol Silverman

When I attended the premier press conference of the first Rom (Gypsy)[1] political party in Macedonia in August 1990, I was struck with the historic significance of the event on many levels-- political, cultural, and emotional. With live *surla* and *tapan*[2] music and participatory dancing announcing the opening, and with a collection box proclaiming that tips were to go to the party, it was clear that Rom politics had entered the level of public consciousness.

This article situates the politicization of the Macedonian Roma in the 1980's and 1990's in economic and cultural terms. In May 1993, Hugh Poulton posed the question of whether the Roma in Macedonia were "A Balkan Success Story?" (Poulton 1993a). I investigate this question through an ethnographic case study of Shuto Orizari (known locally as Shutka), a neighborhood on the outskirts of Skopje, the capitol of Macedonia, with a population of approximately 40,000 Roma, where I lived for five months in 1990. First, I place the contemporary social and political position of Balkan Roma in historical perspective, second, I discuss the economic situation in Shutka and third, I trace the emergence of a political identity by chronicling the events leading to the formation of the first Macedonian Rom party.

At the outset, it must be pointed out that there is no ubiquitous Rom or even Balkan Rom identity nor any two Rom communities exactly alike. Rather, there are a myriad of Rom groups and sub-groups (Liégeois 1986), many of whom live intermixed with other Roma and who differ from each other by dialect, occupations, class, and custom. Nevertheless, Rom intellectuals are successfully forging a pan-European human rights movement based on common historical and contemporary conditions of prejudice and marginalization (Hancock 1993, Gheorghe 1991).

Studying and writing about the Roma are important to me personally for several reasons. I am committed to educating people about and actively improving the position of Roma, who are at the bottom of the social, economic, and political hierarchy in all countries of Eastern Europe. In addition, the case of the Roma poses significant theoretical questions for the study of ethnicity: How does a group dispersed in every country of Europe with a huge array of cultural diversity and with no viable territorial claim create legitimacy? How and why does politicization happen and what are its economic roots and implications? How does traditional culture become mobilized and change during the process of politicization? Although these questions are vast and can merely be raised here, a case study illustrates some of the processes at work in one locality. However, as Verdery (1981) and Beck and Cole (1981) have pointed out, local-level ethnographic study requires historical and economic analysis.[3] This article, then, moves between micro and macro levels in an effort to illustrate the relationship between class, politics, and history.

History

Linguistic evidence reveals that Roma are originally from northern India and that they migrated out of the area sometime between 800-950 A.D. Romany, the Rom language, is descended from Sanskrit and closely related to Hindi. By the 14th century, Roma were established in large numbers throughout the Balkans, some settling and other remaining nomadic (Soulis 1961:152, 163). Initial curiosity about Roma quickly gave way to hatred and discrimination. In the Romanian principalities of Wallachia and Moldavia, Rom were slaves from the 14th to 19th centuries.[4] Slavery was abolished in 1864, but patterns of exploitation have continued (Hancock 1987).

In many countries of Europe Roma were viewed as outcasts, intruders, and threats, probably because of their dark skin, their association with invading Muslims, and their foreign ways (Hancock 1993:17-20). Bounties were paid for their capture, and repressive measures included expulsion, confiscation of property and children, forced labor, prison sentences, and physical mutilation. Assimilation was attempted in the 18th century in the Austro-Hungarian Empire during the reign of Maria Theresa and her son Joseph II by outlawing Romany, Rom music, dress, and nomadism and banning traditional occupations. In the 20th century persecution escalated with the Nazi rise to power. Between 1933 and 1945 Rom faced an extermination campaign which is only now being historically investigated; over 600,000 Roma were murdered by the Nazis and their collaborators (Liégeois 1986; Hancock 1987; Crowe and Kolsti 1991).

During the socialist period in Eastern Europe assimilationist measures aimed at the Roma were enacted in almost every country except Yugoslavia (Helsinki Watch 1991a, 1991b, 1993c; Project on Ethnic Relations 1992; Mirga 1993). In Bulgaria, for example, name changes were enforced in the early 1970's along with prohibitions against Rom music, clothing, language, and Muslim religious customs[5]. In Czechoslovakia, the Roma were considered a "social group" or "problem," and Rom women were forcibly sterilized (Helsinki Warch 1991c:19-35; Project on Ethnic Relations 1992:12-13; Hubschmanova 1993). In all countries of Eastern Europe, including Yugoslavia, Roma were and are the group with the lowest standard of living.

Since the 1989 revolutions, prejudice against Roma and stereotypification of them has increased. They have been scapegoated for all the ills of post-communism: rising prices, unemployment, increase in crime, rise of the mafia, and scarcity of goods. A backlash against Roma has ignited pogroms and beatings in Romania, Bulgaria, Hungary, Slovakia, and the Czech Republic, and anti-Rom skinhead groups are organizing (Hancock 1993). The war in the former Yugoslavia has produced ethnic cleansing of Roma as undesirables (International Romani Union 1992:5). Rajko Djuric, the president of the International Romani Union, was forced to flee to Germany after his home in Belgrade was ransacked.

In 1991 three polls found that Europeans in overwhelming numbers expressed contempt for Rom, e.g. 91% of Czechoslovaks, 71% of Bulgarians (Hancock 1993:8-9). Harassment and rates of unemployment up 80% in some Rom neighborhoods have resulted in a huge refugee population in Western Europe, which has been singled out in violent attacks. Roma are beginning to be deported from Germany, as the objects of a pay-off from Germany to Romania. It is against this historical context that the current politicization movement of the Roma must be viewed.

Shuto Orizari: Class and Community

Until the 1960's, the land on which Shuto Orizari lies was not populated, but rather used for grazing. The community was established after the earthquake of 1963, when the old Rom neighborhoods located in the center of Skopje were destroyed. At that time the government gave Roma the opportunity to obtain cheap housing grants if they would settle in Shutka, which must have seemed to them like a rural wasteland. Many Skopje Roma took advantage of this opportunity, and in the 1970's and 1980's they were joined by Roma from other areas of Macedonia, from Kosovo (which was then an autonomous region of Yugoslavia), and from Serbia. In the early 1990's Shutka had a population of approximately 40,000 people, almost all Roma, almost all Muslim, with a handful of Albanian and Bosnian Muslim families.

Zekir Ismail, a Rom blacksmith born in 1948, narrated Shutka's history as follows:

> Shutka was started in 1964; we came here in 1967, and started to build a house; we started to gather here. It's not only a neighborhood-- it's a little city of 40,000 people. Before Shutka, in 1963 there was a great earthquake, and in all the Rom neighborhoods of Skopje such as Topaana and Madzhare, the houses fell down, it was a great catastrophe. Then we had to find another place to live, to make a good life. The government gave us Shutka. They thought they'd throw the Roma all in one place and they wouldn't have to think about us any more. And that's how we were able to build our houses here. When the people in the big city saw us, they were amazed that we had built such houses, such as they don't even have in the city. However, they think bad things of Shutka, that we are here all together, but it is one of the cleanest neighborhoods in Skopje-- it has the cleanest air.

I call Shutka a community according to the definition by Arensberg and Kimball which stresses shared geographic space, and interdependent social, cultural, and institutional systems (1972:3). Although Shutka Roma are divided into many groups, which differ from each other according to such criteria as dialect of Romany spoken[6], place from which they came, traditional occupation, and religion, they all relate to and many are proud of being residents of Shutka. Living in the same place means that Shutka Roma face common problems, such as unpaved streets, lack of proper sewage, inferior schools, and inadequate medical care. These problems are related to their class position in Macedonian society. I question Puxon's (1973:12) and Poulton's (1993:43) claim that the standard of living is higher in Shutka than in many Macedonian villages; for some Roma, yes, but for the majority, no.

On the other hand, living in such a large Rom neighborhood as Shutka does give Roma the advantage of being able to display their ethnicity with little non-Rom interference. Rarely, if ever, do the police (or other non-Rom administrators) venture into Shutka, and thus there is an atmosphere of cultural freedom. Shutka is saturated with Rom ethnicity and symbolism: Romanes is the language of trade and sociability; Roma feel safe walking around at any time of the day or night; Rom music can be heard constantly, either taped or live; and most importantly, Rom ritual events are celebrated publicly on the street with pride, zest, and impunity. During the four-month wedding season, for example, ten events take might place simultaneously in public space with residents strolling around to watch, comment, and compare.

Class differences, of course, mediate the experiences of Shutka Roma. Shutka is an economically stratified community with a vast majority of lower middle class and poor people, a minority of middle class people, and a fraction of rich people. Some examples illustrate this economic range: the poorest families have flimsy houses with dirt floors, outhouses, and lack inside running water. The income of the poor families might be dependent on intermittent hauling or collecting scrap metal (men's work), or on begging in the streets (often children's or women's work). The few rich Roma, on the other hand, have the means to make their lives easier, such as building big houses, paving their own driveways, installing indoor plumbing and hot water heaters, and owning cars and expensive jewelry. The person acknowledged to be the richest man in Shutka is Hamdi Bajram, a young entrepreneur who is the owner and director of Shuteks (Shutka Textile), the only factory located in Shutka. Three thousand guests participated in his daughter's wedding in Spring 1993.

More common, however, are poor to lower middle class people who have struggled for economic security through extremely hard times. My landlord, Abdula Durak, exemplifies the hard-working mentality of most Shutka Roma. Born in 1932 in the old Skopje neighborhood of Topaana, Abdula grew up working as a physical laborer, hauling things on his back. Haulers typically wait at the central Skopje market place to be hired to transport anything from fruit to televisions to furniture from one place to another. They also wait in front of stores and factories where customers purchase heavy goods. When Abdula accumulated a little cash, he bought a wheel barrow for hauling, then a motorized cart (a motorcycle with a cart attached), and recently, a truck which he uses as a taxi. Every Tuesday and Friday, which are market days, he takes his truck to the central market and waits to be hired. Abdula recounted:

> When I was young we had nothing-- look at my hands-- they know hard work. I carried things on my back, then I had a motorized cart. Now I have a truck. I am the best chauffeur in Skopje. I carry things no one else does--government arms. I'm the one they call when the government people need to go to the airport. Last week the Kocho Racin ensemble called me to transport their costumes. When we were young we ate meat once a month; now my wife cooks meat every day.

In addition to his hauling/taxi service, Abdula is also a storekeeper. In 1988 he opened a corner store on his house property where he sold sunflower seeds and nuts. In Spring, 1990 Abdula expanded the store into a full-fledged grocery, and for this he enlisted the help of three of his five sons, Selvet, Bajram and Dehran (who returned from France expressly for this purpose):

> You see how hard it is for three people to run a store 7 am to 11pm? See how I can't sit down and eat peacefully-- I run back and forth. Selvet has a good head for figures, but Bajram and I are weak in figures. I guess I should wear glasses and use a calculator. Selvet wants to try to earn some money hauling with a motorized cart, and soon Dehran will be back from France. This store requires a lot of work for very little profit. For example, I buy oranges from the government (on credit) for twelve dinars a kilo, I sell them for fifteen dinars a kilo. I spend money on gas to pick them up, plus my own energy. I lose money on oranges. On beer and Coca Cola I make more, but still.... I'm going to try to sell bread now.

Abdula's economic picture is typical of many Roma in Europe and North America because it features a series of adaptable occupational skills. While much of the literature assumes the existence of static group occupations, such as blacksmiths or musicians, the choice of occupation is extremely flexible for many Roma, and a Rom man or woman usually engages in many occupations during a lifetime, and even simultaneously (Salo 1977, Silverman 1988:272). In Shutka, men with fairly regular work as musicians or metalworkers supplement their incomes with trading and marketing. Some families travel to Bulgaria, Greece, and Turkey to purchase goods for resale in the Skopje market. A prominent surla player and his son purchase blue jeans cheaply at factories and sell them in markets. Before the Yugoslav war, they had trading contacts throughout Serbia and Bosnia, but these have been curtailed because of the fighting, and the family's income has suffered greatly.

Abdula's wife, Lebadet, was born in 1935 in Topaana, the same neighborhood of Skopje where Abdula was born, and was very poor as a child. She never went to school, but rather worked as an agricultural worker from the age of nine. "At harvest or planting time, we were hired to work in the fields, even children." Later she obtained a state job as a cleaning lady in an office building. Recently she retired and gave her office cleaning job to one of her daughters-in-law. Lebadet's daughter, many of her daughters-in-law, and in fact, most of the women in Shutka are employed as cleaning ladies. Middle and upper class non-Rom Macedonians often hire Rom women as domestic help. Some Roma have been working for the same families for decades. Other female Roma are cleaning ladies in offices, hospitals, and schools, and on the street.[7] Typical female unskilled and semi-skilled occupations include ironing and cooking in state institutions. I met one of my main informants in the office of administration of the Skopje market. While I was interviewing the male administrator about market patterns, I struck up a conversation with the cleaning lady, who,as it turned out, lived fairly close to me in Shutka, and invited me to her cousin's circumcision.

In general, the advantages of a state job are its regularity[8], the shorter hours, its pension plan, and the vacations offered. The salary tends to be lower, however, than for domestic work in the private realm. Private domestic work is better paid, but there are no security measures, no vacations, no pensions, etc. Some women work six or seven days a week, cleaning two homes a day, and return to do their own domestic work.[9] The average daily salary for domestic work in 1990 was $10, or $250 monthly if a woman works 25 days a month. This was actually quite close to the salary for skilled work usually done by men, such as electricians or low level managers.

In addition to the above occupations, many Shutka women are actively involved in trading. Although they travel much less than men to obtain goods, they often do the selling if it takes place at the local market. When goods are taken to distant markets, men are the sellers. Marketed good are somewhat coded by gender, with women selling clothing, costume jewelry, and dowry items, and the men selling the items they themselves fashion, such as metal goods and scrap metal. On the other hand, both sexes sell certain items fashioned by men such as rope and wooden goods such as cradles, spoons, troughs, *daire*,[10] and sieves.

In 1990 I observed that women in Shutka were more likely to have steady employment than men. This continues to be the case because the unskilled women's economic niche has been less affected by the war, by independence, and by the 1991-1992 disruptions in oil imports from Greece. The economic situation of Shutka Roma must be considered within the total economy of the fledgling independent nation of Macedonia (Poulton 1993b). Poulton is optimistic, claiming that the Macedonian economy has proved more resilient than anyone imagined, and that the average monthly wage is higher than in Serbia. However, with widespread layoffs from state jobs since independence, unemployment has risen for all Macedonians, now totaling 20% (Poulton 1993b:27). Roma have an even higher rate of unemployment, since they are usually the first to be laid off. Because of the decrease in living standards and the widespread fear of the war spreading, some Shutka residents have fled to Western Europe, especially Germany, and even to the United States. Many houses in Shutka are now empty. The German government has begun to construct new housing in Shutka and has promised job training in an effort to persuade Roma to return.

Politics: A Historical View

The former Yugoslavia was hailed by many authors for treating its Roma better than any other East European country (Puxon 1973; Poulton 1989:29). However, this comparison is nothing to boast about considering the deplorable assimilationist measures of other East European socialist governments (see above) and the fact that Roma were still the most oppressed group in Yugoslavia (Liht 1989). Indeed, because Yugoslavia had the largest population of Roma in Europe, plus having a few extremely large population concentrations (in Nis, Belgrade, and Shuto Orizari), the government did pay attention to Roma in important ways. In the early 1970's, the ethnic designation *tsigan* disappeared from print, radio, television, and official documents, and the designation Rom was substituted. Of course, in practice, the derogatory appellation *cigan* continued to be used, but this change signaled some good will on the part of the government.

In 1973, Puxon estimated that in Yugoslavia there were two hundred Roma in the professions, working as doctors, lawyers, engineers, etc., a figure double that of 1953. He claimed that over 50% of Rom wage earners were industrial and municipal workers, 20% were farmers owning their own land, and the rest self-employed artisans and traders (Puxon 1973:18). In the 1980s Romany language radio programs were introduced in Serbia, and a few hours of Romany language teaching was introduced in the primary grades in Kosovo and in Tetovo, a city in Macedonia. By 1990, Macedonian Roma also had a weekly thirty minute television show, although its regularity was uncertain.

From 1981 to 1991, the official political status of Roma in Yugoslavia was that of "nationality." Yugoslavia had a three-level system: the "nations" of Yugoslavia were Croatians, Serbs, Slovenians, Bosnians, and Macedonians; the "nationalities" included Turks, Albanians and Hungarians; the rest were "other nationalities and ethnic groups," such as Vlachs and Jews. In practice, however, most of the republics, which had their own constitutions, considered the Roma to be an "ethnic group." Thus in the 1981 Macedonian census, Roma were still considered an ethnic group (Liht 1989; Poulton 1989:29, 1993a:42). This designation is precisely one of the factors which mobilized Macedonian Roma to political action in the 1980's.

As early as 1948, the Roma of Skopje began to organize politically and culturally. They obtained seats on the town council and formed their own cultural association, *Phralipe* (Brotherhood), whose title fit in quite well with the socialist motto *Bratstvo i Edinstvo* (Brotherhood and Unity). During the socialist era, Rom social and cultural organizations such as soccer teams, boxing clubs, drama clubs, and music and dance ensembles proliferated in Skopje. The amateur folk music ensemble, also called Phralipe, travelled throughout Europe to rave reviews. Regarding music, it is important to note that the 1970s also represented the first success of Roma in the world of professional non-Rom commercial recording (Silverman, forthcoming). Some Rom singers and instrumentalists became famous performers, achieving notoriety both in Rom and non-Rom circles.

After Shutka was settled in the late 1960's, it quickly became a center for cultural and political life; a Rom town council was formed and a representative was elected to the Macedonian Assembly. There were, however, many negative consequences for Roma who were politically active. Faik Abdi, a town council member from 1969-1974 (and later president of the Rom party, see below) had his passport confiscated for five years, meaning that he could not travel outside Yugoslavia during that time. And of course, in the greater Macedonian society, discrimination in employment and social services continued.

In order to understand the emergence of Shutka as a site of relatively successful political organization, we must consider the larger historical context of European Rom political activism and the role of Yugoslav leaders (Hancock 1991). In 1971, the first World Romani Congress was organized in England, and its chair was a Serbian Rom, Slobodan Berbeski. The second Congress in 1978 in Geneva lead to the formation of the International Romani Union, which today claims over seventy regional and national Rom organizations in some twenty-eight countries. The third Congress took place in Göttingen in 1978, where Sait Balic, an engineer from Nis, was elected president and Dr. Rajko Djuric from Belgrade was elected secretary. The election results caused Jean Liegeois to remark about the "Yugoslav influence at Göttingen" (Liégeois 1986:163). The fourth Congress took place in 1990 in Warsaw, a site selected to highlight the emerging leadership role of East European Roma, and Rajko Djuric was elected president (Hancock 1991:145-148).

The prominence of Yugoslav leaders in European Rom politics of the last twenty years was surely striking to potential Shutka activists. Models for Rom activism proliferated all over Eastern Europe after the 1989 revolutions. Rom parties, unions, and cultural and business organizations were formed in Bulgaria, Romania, Czechoslovakia, Hungary, Poland, and after 1991, in the former Soviet Union. Closer to Shutka, A Serbian Rom party was formed in 1989 and the first International Rom Summer School was held in Belgrade in July 1989 (Djuric 1989). Four prominent Shutka men attended the Romani Congress in Warsaw, just four months before the premier of the Rom party.

The Formation of PSER (Partijata Za Tselosna Emantsipatsija Na Romite): Politicization in Process

When Iljas Zendel, Saip Jusuf, Gjunes Mustafa, and Saban Iljas returned to Shutka from the World Romani Congress in Warsaw in April 1990, many people in Shutka, including me, were curious to see the videos and printed materials which they brought home with them. As I watched videos of the Congress at Gunes's home, he told me that many Roma were sick and tired of seeing themselves stereotyped in television series and films.[11] He hoped my research would counteract these stereotypes. Gunes worked as an orderly in a hospital and also led an amateur youth theater group in Shutka which performed plays in Romany about Rom life. One such play depicted their Indian origins, the period of Romanian slavery, and their struggle for freedom. For the youth in this group, acting became an act of politicization.

During April 1990, Rom leaders were preparing for the visit to Shutka of Vasil Tupurkovski, the Macedonian member of the Yugoslav collective presidency. Never before had such a high ranking official ever visited Shutka, plus this visit coincided with one of the most important Rom holidays, *Erdelez* (St. George's Day).[12] Although it is beyond the scope of this paper to analyze the rituals of this holiday, it is important to point out that Shutka Roma viewed Tupurkovski's visit both as an honorable political act and an appropriate ritual act, since on *Erdelez*, guests become part of family and community life. In addition, the visit underscored the relationship between Rom culture and politics: Tupurkovski was greeted with a dance and music performance, given bread and salt by a Rom woman dressed in *shalvari* (Rom traditional clothing consisting of wide billowing trousers and matching jacket), given food, and then paraded throughout Shutka with traditional Rom processional music (*surla* and *tapan*). He delivered a speech outlining his commitment to Rom progress and finished up the afternoon digging a shovel-full of dirt for the foundation of the new Rom factory, Shuteks. Moreover, hundreds of Roma turned out to see and hear him, despite the rainy weather. Perhaps insignificant as an isolated event, Tupurkovski's visit mobilized the leadership of Shutka, demonstrated that they could successfully orchestrate a large political event, and gave them an inkling that ordinary Roma would take an interest in politics.

About a month later, on 25 June 1990, a meeting was called for the educated youth of Shutka. The meeting was chaired by Faik Abdi, an advisor in the economics and planning division of the Skopje factory, Komuna. Forty young people showed up, twenty five men and fifteen women, and the air was thick with anticipation. Even before the meeting began, a great deal of political consciousness-raising had been accomplished just by assembling these educated young people and providing a sense of belonging to a group of future intellectuals.

All these students and former students (and those not present) had experienced many forms of discrimination in school, like receiving poor grades in spite of doing good work, being tracked away from academic subjects, being discouraged from continuing their education, and being socially ostracized. One teenager described how she was consistently undergraded in comparison to her peers and how her teachers refused to see her during office hours. In addition to these problems with non-Roma, these young people were often chided by other Roma for continuing their education. Since there were no high schools in Shutka, attending high school meant travelling long distances in non-Rom environments. Young people were needed by their parents for work, and education was not a priority in many families. Rom families, of course, differ greatly in their philosophy about education. Sabo, the father of Trajko Petrovski, who, with a Master's degree is the only Rom ethnographer in Macedonia, boasted to me that "with this cart I sent seven sons to school." Indeed, even though he is an illiterate trader, all his sons (but not daughters) finished eighth grade, and a few studied further. Girls especially were under great pressure to leave school in order to marry and have children or to help with domestic labor. A sixteen-year old girl studying nursing with whom I traded English for Romany lessons remarked that "women's liberation doesn't exist here." [13]

Faik Abdi opened the meeting with a query about whether to conduct the meeting in Macedonian or in Romany, since Shutka Rom are fluent in both languages. The unanimous response was Romanes, affirming the separate identity of Roma. After the leaders introduced themselves, the young people identified themselves and described their education. They spoke passionately of their ambitions to be teachers, journalists, nurses, doctors, engineers, economists, historians, lawyers, business people, etc, and documented their frustrations related to lack of opportunities and meager economic resources. One young woman said she couldn't go to college because her parents couldn't afford it, and Faik suggested that they create a communal education fund to aid all people with her predicament. Plans for introducing Romanes into the primary grades were discussed. The meeting ended with a lecture by Saip Jusuf on the history of Romanes.[14]

The next youth meeting was scheduled for a week later, but never really materialized. Ten women waited for thirty minutes, but only two of the organizers showed up, without the key to the meeting room. The rest of the men were watching a major soccer game which was scheduled for the same time. As people gathered informally outside, they complained about the competitive attitude of some of their leaders. Saip Jusuf took the floor and continued his lecture on the history of Romany. This meeting, or lack of it, illustrates some of the problems in the process of Rom politicization: disorganization, lack of coordination and competition among leaders. These were somewhat addressed in the preparatory meetings to the first press conference of PSER.

On 7 August 1990, approximately thirty young people, mostly men, plus the leaders of PSER attended an organizational meeting. The tenor of the gathering was reminiscent of the meetings I attended in the early 1970's at City College of New York to protest United States involvement in Vietnam and demand the creation of a Black Studies Program. The room was pregnant with possibility, yet also with hesitation. Faik stressed that now was the time to organize PSER in order to eliminate discrimination. Some in the room were hearing of the party for the first time. Some were hearing the term discrimination for the first time, because, as an international term, many Roma were not familiar with it even though they experienced discrimination every day of their lives. In essence, Faik was establishing a discourse, a vocabulary of words and a style of expression to present to the non-Rom world. This discourse, developed later in the party platform and other documents and interviews, played an important role in the process of legitimation of Rom political identity.[15]

Faik described some of the points of the party platform, e.g., schooling, publishing, and radio and television programs in Romany, and why they were important. He emphasized how political organizing is happening among Roma in other parts of Yugoslavia. He asked them to visit the homes of their relatives, friends and neighbors to encourage them to attend the premier press conference of PSER on 12 August. He encouraged more women to become involved and said they needed women to sit on the dais for the press conference. He suggested meeting at eight every night to report their progress. Bajram Hamdi asked how they should respond if people are afraid of repercussions; Faik stressed that they have "the right to organize. It's up to young people to decide their future."

By Sunday 12 August the rehearsal space of the amateur theater group had been cleaned and decorated for the press conference. A huge hand-lettered banner bore the party's name, and three flags flanked the dias: the flag of Macedonia, the flag of Yugoslavia, and the Rom flag. The Rom flag was adopted in 1971 at the first World Romany Congress; it consists of a blue field above a green field with a red wheel in the center, symbolizing sky and earth, nomadism and the journey toward the future. The Rom flag was situated on the same level and between the other two flags, a significant signal indicating that the Rom party was a patriotic component of Macedonia and Yugoslavia, not separatist, and not oppositional. This theme of patriotism was echoed in the party platform (see below).

Well-known Rom musicians had been hired to play *surla* and *tapan* for dancing, and as the leaders danced, others joined. Many people who knew nothing about the press conference were attracted to the scene by the sound of the music. It was a brilliant publicity idea and also a quintessential polyvocal symbol. *Surla* and *tapan* are associated with Roma in Macedonian culture since Roma hold a monopoly on these instruments (Rice 1982 ; Silverman, forthcoming). The association is stereotypical but positive since Roma are highly valued by Macedonians for their musical talent. In addition, within Macedonian Rom culture, *surla* and *tapan* serve the function of announcement.[16] Thus when Faik Abdi arrived in his car, the musicians played a melody commonly performed when important guests arrive at weddings, circumcisions, soldier-send-off celebrations, etc. The Roma had, in effect, infused the press conference (an event they imported from non-Rom) with Rom culture, saturated it with in-group symbols which also simultaneously served as emblems of Rom culture for non-Roms (who were also in the audience). Furthermore, the traditional custom of musicians receiving monetary tips for playing requests was replaced by a collection box near the musicians labeled PSER. Traditional culture was, then, appropriated for politics. Politicization, then, proceed simultaneously in two complementary directions: the use of tradition in politics, and the use of politics in tradition.

By the time Faik called the press conference to order, two to three hundred people had gathered, mostly residents of Shutka, but also the press. Over 90% of the participants were male, but there was one female journalism student on the dais, the same woman who read the news in the weekly Romany television shows. The entire press conference was conducted in Macedonian, obviously, the preferred language for politics because those in power speak it. Faik delivered a passionate opening speech which touched on the question of assimilation:

> In other neighborhoods of Skopje outside of Shutka, and in other cities like Kumanovo and cities in Eastern Macedonia, where there are smaller concentrations of Roma, emancipation has proceeded faster than here. But also, many Roma in these neighborhoods and cities don't say they are Gypsies; they say they are Turks, Albanians and, most recently in Ohrid, Egyptians.[17] I know Turkish perfectly, but I'm not a Turk. I'm Muslim, but I'm not Turkish. I am a Rom.

Many young Roma in the audience spoke about the frustrations and prejudice they have experienced. One young man commented, "People think we Roma have comforts. A paved *korzo* (the street on which the daily evening walk takes place) was promised to us years ago and was all talk." Strong sentiments were expressed, and people spontaneously yelled out "PSER" and "Abdi Faik." An emotional speech was given by Rahim Burhan, the director of the internationally famous theater company Phralipe which had just been forced to vacate its premises. A few months later, Burhan and the company moved to Muelheim, Germany (Trappmann 1992).

The press conference concluded with a reading of the party platform, the only time a woman's voice was heard. The platform is described below. As the first event in a series of meetings, this press conference inaugurated the public presence of Rom politics. By September 1990, PSER claimed 8500 members, and on 28 October 1990 a rally in Shutka attracted 5000 Roma (Kochkovka 1990, Nova Makedonia 1990). By April 1993 PSER had grown to 36,000 members with local branches throughout Macedonia. Faik Abdi has remained president and also currently serves as a member of the Macedonian parliament. In early 1993 Gunes Mustafa formed a rival spin-off party, but PSER continues to be the main vehicle for Rom political action (Trajko Petrovski, personal communication; Poulton 1993a:44).

Lest the reader erroneously think that a huge majority of Shutka Roma were quickly mobilized, I must present a typical view of many Shutka residents who had either no interest or outright scorn for public politics of any variety. For example, while I attended the first press conference, not one person in the dozen or so houses surrounding mine even knew of the event, and when I told them, they just laughed. Gjulizar Dzheladin explained to me her reluctance to trust the leaders,

> We have all the freedoms we want already, we are better off in Yugoslavia than anywhere else. When you see Roma who don't send their children to school, who don't work, it's their own fault.... I am afraid that people will laugh at the new party. We don't have enough educated Roma. I'm not educated, neither are my three sons and three daughters. Even the leaders aren't well-educated. The leaders want to be big men--it's only for glory. There is a lot of jealousy. There have been organizations before and nothing came of them. We'll see.

It is useful to see Gjulizar's comments in the light of her own personal history. The daughter of a Rom partisan fighter in World War Two, she was raised in a home dedicated to the unity of Yugoslavia. In spite of being illiterate, she received an honorary diploma from a Marxist evening school for her patriotic activities. She married and became a member of one of the richest families in Shutka due to her husband's tailoring and trading business. Perhaps, then, she has the luxury to ignore politics.

PSER: Platform and Progress

The 1990 platform of PSER was conceived when Macedonia was still a socialist republic of Yugoslavia, thus it is filled with deference to socialist ideals and patriotism for Yugoslavia.[18] Since the breakup of Yugoslavia, these socialist goals have been abandoned, but the essential platform remains. Declaring that "Roma are truly the least emancipated people in Macedonia," the platform stresses education, language and media rights and access. Section I deals with education and specifically advocates bilingual (Romany and Macedonian) classes in elementary schools in Rom neighborhoods, the training of bilingual teachers, the founding of a department of Romany Studies at the University of Skopje, improvement of access for Rom students to high schools and the university (with the development of quotas), and the infusion of Rom history into the curriculum. Many of these goals are already in sight. A Romany primer has been prepared and two hours a week of Romany education will be introduced in grades one through eight. A Department of Romany Studies at the University will be inaugurated in October 1993, and a seminar was convened by the Ministry of Education to study the educational needs of Roma (Poulton 1993a:44).

Section II deals with culture and media, advocating government support for the creation of a Romany newspaper, the upgrading of radio and television broadcasts in Romany, the strengthening of ties with India and with Macedonian Roma in other countries, and the construction of a Rom mosque in Shutka. None of these goals have been realized except for the regularization of a weekly thirty minute Romany television show which features news, cultural events, and music.

Section III deals with the use of the Romany language, advocating its equality with Macedonian for all official purposes, and encouraging the dissemination of Romany literature. This goal is still in the future, but will surely be aided by the educational mission outlined in Section I, and by the publication of a Macedonian-Romani dictionary now in progress. Section IV deals with the recognition of Roma as a nationality, not merely an ethnic group. This has not been accomplished, but the issue of nationalities/ethnic groups is being raised in parliament by the Albanian party, which wants the constitution rewritten to include them as equal citizens(Poulton 1993b:24). Section V deals with increasing the number of Rom representatives to city, regional and national government bodies, another long term goal. Finally, Section VI advocates working to end all forms of discrimination.

Conclusion

A number of factors have lead to and continue to lead to the emergence of Shutka as a site of relatively successful political organization. First the emerging human rights and political movements of the Roma of other East European countries serve as a model of what to do and what to avoid. Secondly, the large population of Roma in Shutka allows a critical number of intellectuals and future intellectuals to assemble. Third, the relative economic stability of many Shutka Rom instills a sense of security in their community. Fourth, the unthreatened display of Rom ethnicity in Shutka fosters a sense of cultural pride and worth. All these factors promote residents to realize the viability of their community to serve their interests and deal with their problems. Evidence that Shutka Roma have the confidence to act more globally occurred in March 1993 when PSER called for the establishment of "Romanistan." Asking for a Romany nation, perhaps more metaphoric than real, was done to underscore the plight of Roma as a people without a territory. PSER's letter to the United Nations with this request encouraged the United Nations to pay attention to the plight of Roma all over Eastern Europe.

Whereas it may be overly optimistic to label the situation of Macedonian Roma "a success story," the accomplishments of Macedonian Roma are notable in the areas of education, media, and politics. Even president Kiro Gligorov has shown sympathy for their plight. On the other hand, all class indicators point towards continued discrimination: they have the lowest standard of living of any ethnic group, and they are still the least educated, least healthy, and most socially and politically marginalized portion of the population. On the positive side, in Macedonia there has been no backlash against Roma and no incidents of violence (Poulton 1993a:42), unlike other East European nations. For many Macedonians, the major ethnic question is about the rights of the Albanians, the largest minority, not the rights of Roma (Poulton 1993b; Perry 1993). Ironically, the fact that the Roma have not aligned themselves with the Albanians may be a political plus; by distancing themselves from the perceived "Albanian threat," the Roma are viewed more sympathetically or more harmlessly in the eyes of many Macedonians. In the future, the fate of Kosovo Albanians will indirectly but profoundly influence Macedonian Roma vis a vis the Albanians of Macedonia.

Notes

1. I have chosen to use the adjective Rom (plural noun, Roma) rather than Gypsy because that is what many Rom people call themselves. The term Gypsy, along with its cognates Gitan (French), Gitano (Spanish), Yiftos (Greek), and Egjuptsi (Macedonian), is an outsider's term with strong negative connotations. It derives from the false conclusion that they originally came from Egypt. Other labels given to them by outsiders such as Bohemian (French) and Tatar (German) reflect equally false origins. The Slavic, Romanian, Hungarian, Albanian, German, Italian and Greek versions of the label Tsigani (e.g., Ziguener, Zingari,) come from the Greek Atsingani, a heretical sect active during the Byzantine period (Soulis 1961:145-146). Among themselves, Rom use regional, occupational, religious, or tribal names such as Sinti, Manush, Romanichals, Kale, Lovari, Kalderash, Horahane, Arliji, Dzhambazi, etc. Rom or Romani has become somewhat of a unifying term in the 1990's.

2. *Surla* is a double-reed wind instrument and *tapan* is a two-headed cylindrical drum; they are played at important life-cycle and calendrical rituals. Only Roma play *surla* and *tapan*, and they are learned by males in kin-based groups, thus their association with Rom

ethnicity is strong. See section below on the first press conference of the Rom political party.

3. In 1981 Verdery wrote, "It is my belief that insofar as one is to make sense of ethnicity in Southeastern Europe, one must necessarily supplement the standard local-level ethnographic study with detailed analysis of history-- not merely local history, but the history of political and economic organization at progressively more inclusive levels of the socio-spatial system relevant to one's local concerns" (1981:1). Her later work (1983) ably follows this advice.

4. As bonded serfs owned by noblemen, landowners, monasteries, and the state, they were sold, bartered, flogged, and dehumanized; even their marriages were strictly regulated. As slaves, Rom were an important labor and artisan source, providing skills in goldwashing, bear-training, woodcarving, blacksmithing, and music (Hancock 1987; Crowe and Kolsti 1991).

5. See Silverman 1988 and 1989 for a discussion of how Bulgarian Roma responded to these measures.

6. See Friedman 1985 for analysis of the problems of creating a Romany literary language.

7. A typical conversation with a group of Rom women went as follows: "Where do you work?" One answers, " The Institute of Geology," another "The Institute of History," another, "The central hospital." What do you do there?" "We are cleaning ladies."

8. Regularity is somewhat relative; since the beginning of the Yugoslav war and especially since the declaration of Macedonian independence, many state jobs have been eliminated and the payment of state salaries have been delayed.

9. It is beyond the scope of this article to discuss the important sphere of non-wage labor, such as cooking, cleaning, and the labor of ritual work.

10. A *daire* is a tambourine with a skin face, wood frame, and jingling metal pieces. It is used by the local Muslim population.

11. In 1989 the film Time of the Gypsies received the prize for best direction at the Cannes film festival. Photographed partly in Shutka, many residents were very opinionated about the film.

12. St. George's Day takes place for three days beginning May 6, and is the most important calendrical holiday among Muslim and Christian Roma in Macedonia.

13. The issue of Rom women's subordination and the negotiation of female power is extremely complicated and cannot be treated here. For comparative analysis of American Rom women's power, see Silverman 1981 and Sutherland 1986.

14. Saip Jusuf is a Rom leader who is a self-trained linguist and a former physical education teacher. In 1980, with non-Rom Macedonian linguist Krume Kepeske, he published *Romani Gramatika/ Romska Gramatika*, an attempt to create a standard literary Romany language. Problems with this book are discussed in detail in Friedman 1985. I noticed that at the meeting just described, the young people found Saip's lecture boring and this somewhat doused the activist sentiments generated by the gathering. The young people were more interested in sharing their common problems than in hearing about which Romany words were closest to Hindi, and therefore, supposedly older.

15. The question of discourse cannot be adequately discussed here, but informs political conceptions. Gheorge has struggled with this problem in writing documents for UNESCO and other European bodies. A major question is whether to conceive of Roma right as civil or collective i.e., group) (Gheorghe 1991).

16. For example, at weddings, the important processions, such as the groom's family arriving at the bride's house, are accompanied by *surla.*

17. A group of Albanian-speaking Roma in and around the cities of Ohrid and Struga call themselves Egjuptsi, deriving from a mistaken notion of where others thought they originated. In 1990, however, their leaders publicly claimed they were actually from Egypt in an effort to disassociate themselves with Roma, and thereby raise their social position. (See Sudetic 1990 and Mukerem 1990 On the larger question of Macedonian Roma identifying themselves as Turks or Albanians, see Poulton 1989:5 and Poulton 1993a:43.

18. Since the breakup of Yugoslavia, the Macedonian socialists have reorganized into the Social Democratic Union of Macedonia, which now controls parliament (Perry 1993).

References

Arensberg, Conrad and Solon Kimball. 1972. Culture and Community. Gloucester, MA: Peter Smith

Beck, Sam and John Cole, Eds. 1981. *Ethnicity and Nationalism in Southeastern Europe.* Amsterdam: University of Amsterdam Antropology-Sociology Center.

Crowe, David, and John Kolsti. 1991. *The Gypsies of Eastern Europe.* Armonk NY: M.E. Sharpe.

Djuric, Rajko. 1989. "Jezik-Knjiga Mudrosti i Svesti: Prva Medzhunarodna Letna Shola Roma. *Ilustrovana Politika* 1604, 1 August:50-51.

Friedman, Victor. 1985. "Problems in the Codification of a Stadard Romani Literary Language". *In* J. Grumet, Ed. *Papers from the Fourth and Fifth Annual Meetings.* New York, NY: Gypsy Lore Society, North American Chapter. Pp. 56-75.

Gheorghe, Nicolae. 1991. Stat*ement of the Representative of the Romani International Union to Commission on Human Rights*, UNESCO, 5 March. Report, International Romani Union.

Hancock, Ian. 1987. *The Pariah Syndrome: An Account of Gypsy Slavery and Persecution.* Ann Arbor: Karoma.

____. 1991. "The East European Roots of Romani Nationalism". *In* David Crowe and John Kolsti, Eds. *The Gypsies of Eastern Europe.* Armonk NY: M.E. Sharpe. Pp. 133-150.

____. 1993. "Anti-Gypsyism in the New Europe." *Roma* 38-39 (January/July 1993): 5-29.

Helsinki Watch. 1991a. *Destroying Ethnic Identity: The Gypsies of Bulgaria.* New York: Helsinki Watch.

____. 1991b. *Destroying Ethnic Identity:The Persecution of Gypsies of Romania.* New York: Helsinki Watch.

____. 1992. *Struggling for Ethnic Identity:Czechoslovakia's Endangered Gypsies.* New York: Helsinki Watch.

Hubschmannova, Milena. 1993. "Three Years of Democracy in Czechoslovakia and the Roma." *Roma.* 38-39 (January/July 1993): 30-49.

International Romani Union. 1992. *Romanis and the Helsinki Process: Current Standards, Achievements, Shortcomings and Further Improvement.* Manuscript.

Kochovska, Juliana. 1990. "Na Najniskoto Skalilo na Zhivot." *Nova Makedonia,* 24 September 4.

Liégeois, Jean-Pierre. 1986. *Gypsies: An Illustrated History.* London: Al Saqi Books.

Liht, Sonia. 1989. Yug*oslav Roma Between Authoritarian and Democratic Emancipation.* Belgrade: Center for Studies in Cultural Development.

Mirga, Andrej. 1993. The Effects of State Assimilation Policy on Polish Gypsies. *Journal of the Gypsy Lore Society*, series 5, 3(2):69-76.

Mukerem, Arifi. 1990. Romite Se Egipkjani. *Nova Makedonia* 13 June:11.

Nova Makedonia. 1990. Romite Aktiven Politicheski Subject. *Nova Makedonia*, 29 October:2.

Perry, Duncan. 1993. Politics in the Republic of Macedonia: Issues and Parties. *RFE/RL Research Report* 2(23), 4 June:31-37.

Poulton, Hugh. 1989. *Minorities in the Balkans*. London: Minority Rights Group.

____. 1993a. The Roma in Macedonia: A Success Story? *RFE/RL Research Report* 2(19), 7 May:42-45.

____. 1993b. The Republic of Macedonia after UN Recognition. *RFE/RL Research Report* 2(23), 4 June:22- 30.

Project on Ethnic Relations. 1992. *The Romanies in Central and Eastern Europe: Illusions and Reality*. Princeton NJ: Project on Ethnic Relations.

Puxon, Grattan. 1973. *Rom: Europe's Gypsies*. London:Minority Rights Group.

Rice, Timothy. 1982. The Surla and the Tapan in Yugoslav Macedonia. *Galpin Society Journal* 35(3):122-137.

Salo, Matt and Sheila Salo. 1977. *The Kalderash in Eastern Canada*. Ottawa: National Museums of Canada.

Silverman, Carol. 1994. "Rom Music." *Garland Encyclopedia of World Music: Europe*. New York, NY: Garland.

____. 1989. "Reconstructing Folklore: Media and Cultural Policy in Eastern Europe. *Communication* 11(2): 141-160.

____. 1988. "Negotiating Gypsiness: Strategy in Context." *Journal of American Folklore* 101(401): 261-275.

____. 1986. "Bulgarian Gypsies: Adaptation in a Socialist Context." *Nomadic Peoples*, (*special issue, Peripatetic Peoples*) 21-22:51-62.

____. 1981. "Pollution and Power: Gypsy Women in America." *In* Matt Salo, Ed. *The American Kalderash: Gypsies in the New World*. Centenary College, New Jersey: Gypsy Lore Society. Pp.55-70.

Soulis, George. 1961. "The Gypsies in the Byzantine Empire and the Balkans in the Late Middle Ages. " *Dumbarton Oaks Papers* 15:141:166.

Sudetic, Chuck. 1990. "Pharaohs in Their Past? So the Yugoslavs Say. *New York Times* 21 November:A4.

Sutherland, Anne. 1986. "Gypsy Women, Gypsy Men: Cultural Paradoxes." *In* J. Grumet, ed. *Papers from the Sixth and Seventh Annual Meetings*. New York, NY: Gypsy Lore Society North American Chapter. Pp.85-96.

Trappmann, Klaus. 1992. "Dramaturgie der Emotionen:Roma-Theater Pralipe Gastiert mit Lorca und Shakespeare." *Musik Und Kulturtage der Cinti Und Roma*, Berlin, 1-11 October.

Verdery, Katherine. 1981. "Ethnic Relations and Hierarchies of Dependency in the Late Hapsburg Empire: Austria, Hungary and Transylvania. *In* Sam Beck and John Cole, eds. *Ethnicity and Nationalism in Southeastern Europe*. Universiteit Van Amsterdam: Antropologisch-Sociologisch Centrum. pp. 1-28.

____. 1983. *Transylvanian Villagers: Three Centuries of Political, Economic and Ethnic Change*. Berkeley: University of California Press.

13

Social Change as Reflected in the Lives of Bulgarian Villagers

Radost Ivanova

The resignation of Todor Zhivkov as president and leader of the Bulgarian Communist Party on November 10, 1989 is widely regarded as the turning point which placed Bulgaria on the road to change. Though those events are fairly recent, the situation in the country has drastically altered. Along with the political polarization accompanied by mass protest rallies, the transition from socialism towards democracy and a market-oriented economy has been extensively furthered. There is hardly a person who could predict how drawn out and painful this transition was to be, how profound the transformations it would bring to the political and economic life of the country, to its people as a whole, and to every single individual. This time of change is not only visible in society but is also taking place in the very mentality and actions of every Bulgarian.

Different layers of society accept in different ways the realities of this transition. Furthermore this process is highly individualized. Very frequently it is a function of the personal fate of the individual, of his or her past and present, of their social position, education and age, of one's political ideas and party affiliation. In this transition towards the market economy Bulgarian villagers especially face new challenges, especially changes in agriculture which occupied the leading role in the Bulgarian economy until the end of World War Two.[1] It is a fact of common knowledge that agriculture is not only a means of livelihood but a way of life as well. For this reason the various political and economic changes have much more profoundly marked the life of the rural population than their urban counterparts.

My principal goal here is to depict the influences of social, political and economic changes on the life and mentality of Bulgarian villagers, to relate the moods which these changes produce, and to describe villagers' reaction to the events taking place around them. To consider these questions I will use observations and interviews from 1992 field data from the Sliven region of the Thracian valley of southern Bulgaria. The region is famous for its agricultural profile. Thanks to the assistance of my colleague of Vesselina Savova, who works for the Sliven History Museum, I was able to witness the liquidation of a collective farm[2] located in the village of Panaretovo and the distribution of its livestock to its members from Panaretovo and four neighboring villages: Samuilovo, Gloufishevo, Metchkarevo and Guergevets, which together formed a single APK.[3] In addition observation I managed to interview other farmers in their homes and at my village residence. Thus I was able to record not only the spontaneous comments made during the event but also a number of stories of farmers of different generations, different social status and political affiliation.

All these villagers derived from a homogenous environment based on a single complex of social structural relations (Bertaux 1993:21). Their stories are full of biographical narratives with comparisons between contemporary events and those from the past, especially the ones which accompanied the collectivization process following the so called "socialist revolution" of September 9, 1944. They are also full of descriptions of their attitudes towards these events, and of the character of their work under the system of socialist cooperation.

While doing field work I never forgot the importance of the spirit of cooperation necessary between the interviewer and informant (Kirshenblatt-Gimblett 1988:142-143). My approach was based on the idea that the interviewer should always maintain neutrality while at the same time also feel free to speak about what is on their mind and not what one is supposed to say. All the time I felt that Bulgarians had lost the ability to speak out with sincerity in front of strangers, especially about politics, economics, and society in general. In this sense my informants fell into two groups. The first group supported the political formation in power at the moment, e.g. the Union of Democratic Forces. Its members responded in a free, unconstrained manner to my questions while stating their views and attitudes. Things were much different in the second group, those who supported the Bulgarian Socialist Party, heirs to the former Communist Party. These people tried to keep our conversation within the frame which they considered necessary in the face of strangers. They showed more restraint in their answers as well as in their personal assessments of the events.

The Event in the Comments

The distribution of livestock at the Panaretovo collective occured on the 14 and 15 of October 1992. It was this event that especially provoked local emotions which then gave rise to the local commentaries on which this paper is based. Early on the 14th the village of Panaretovo seemed deserted, itsstreets, houses and yards empty. However, in contrast to the emptiness of the village, a huge crowd of people of all ages had literally besieged the buildings of the farm located in the northeastern side of the village. Villagers from five settlements, most members of the agrarian-industrial complex, had gathered there. As they mulled about, every so often two or three men would come out of the barn pulling a cow. The human uproar was complemented by the lowing of cattle as the animals tenaciously resisted new owners' attempts to take them from the herd to their homes. The cows' disobedience challenged the impatient, unrestrained villagers who started to push and beat the animals. Some of the cattle were hurt and their blood left traces on the paths towards their new homes. Not only was the scene unpleasant to view but it suggested a brutal attitude toward the animals.

Thus were the agrarian-industrial complex cattle distributed. According to the members of the collective farm, before the distribution the collective had some 680 animals, all of a select breed bought in Germany for hard currency in order to create a state-of-the-art dairy farm. Though every cow had a numbered metal plate attached to its ear, the villagers forced their way into the barns to pick animals of their choice in a random, disordered way.

Many villagers commented critically on the sight of their co-villagers acting so outrageously. These animals, some said, lived in freedom since their birth and had never been tied to any object. Hence they now disobeyed their new owners. Other disapproving comments were interspersed with details about raising cattle, milk yields, and so on. The brutality toward the animals particularly evoked criticism. However, since not all the assembled people were opposed, I wanted to evaluate some of the event's details for myself including peoples' attitudes and personal assessments.

Those who approved the distribution unconditionally were mostly women. They reacted in a spontaneous and emotional way under the influence of their impressions from what they had seen and what they had heard. "Why shouldn't we celebrate this?," said Iovka Slavova, one of the participants.

> What is good about having a collective farm anyway? Some steal while others stay hungry! Our leaders, our president, the bunch of guys around them, weren't they all poor as lice? Now they have become millionaires! They are just making fun of the people.

As she spoke Stephana Slavova's mood gradually changed from simple satisfaction to open happiness as she thought of the new cow that now belonged to her household. While taking it home, the animal was so wild that it bumped into a trailer and wounded itself.

> I didn't sleep the whole night... I woke up seven times to see if it would live. I prepared some sumac infusion for her; even brought her candy... I am trying to teach her, I caressed her, because she was so fiery yesterday... And she looks at me in a way as if she wants to tell me something. One of our cows was named after our elder daughter, Nella. The other was named after our younger child. I also have a grandson, Petar, so I will name this one after him, Pepa.

Unlike the women, the reaction of the men, although also negative towards the collective farm, was nonetheless somewhat more restrained and rational. As one said, in reflecting on his reestablished economic independence, "I am happy because I am going to work on a job of my own, and I'm going to get what I've worked for. I'm never going to sell out my labor to anybody else again."

The most negative responses to the collective farm (but positive about the distribution of cattle) came from men and women who, prior to collectivization were owners of large estates and numerous cattle, and who were regarded by co-villagers as rich or middle-class. Such people were also often open supporters of the Union of Democratic Forces, the ruling political force at the moment. At the other extreme were supporters of the opposition Bulgarian Socialist Party. Such people were often land-poor or landless in the past and assisted the establishment of the collective farm in 1950. For them, the liquidation of the collective farm and its property had no meaning other than a return to their earlier condition. Hence most of them saw collective farming as a good form of organization for agricultural labor. "The collective farm wasn't that bad. Whoever you'd ask, nobody would tell you a bad word about it. The people were satisfied," said Krastio Ganev, 65, a former farm leader. He personally preferred the farm because he thought that the "work went better under it." He expressed his reservation towards other options (e.g. to create new cooperatives of owners) saying, "I don't know how things will go." In his view, future cooperatives will be formed on the basis of political affiliation. According to him only those whose family had maintained a good reputation in the village throughout the generations would not go for the new cooperation.

Dobri Peev, 72, the former president of the collective farm, shared a similar view on these issues.

> They would have done much better to have left the animals here... However once the orders to break up the farms came from above, they must follow them. They might have studied a lot (before making this decision) but they are unaware of what's happening here, in the countryside...

Further, Peev tried to analyze the situation to find an answer for the liquidation of the collective farm.

> When it was only a collective farm, so far so good. When it became an agrarian-industrial complex, and those guys (i.e. the bosses) got into their limos...What

happened next? Things were going in such a way that no doubt something was about to happen.

The former president thus saw the collapse of the collective farm as due to the integration of many farms into agrarian-industrial complexes. In Panaretovo an agrarian-industrial complex was formed in 1969, which incorporated the collective farms of five villages. Later it grew to include a total of thirty villages. "And this was the worst that could be done," says Mr. Peev. The members of the complex were happy at the beginning since they received both cash and kind payments in remuneration for their work. Later when the situation changed everyone deserted the farm, leaving only the gypsies and a small number of Bulgarians as workers. "I stated this at the Party's regional Committee. Once we took this way, we ended up in the middle of nowhere," Peev concluded.

The narratives of villagers with a non-committal view of the cattle liquidation were of the greatest interest. Their evaluation seemed to reflect the reality of the event in its complexity and diversity. However, they generally concluded that the collective should take a different tack. For example, Christo Paskalev, 70, an heir to generations of rich farmers who owned 700 decars of land in the past said that the distribution of the cows and the destruction of the barns was incorrect:

> I think there couldn't exist anything stupider than this. People cannot understand that they must preserve everything. The former system didn't do much good, but whatever it built up should be kept intact so that the new private owner can reap his harvest. For if I have 300 decars of arable land, for example, and I don't have a dry house or a dry room where to dry my harvest, I'll have to start over again with the threshing board, which is the same as to go fifty years back in the past. Because there is machinery now, isn't there, but they are destroying it. In my opinion everything must be preserved.

Later commenting on the cow distribution, Paskalev continued:

> They should have given them to those who used to be owners, that is, who gave their animals away (i.e. the animals given to the collective farms at their formation) and who will take care of them and will produce milk and meat... Now most of the people who are taking the animals away, especially those communists who established the collective farms, are just grabbing them to give them to the gypsies who will take them directly to the slaughter house. Next year we won't have either milk or meat, as they will annihilate private property... just staging a boycott. For me this is a simple boycott. To take the cows away and get them slaughtered. This should be restricted. The females especially should not be given away under no circumstances.

The decision to break up the collective farms and return its animals to their rightful owners was both expected and unexpected. It was expected as forty five years of socialist cooperation failed to eradicate the desire for private property among the villagers. It was unexpected because the former owners were elderly and most of their children and grandchildren had left the village for the cities in the search of jobs and happiness. The suddenness of the distribution thus created a great deal of confusion and uncertainty as early as the day after it occurred.

One of the biggest problems related to the cattle distribution was the severe forage shortage. This was because the distribution of the cattle occurred in October, when the forage was wet from the rain. Furthermore the land was still at that time collective property, a fact which raised serious doubts as to whether any forage would be available for the year to come. Consequently, even those people strongly in favor of the distribution pondered whether to take one cow or two while others were hesitant to take any at all.

Other problems posed by taking care of cattle were no less serious. Many villagers, especially the elderly, did not feel able to deal with the heavy demands of stock-keeping. Further, they were uncertain whether their children would return to the village to help them. Some young people from the town of Sliven, thirteen kilometers from Panaretovo, used to spend their leisure time with their elderly parents, giving them a hand in the agriculture. Thus they simultaneously ensured an additional quantity of foods for themselves. Now, however, their return was somewhat problematic.

The restitution of cattle combined with the reappropriation of land encouraged some of the younger people who had spent most of their lives in the cities to return to the village and take over the management of their parents' estates. In fact, the return of village youth actually precipitated the liquidation of the collective farms. Many came back after being let go from urban employment and pressed for economic independence. Stephanka Slavova from the village of Gloufishevo thus suggested:

> My children were in the city. My elder daughter worked in the knitwear factory, the younger one in a warehouse. However, both of them are now laid off and since they returned to Blatets,[4] they are now working forty to fifty decars of land, raising hogs, and also some sheep. They also brought their husbands to the village. One of them recently told me: 'Mom, I had enough of the alarm clock every morning. Now I feel so great that I wake up whenever I want, and I raise whatever animals I want, and we've already stuffed up our winter supplies.' Now they both feel perfect.

The restitution of the animals was not as welcome in families where the younger generation was relatively independent of their parents. Thus Dina Paskaleva, 60, did not think her life will improve after the restitution since her family did not have the labor power to care for cattle in any case. In addition she said:

> The young won't come back. I've got two daughters and neither will return. They dropped by yesterday only to laugh at the milk, the strainer... They left us when they were very young so it's going to be very hard to make them come back. As one of them said: 'I didn't say you should take any cows.'

The hope of this latter group of farmers lies in their remaining relatives in the village, their brothers, sisters, etc. With these transformations, then, both family ties and attitudes towards property which have never really lost their importance in the lives of Bulgarians are now likely to gain a new life.

Attitudes Towards Property

A Little Bit of a History

Prior to the end of the last century the historian of Bulgarian law, P. Odjakov (1893:8), wrote:

> Each Bulgarian considers himself morally obliged to have a legal marriage and children from it, who are to preserve the existence of his family and offspring and make it multiply in numbers over the generations. Hence he considers it his civil feat to marry in timely fashion in order to be able to build up and leave a home and household to his followers. This is his final goal and what he accepts as his lifetime mission: to work for his offspring. The curse 'Let God deprive you of children, let Him efface your family; let you not see a beast of your own in front of your door...' is a most dreadful malediction among Bulgarians.

Thus, "family" and "household" are the two most outstanding and defining features of the patriarchal Bulgarian which give him the moral right to regard himself as a human being. No matter what form "home" and "family" have taken over the years, and without regard to the changes in households, these values and institutions have both survived the centuries as key symbols in rural Bulgaria.

In the traditional patriarchal community until the liberation of Bulgaria from Turkey (1878), "family" and "household" constituted a single unit. Under the leadership of the eldest and most capable man called "elder" *(starshina)*, or "master" (*gospodar)* (Gueshov 1887: 428), the household formed a kind of family corporation which effected common use of resources and income. The continuous existence of the patriarchal community from the Middle Ages left a permanent trace on the spiritual make-up of the Bulgarian. It played a major economic and moral role in Bulgarian survival especially during the five centuries of Turkish domination. According to Gueshov its main advantages were its common possession of land which enabled the most rational use of agricultural machinery, its division of labor on the basis of age and sex, and the economic equality of all of its members (1887:445-446).

Along with its advantages the patriarchal community undoubtedly had some drawbacks. First it dampened the economic initiative of its members, making them machines simply executing the orders of their master. The work ethic was also diminished as members of the community enjoyed equal rights with regard to food and clothing. Finally, as the patriarchal household occasionally enabled labor specialization, those among them who specialized were often unable to successfully cope with learning the diversity of farming activities (Gueshov 1887:447).

According Ivan Hadzhiiski, until the end of last century the patriarchal community secured "long periods of calm, peaceful, quiescent, monotonous and uniform life...with a closed natural economy in which people lived who had only heard of murders, thefts and fraud. (Hadzhiiski 1966: 33)." These people were inspired by the spirit of collectivism, reflected in their desire "to be like all other people," "to not stray from the people," or otherwise, "what would people say, wouldn't that be a shame in their eyes." Thus, the villager knew that he was nothing outside his community. He was rich through it, he was strong with it. He was proud not with himself but with his community (Hadzhiiski 1966, I: 76)."

The typical mentality of the villager from this period is reflected most distinctly in his understanding of life and his attitude towards work and pleasure. Work, was the care he took for his land and his animals. Pleasure always passed through his stomach, with what he ate and drank. The pleasure was considered full and complete when one sat at the table with friends and relatives during engagement ceremonies, weddings or village reunions, and listening to songs, music and watching folk dances (Hadzhiiski 1966:55).

This is the general picture of the heritage with which Bulgarian villagers now confront the last years of the Twentieth Century. Newly re-instituted capitalist relations, not to mention the inheritance of socialism, are quickly demolishing this patriarchal idyll. Thus, many rural Bulgarians are often unable to adapt to the new economic and moral conditions. This results in the transitional forms which have emerged that link the patriarchal community with private property on land, in which a significant role is played by kinship ties. The collective land cultivation by brothers who were previously economically atomized could serve as an example. Furthermore other forms of mutual labor assistance, some of which exist even today in some villages, also appear (Krastanova 1986).

Following Bulgaria's liberation from Turkish domination and ending with World War One, the "blood" link of the villager with his land and animals was cemented, and villager identification with private property was born. Furthermore, a specific cult towards this property developed especially with regard to domestic animals who were treated equal to (and often even better) than other family members. Ivan Hadzhiiski mentions a number of cases of village fires where householders, in their attempt to save their animals and their property, totally forgot about their children. He also provides some examples where the feeling of love towards animals dramatically exceeded what is usually considered to be a normal attachment toward property. There is, for example, the tale of the villager who took two prescriptions to a drugstore, one for his wife, the other for his cow. "Watch out," he said to the chemist, "and don't confuse these because I don't want to poison my cow. What would I to do without it (Hadzhiiski 1966-I:208)."

Similarly, a popular song from that time is still sung in company at meals:

Mango's hut one day caught fire,
And his wife is crying:
"Please, save my kid!"
"Let the kid go but save the donkey.
We'll make another kid,
But we can't make another donkey!

In the past moral deviations were extremely rare and penalized by exceptional sanctions. However, in the current period envy, theft, and dishonesty are increasing. Theft is most directly related to property. Before what theft existed was petty, focussed mainly on animals, and took place in border regions or in larger cities (Hadzhiiski 1966-I:110-118, 1966-II:123). Thieves were punished in a traditional way. If someone was caught stealing he would be "decorated" with some of what was stolen and, under the beat of the drum, led through the village from one end to the other, (Videnov 1991:180). Following this the thief became *persona non grata* and was urged to leave the village. Such severe sanctions thus maintained the high level of village morality, and, until recently, house doors in villages and small towns were always left unlocked.

This short historical review outlines the formation of two types of sentiments toward private property among Bulgarian villagers. The first concerns that of collective property, which developed in the centuries before the advent of capitalism in Bulgaria. It was preserved in various customs and degrees among all villagers even after this period. However, it was most obviously characteristic among the poor and smallholding peasantry. The orientation to collectivism, in fact, partially explains the development of the rural cooperative movement in Bulgaria, especially during the 1930s. The second type, the orientation to private property, is a relatively new feeling. For the period until the beginning of World War Two, however, it managed to develop and strongly define the thought and actions of the private proprietor. The more labor invested and the greatest extent of property owned, the stronger this feeling was. Thus, the end of World War Two found the larger part of Bulgarian villagers as small owners, with a well developed sense of property, and firm attachment to the land and animals.

The Effects of Socialist Collectivization on Villager Mentalities

Socialist collectivization also left permanent traces in the mentality of Bulgarian villagers. The forty years of the reality of socialist agriculture to a great extent, rid many people of their affinity for collectivism. In fact, the recent economic difficulties experienced by the transition to democracy intensified the bitterness toward collectivization especially among those who favored it during the 1950s. The inhabitants of Panaretovo and the other four villages from the Sliven region are a case in point. Their comments and narratives typically express the prevailing moods and feelings of the collectivization period.

In fact the concrete experience of the distribution of cows, refreshed villager memories of this time and reinforced their dim view of collectivism. In speaking of this time the people of Panaretovo recalled how they considered themselves to be *babaital,* i.e., large, strong, brave, and resolute people who don't give in easily. Citing this characteristic they compared themselves favorably to other villages and claimed they were the last to enter the collective farm system and the first to start the liquidation process. The actual reality, however, was something else. Thus, the first collective farm emerged in the village in 1950 with nineteen of the poorest village families the initiators. The first president of the new collective farm, Dobri Peev, gave all his twenty decars of land to the farm. The response was quite different, though, among owners of middle and large estates. Their well developed sense of private property did not allow them to part easily with their inherited land and animals. This resulted in a period of hidden or open resistance which ended in 1956 with the full defeat of private ownership.

It was officially announced that the cooperation of farmers was a process taking place voluntarily. Indeed, among the villagers interviewed all responded that no one obliged them to enter the collective farm. Those who remained outside it after 1950, however, were exposed to enormous indirect pressure, exercised mostly by the so called "order." The latter was an official regulation requiring the delivery of such a large quantity of agricultural produce by each farm, that it was beyond the powers of any individual farmer to comply. Thus, for example, Slav Slavov, 65, remembers how he once took his "ordered" delivery to the neighboring village of Carmen. The time of the delivery was so important that those who had failed it had to pay a 100,000 Leva fine, plus interest. In response to my question whether the process of collectivization was really a voluntary one, Vassila Slavova, 84, responded: "Well, once you see that all others joined in, what else could we do? We did the same. We jibbed for a while, it's true, but we joined in, too. Two tons was our order... How could one make it?"

The huge quantities of mandatory deliveries were later supplemented by the force of the public opinion both from local authorities and from those who had already joined the collective. Stephana Slavova from the village of Gloufishevo, for example, shared her memories of how their lands and animals were taken away in 1954. Her father-in-law had 200 decars of land. Both she and her husband were so attached to their animals that even after their joining the collective farm they wanted to raise cattle. Not only were they not allowed to, but they were harassed, treated as fascists, and so on. Unable to stand this psychological pressure they left the village. Her husband became a mason in the town of Sliven and she became a cleaner.

The economic and psychological pressure resulted in an active resistance on the part of some farmers. In 1951 there were already people who had accrued immense fines and interests. Eleven persons from Panaretovo and the nearby villages who prepared to escape to the nearby forest became known as *goriani* (foresters). Their resistance came as a spontaneous response to the pressure. Most of them were members of the opposition wing of the Bulgarian Agrarian Union, lead by Nikola Petkov, which came under attack and persecution by the communists after 1945. One person among those who survived the persecution is Iordan Penev from Panaretovo. He was forty-one years old when he joined the *goriani*, whose number, according to him, amounted to as many as 130 people. They intended to make their way to Greece or Turkey when they had an opportunity. However they were renounced to the authorities by an informer, following which they were all arrested and sentenced to prison.

Regarding the establishment of the collective farm I. Penev responded emotionally about the seven years he spent in the well-known Bulgarian concentration camp of Belene. According to him he joined the *goriani* for political reasons as he was angered by the arrest and killing of the agrarian leader, Nikola Petkov, in 1947, and the persecution of his followers. His escape to the forest, however, was used as a pretext by authorities to take away his family's flour, plunder his house and burn his documents providing proof of his ownership of his lands. Full of grief he remembered how, after he was sentenced and sent to jail in Belene, his father was compelled to join the collective farm in 1956, and his wife was constantly harassed.

The fate of a family left by a "man-of-the-forest" is also reflected in the story of Dina Paskaleva, 60. She was eighteen when her father joined the *goriani*. After that her mother and brother were not allowed to join the local collective farm, her brother felt compelled to leave the village and become a miner, and her mother was constantly harassed, summoned for interrogations, and so on. When they failed to pay their taxes their animals (eighteen sheep and a horse) were expropriated. Finally her mother suffered a nervous breakdown and hanged herself at the age of sixty-two. Her brother returned from his job as a miner and was rejected for a second time for admission into the collective farm. Thus all their property was confiscated by the collective even as they were prevented from benefitting by membership in the organization. In this way the 1960s was the period when the villagers, from the Sliven region and from the rest of Bulgaria as well, were deprived of their lands, animals, and agricultural machinery and became wage workers on their own property. The first, most decisive steps towards the economic levelling of the villagers occurred. Henceforth all problems had a different character.

The "Errors" of the Socialist Collective Farm

The so-called "errors" of collectivization are much more complex than those which I discuss below. However, those singled out here have been selected since they are the one most frequently mentioned by people and, as such have left the greatest impression in popular memory. The first "mistake," which cooperative farmers have never come to terms with, was the levelling of labor requirements and remuneration. Traditionally Bulgarian farmers have always been hard working. During the period of the patriarchal community they regarded their work as a moral obligation and necessary for the mutual success, of their family and community. Later, during the time of capitalism, their existence depended entirely on the quality and quantity of their own work. Lingering sentiments of property ownership, the rural ethic, and commitment to family and community even managed to keep this enthusiasm alive in the first few years of collective farming. However, this situation soon changed for a number of reasons. First, the collective farm eradicated the boundaries between the separate properties from which it has formed, and thus alienated villagers from their former land. Furthermore, they were deprived of their animals, and prevented from future stock ownership. Consequently, the empty barns were soon neglected. Second, collective farm remuneration was low and received on the basis of labor-days, without regard to actual accomplishment. Even today, after eighteen years of work within his collective farm Petar Petrov from Gloufishevo remembers:

> Once we were about to work I wanted to work hard. But when we were to pick up peaches my fellow workers would lie down and do nothing for the whole day, or break them, destroy them. I could't take this chaos. I would like to see everyone pickingup his own line. One person would pick up 13 peaches, I would pick up 40, and yet we were paid equally. I felt like talking to the administration.

To determine collective farm labor compensation, a committee was formed with the participation of the farm's agronomist, and only if this committee granted a high grade to the quality of one's work would that person be paid what he deserved.

The collective farm gathered under its roof all sorts of people, with different work capabilities and desires. Consequently, it alienated many from each other. The attempt to level farm labor with that of the urban worker forced the villager to modify his views on life and influenced in a decisive way his fate and morality. The energy which had been accumulated during the centuries for the creation and affirmation of his own farm gradually evaporated as it started loosing its sense with the establishment of the new relationships among the people.

Urban migration following collectivization grew significantly, especially following the transformation of the collective farms into agrarian-industrial complexes. Over time power became increasingly centralized. Conditions were created through which vices traditionally sanctioned by society like theft and sloth mushroomed. The more the individual was deprived of the chance to defend his rights and interests by the unlimited power of the state, the deeper the demoralization of society grew.

Of all the vices that emerged with collectivization theft was the one hardest to accept and the one most frequently cited for the failure of collective farming. Its dimensions, however, were different at different stages of collectivization. According to the farmers themselves, immediately after the establishment of the collective farm in Panaretovo everyone was concerned about the preservation of farm property. The villagers maintained their spirit of proprietorship for a while. And the exceptions, in fact, were punished severely. Thus, Dobri Peev remembered that during the first years after the start of collectivization a villager was sentenced to three years in jail for stealing an iron coil. "But at that time work was done by hand and honestly," concluded the former president of the cooperative farm. The other farmers also remember that during the first years they were not allowed to take a kernel grain from cooperative. Moreover, farmers harvesting in the fields were frequently inspected.

The stories told by the members of the cooperative farm about theft leave the impression that the evil originates not from ordinary workers but from a certain category of individuals. Among the categories of people most frequently identified as thieves are the rulers, the "insiders," those who used to be poor in the past, communists, and gypsies. The first four groups, in fact, overlap each other. They are just different names for the strong and powerful of the day. Here are a few comments:

"They have been stealing for quite awhile! They had nothing and became rich. And we who gave everything, lost. That's what made us go to the cities to look up for jobs. We left them free and they now want to take more! (i.e. of the cows). "The communists weren't able to lead the people, because they started stealing. They were stealing day and night..."

It is interesting to note that some people made a distinction between theft of private property and theft of cooperative property. To my question whether stealing from cooperative property was considered theft Maria Vassileva responded: "No, this wasn't regarded as theft, it was even considered with pride. If somebody stole from a person, this was more likely to be viewed as theft. When somebody stole from the cooperative it was as if they were taking from their own."

All my informants in Panaretovo maintained that there were no thieves in the village, but just theft from the cooperative. This suggests that the latter form of theft had become a semi-legal form of remuneration during the last decade, a moral norm as affirmed in the proverb that: "One can't steal from his own father and government." Even the president of the cooperative farm himself proved unable to oppose the "norm": As he said: "I watched them with my own eyes (i.e. the thefts). I'd warn one or another person against it but nobody paid attention. People would take an animal that weighed forty kilograms and pay for a five kilograms animal. As the former president indicates, the fictitious sale was one of the main mechanisms of theft. And he went on to say: "Errors and theft killed the (socialist) system."

Kinship as a Balancing Force

Initially the start of the collectivization process had an unwholesome influence on the positive aspects of kinship in Bulgarian society. During the 1950s and 1960s the mass urban migration especially facilitated weakening of kinship as an organization of principle (Smollett 1989:128). The division of labor on one's own farm according to the sex and age of family members was completely displaced by collective farm team work.

The new social and economic structures had the strongest impact on women. Their isolation at home was shattered and they now had to face the hardships of life along with men. Working outside their homes, for the first time they were now exposed to insults and curses; for the first time they experienced vulnerability and defenselessness in the face of strangers. The words of Maria Slavova, setting family morality against work at the collective farm, especially evoke this situation.

> We were a big family of 13 children, but I was totally unused to such talk (i.e. on the collective). People spoke with their asses. All day long they spit out moronic stuff. They did some work, however they were very simple and had no discipline whatsoever. I had to have guts to tolerate this all day long.

Undoubtedly, the disintegration of kinship could not persist for long in a society where the individual was defenseless in the face of rulers and authorities. As Smollett notes, the 1970s and the 1980s saw the revitalization of ties between villages and cities and also among relatives from several different cities or different families within the same city. Contacts during this period were facilitated thanks to the car and telephone (Smollett 1989:128). In the village itself social ties were further strengthened by the economic interdependence which flourished during times of family crisis or at the rites of passage. In other words, having survived the crisis of change and transformation of the 1950s and 1960s kinship ties entered a new period of intensification, which has persisted to this day. This is even visible at the cow distribution in Panaretovo. Almost all the people interviewed maintained that the best cows were given to the "insiders" and their relatives: "...they would come, tie their tails (i. e. mark them) and lead them away; all of these are people of their own relatives. And all other strange people including us here are just watching and taking the garbage," said Vassil from Panaretovo.

Judging by the words and actions of the inhabitants of Panaretovo, kinship is a phenomenon on which Bulgarian agriculture will have to rely for an indefinite future. Some politicians think in a similar way. Considering the restitution of the technical inventory of the collective farms the Honorary President of the Democratic Party declared: "I am against the excessive fragmentation of ownership of agricultural machinery. I think that it could be owned by a single kin or several families mutually cultivating their land (Kiurktchiev 1993:12)."

In Panaretovo at this moment of transition when land has still not been restored to its rightful owners and the new type of cooperations do not exist yet, the first three informal labor associations have already emerged. Their members are united mostly on the kinship principle. No doubt, while society is experiencing a crisis, and while the people are facing economic shortages, lack of satisfaction and alienation, the kinship will continue to play the key role of balancing element for survival.

Conclusion: From Repudiation to Prudent Optimism

Bulgarian villagers are still at a crossroads. The clearer the perspective that they could now own not only animals but the land as well makes the village of nowadays a potential center of attraction for some of those who had left it earlier. The restoration of the "blood" link with the land is that crucial factor which will determine the villagers' future: whether they will look for their fortune far from the places where they were born or to weed out the road of their ancestors and take it anew.

I revisited the village of Panaretovo in January 1994 at which time I had the opportunity to meet some of my previous informants. Fifteen months had elapsed since the day when they received cows from the local collective farm. The euphoria which had accompanied the distribution of the livestock was long since gone. Half the animals had been sold or sent to the slaughterhouse, eaten, and forgotten. At this point each family had a single cow, and the new born calves were for sale or slaughter.

All the above is easily understandable since most of the inhabitants of Panaretovo are now past retirement age, which makes it impossible for them to expand their animal holdings. Furthermore, the cost of raising a cow is greater than its value. That is, its fodder and care exceed the earnings from milk sold on the market. All the villagers whom I had questioned were unanimous about the lack of economic incentive to raise animals except for their own subsistence needs for milk, butter and cheese. According to them, the cause of this is due to the low price for milk now offered by the Serdica State Enterprise. Until recently it had monopoly on the purchase of milk produced in the country and paid only LV 3.57 per liter. Milk prices varied from LV 8 to 10 on the market.

Just a few days before my second visit the villagers learned why the purchase price offered by Serdica was so low. They claimed that the company had large amounts of cheap powdered milk from the Commonwealth of Independent States, which it processed adding only 10.5% of natural milk to it. It thus satisfied the needs of the market without buying large amounts of milk from the villages. Regardless of the low production costs of this milk Serdica sold it for the same price as that of natural milk, thus making large profits in a short time. Apparently this is just one example of the diverse kinds of corruption currently affecting the Bulgarian economy and hindering its agricultural reform. Undoubtedly, corruption is one of the key factors that explains the villagers' recent pessimism about the future of stock-breeding in this region.

However, in a most recent development a new private company from the the neighboring town of Nova Zagora expanded its business into Panaretovo. It offered a better purchase price for the milk of LV 5.50 per liter. Very naturally, all the local producers sold to the new company leaving Serdica without suppliers. This slowly emerging competition creates a beam of hope that one day things will fall into place for people in places like Panerotovo.

Indeed, there are now a few optimists among Panaretovo stock-breeders. The brothers Hristo and Ivan Paskalev belong to this small circle. In a short time following the distribution of the animals they managed to start up a dairy farm of their own, now housed in one of the buildings of the former collective farm. Immediately after the end of the distribution campaign of October 1993 the two brothers started buying their neighbors' cows. Along with those they already owned and newborn calves, they now have twenty-six animals. Both Hristo and Ivan clearly recognize that they are losing money. However, they both think that animals are indispensable. Said Hristo: "I wouldn't give up the cows; they shouldn't all be slaughtered. If we end up slaughtering all of them, what will our people do after that?"

Both brothers hope that things will get better. "Well, it will take two, three, probably four more years until we get on our feet," forecasts Hristo. But both are now working for the future while trying to offset their losses by gains from other sectors, such as gardening. This year they will do what they did last year, and plant watermelons, carrots, potatoes and use their greenhouses for early cucumbers and tomatoes. Later during the year they expect some profit from peaches, which they will invest in technology for their new farm. Says Hristo: "No, I haven't lost hope. I only regret one thing: my age. Why didn't this happen at least twenty years ago... If I could only be at least fifty now! And I am already seventy-two."

In spite of their advanced age the Paskalev brothers succeeded in buying at auction for the price of LV 7 million the spacious and technologically well-equipped barn of the former collective farm. Asked how they would pay this large sum of money, Ivan responded that they were currently negotiating with a Kuwaiti company which had promised them a loan against exports of finished products, e.g. milk, butter, cheese. Both brothers are convinced that agriculture will become profitable as soon as it supplies high-quality products for the Western market. "There was time when we used to do business with the Soviet Union since they bought produce of poorer quality. However, said Hristo, "to do business with the West we now need to start producing otherwise."

The restitution of land is the other big concern on villagers' minds. The actual amount of land people previously owned has not yet been returned to its former owners, but only an approximation of what they possessed before collectivization. This is a serious cause of tension and insecurity as it plays havoc with local planning, for both the present and the future. Furthermore, for most of the villagers the precise restitution of the land in its former boundaries would mean its extreme fragmentation, thus preventing the use of modern technology, among other problems. In this sense the attitudes towards restitution vary widely. Thus the owners of small amounts of land claim that it is neither possible nor necessary to stick strictly to the previous boundaries of their property. They prefer to receive more compact lots. On the other hand, large landowners insist on receiving the lots they once had. "If only one can run faster than the bullet he will be able to get my land," claims Hristo Paskalev.

Notwithstanding its provisional character, a cooperative of small landowners already exists in Panaretovo. It has one hundred and ninety members who own about 3,000 decars of land among the six thousand eight hundred decars of the village's total arable land. The cooperative membership exceeds the number of families in the village, (a total of one hundred and thirty) since many are not the actual former owners of the land, but rather their heirs (e.g. sons and daughters, or even grandchildren), many of whom live outside the village. This provisional solution of the land problem blocks any further sales or purchases of land, and further prevents its owners from planning for the future. This situation negatively affects both the personal intentions of each owner, as well as on the process of reform in agriculture as a whole. It explains why the inhabitants of Panaretovo now mostly rely on earnings from perennial plants, such as peaches, for example, and from vegetable production grown in spacious village yards.

The small pensions the villagers receive hardly cover their taxes and monthly expenses for electricity, water, heat, and so on. They sustain their families mostly on earnings from their garden production with the remaining surplus sold on the market for an insignificant additional income. This group of owners does not forsee developing modern farms in the future, since they do not expect their children or grandchildren to come back to the village. Also, as they are sufficiently satisfied in material terms, they refuse to entertain any kind of large-scale change. Though most are cooperative members they do not work for the organization but rather invest small amounts of money for the purchase of seeds, machinery rental, and so on. In return they receive revenue mostly in kind (e.g. grain).

Somewhat earlier rumors abounded in the village about two families, the above-mentioned Paskalevs and the Droumevs, who were considered rich. They had large accumulations of land, more numerous head of livestock, farm machinery, etc., which they received as a result of the liquidation of the collective farm. Though forty years of socialist collectivization did not eradicate the work ethic and entrepreneurial skills of these lively Bulgarians, their fellow-villagers regarded their sudden "enrichment" of these two families with envy. The villagers claimed that they had plundered the property of others in the village, and treated them with an open hatred. To many it was strange that yesterday's equality had all of a sudden given way to the drastic differences observed. Some villagers even refused to greet members of these two families when seeing them on the street. Still, for some this initial disdain was quickly overcome, and now the esteem for the labor and entrepreneurial skills of the two families continues to grow. The question of richness and poverty is treated by Hristo Paskalev in a rather simpler way. "Now there exist two groups: those who are good for nothing, and those who work. Later on we will have people who are starving and people who are full."

The "wealth" of the two families can also be explained by their stable kinship ties within the village, and in the readiness of those of their kin who had left the village to return to work the land. Hristo Paskalev even now regrets having allowed to one of his daughters to go to university and earn a graduate degree in history. But, as he says, times were different then. "What could she have aimed at in the village? Now it is different. (To leave the village means) a loss of money. Money is what makes your life." He is convinced that his daughters and grandchildren will agree to come back: "My heirs will return, so I am trying to attract them, to teach them. Now there is enough work from sunrise to sunset."

All villagers remain unanimous that many errors were committed with the liquidation of the collective farms. Most often they blame these on the blunders of various political parties, their respective leaders, and the parliament. Unlike during the first days and months after the fall of Zhivkov when everyone followed the news on the TV and the radio attentively, now this is considered to be time lost. Nobody cares anymore about "those above," who are only able to trifle away with "stupid things." Most of my informants expressed their categorical determination to abstain from voting during the next elections.

I had just finished interviewing Hristo Paskalev when he told me that he was once invited to participate in a meeting of the Agrarian Union with its leader, Mrs. Anastassia Moser, which was to take place in the nearby town of Sliven. He expected to see in her person the charm and intelligence of her father, G. M. Dimitrov, whom Hristo knew personally. "She looks as if she has been adopted," he exclaimed, "she doesn't understand anything about agriculture." She had given him the advice to increase the size of his land up to seven thousand decars. "In what way am I supposed to increase the size of my lands to seven thousand decars? This is the total size of the lands of the village. Who is the one who has so much land in Bulgaria?"

As a veteran member of the Nikola Petkov Agrarian Union Hristo Paskalev was severely disappointed with the leadership of his own party. In his view, the leaders who are supposed to deal with the fate of the ordinary people are unfamiliar with their problems. Moreover, they are in constant conflict among themselves. It is true there are significant differences between the agrarian unionists belonging to the two agrarian parties, and that the "red" agrarians have always been "authorities' informants" during the totalitarian period. However "a single stone does not build a house." For this reason Hristo thinks that unless the agrarians unite and take their well-deserved place in parliament, there will be no improvements in Bulgarian agriculture. As of now, however, only the inertia of the reform process currently on-going in the villages provides people with some optimism. As Hristo believes "This (reform in agriculture) will never stop!" Thus hesitatingly, and sometimes with a lot of guess-work, the movement forward continues.

Notes

1. According to statistics in 1946 the share of the rural population as part of the total population of Bulgaria was 75.3%. Of these 62% owned up to fifty decars of arable land, 27.3% from 50 to 100 decars, 9.2% from 100 to 200 decars, 1.4% from 200 to 500 decars, and 0.1% over 500 decars. This clearly indicates that the rural poor were predominant in Bulgaria. The processes of rapid industrialization accompanied by collectivization of lands which followed 9 September 1944 led to subsequent massive urbanization. As a result the population structure was heavily unbalanced in favor of urban settlements. According to the 1975 census figures the rural population comrpised 42% of the total. The social structure itself of the rural population, however, has also been changed. Thus, 62,2% were registered as workers, 8.2% as employees, 1.5% were involved in other professional activities, and only 28.1% were cooperative farm members. For more information refer to Entsiklopedia na Bulgaria, vol.6, Sofia, 1988: 153-154.

2. Here I would like to acknowledge Vesselina Slavova and her parents for the assistance that I received during my work in the village of Panaretovo. The interviews there were recorded and subsequently archived with the Audio-archives of the Institute of Folklore with the Bulgarian Academy of Sciences under call numbers 1097, 1098, 1099, 1100 and 1101.

3. An agrarian-industrial complex is a conglomerate of agricultural collective farms joined with other units that provided them with technical services.

4. A village located in the vicinity of Sliven.

References

Bertaux, Daniel. 1993. "The Biographic Approach: Methodological Value and Perspectives. " *Bulgarian Folklore* 2: 19-29.

Gueshov, Ivan. 1887. "Zadrugata v Zapadna Bulgaria." *Periodichesko Spisanie na Bulgarskoto Knizhovno Druzhestvo v Sredets* XXI-XXII: 426-449.

Hadzhiiski, Ivan. 1966-II. *Optimistichana Teoria za Nashia Narod.* Sofia: Bulgarski Pisatel.

Kirshenblatt-Gimblett, Barbara. 1988. "Authoring Lives." *In* Tomas Hofer and Peter Niedermuller, Eds. *Live History as Cultural Construction/ Performance*. Budapest: Ethnographic Institute of the Hungarian Academy of Sciences.

Kiurktchiev, B. 1993. "Selianinut Iska da Znae Kude e Zemiata mu i Kude e Sinurut i." *24 Chasa*, 10 September: 12.

Krastanova, Kipriana. 1986. *Traditsii na Trudovata Vzaimopomosht v Bulgarskoto Selo.* Sofia: BAN.

Odzhakov, P.V. 1893. *Istoria na Bulgarskoto Pravo.* Chast Vtora. Kniga Purva. Russe.

Smollett, Eleanor Wenkart. 1989. "The Economy of Jars: Kindred Relationships in Bulgaria-An Exploration. " *Ethnologia Europaea*: XIX, 2: 125-140.

Videnov, Mikhail. 1991. *Godechaninut.* Sofia.

14

A Rural Business Class in Transition: Observations from a Polish Region

Joanna Smigielska

Defining Rural Entrepreneurs

A period of systemic transformation is a most interesting time for researchers of everyday life. Things that used to be self-evident and established now undergo rapid change, quite often of a radical nature. Practically overnight new principles of community organization and operation enter into force even as people's attitudes and concepts of the world are changed. This chapter focuses its observations on a sample of individuals representative of rural business interests and shows how such individuals have changed under the new conditions. What the observations make especially clear is the irrationalism of the former system of *Realsozializmus* but the inability of individuals to break totally away from these conditions.

My observation was conducted in central Poland, in Plock province. The villages which I examined surround a town with the population of about fifty thousand, approximately 120 kilometers away from Warsaw. The region, called the Mazovian Plains, has a flat landscape and rich soil. The settlements are situated along communication routes and have a compact form. An average farm consists of a brick house, at least one farm building, and a garden. The yard is rectangular. Each village has at least one department store, with larger ones with fire and police stations. Of particular importance in the region, is that the land is not too fragmented; the average farmer owns about five hectares. The selected micro-region included four villages of about 800 inhabitants and a total of 193 farms. Of these, nineteen farms whose owners exhibited features of a rural business class, were selected for study. My respondents were aged forty to fifty and one of two had a rural background.

My choice of this region for observation was based, first, on my many years' acquaintance with the region and the area, and my knowledge of the financial standing of the individuals selected for examination. My criteria included the living standards and possessions of respondents. To confirm the representative nature of my sample students of two nearby secondary schools were asked to name those of their neighbors who could be called rich. Student respondents were also asked to define the criteria of their choices. I had no trouble whatever guessing the identity of the described farmers. Based on particulars as to type of trade, appearance of the farm, house, and farm buildings, number and make of cars and agricultural machines, I could easily identify my future respondents. During the subsequent interviews, I focussed mainly on today's problems of the leaders of rural business. In this way, I could find out about certain new trends among this group.

A trait the respondents had in common was the date of origin of their wealth. Instead of having only grown rich in the recent years, they had already been prosperous in the 1970s. The question arises, how could such farms emerge and function under communist rule? The answer is that early in the 1970s, on January 1, 1970 to be exact, compulsory annual supplies of agricultural products were abolished and farmers freed of the duty to sell definite quantities of such products (grain, cattle, etc.) to the state. It was then that the situation noticeably improved in rural regions. Some farmers were very quick to adjust to the requirements of modern farming. A trend developed where many abandoned traditional farming, which involved no specialization, and became specialized in either plant or animal production. Furthermore state policy also encouraged people to take up farming by providing extremely cheap credits for manufacturers of food, and just as cheap investment credits.

Sources of Rural Wealth Prior to the Transition

The examined population can be divided into three categories according to their specific ways of growing wealthy. The first group are farmers who had previously owned farms that specialized in a definite area of production (e.g. fruit-growing). The second group had traditional non-specialized farms (plant and animal production) and chose a specific type of farming. The third group within the sample are people who either took up farming (for economic reasons or availing themselves of the favorable circumstances), or had just graduated from agricultural colleges or schools and decided to work on their own farms. In this latter group, there are also persons who considered farming their passion. A typical successful member of the first group is Adam. He received ten hectares of land from his father, complete with an already organized apple orchard, a three-room house and farm buildings. His family were fruit growers by tradition. Adam graduated from an agricultural school and says he had never considered the possibility of earning his living any other way than through farming. From childhood his ambition had been to work on a farm of his own and to take the responsibility for his actions. He had been well acquainted with the strong and weak points of the trade of his choice. His first step as independent farm owner was to take an investment credit. This proved rather easy as his father had always been highly thought of at the bank, made all payments on time and managed the farm well. Adam used the credit to buy additional land and to set up a new orchard with the latest apple-tree varieties. He also made additions to the farm buildings, raised a cold storage plant and modernized the maintenance building. Later on he proceeded to rebuild the house and purchased all the necessary agricultural equipment, machines and appliances. He now sees those years as the most beautiful period in his life, a period of construction and creation even if it was also one of hard work. Due to market shortages, the people incessantly had to make considerable efforts to "organize" the things they needed. Practices such as using one's "connections", incessant giving of "presents" (actually, bribes), and rendering numerous services to the person who was competent to okay your request, were all in the day's work.

Adam's farm is decidedly superior to those of his neighbors. The large house is tastefully appointed and the stylish furniture from Swarzedz[1] looks especially attractive in the spacious rooms. A beige woolen rug, flower vase and a 19th century chandelier purchased at a DESA shop,[2] as well as an annex full of green plants, together make the interior cozy and far from pompous. The kitchen has all the available appliances that make work there easier. Children's rooms and bathrooms are situated upstairs. The yard is clean and well cared for, the lawn mowed regularly, and the bushes trimmed. Adam owns Western passenger cars and trucks. In the summer Adam's wife takes the children on holiday and in the winter the whole family goes to the mountains. This standard greatly exceeds an average farmer's material standing. According to Adam, the factors that contributed to his success were first of all: the possibility of investing, and production of top-quality apples. Producing top quality produce, however, was difficult to achieve. As Adam said: "It's quite easy to grow just apples, but it takes a lot of hard work and money to make your apples fine and available the year round." Adam realized that if he was to achieve his planned living standard, his production had to be not only large but also high-quality but he also had to enter Western markets. He saw clearly that exporting would stimulate production, but export had to consist of highly desired products and not merely focus on the disposal of any kind of surplus, as was the case with exports to the former Soviet Union. With his high quality produce Adam gained a strong position on the market. He was always able to sell his fruit and had regular customers. What he earned was enough to pay for both investments and consumption. He knew that he was rich and had invested his money well. Moreover, he derived satisfaction from his work; first, he liked his trade, and second, he saw he was good at it. He knew that success resulted from hard work on the farm.

Bogdan is an example of a farmer who turned a traditional farm into a specialized one. He graduated from a Secondary Technical School of Farming and Animal Production and joined his father on the family farm. The father believed in traditional farming, and consequently had no focus as such. He sowed corn, grew vegetables, produced seed, and bred hogs and calves. Bogdan decided to specialize in breeding calves and milk cattle. To this aim, he sought credit to build and furnish a cow barn. It was a large-scale investment which many farmers feared at that time, and Bogdan's neighbors eyed his doings with mistrust. But animal production started to yield good results, and Bogdan soon had many followers. Parallel to work on the farm, Bogdan had to "organize" all the necessary means of production. This involved repeated visits to the commune council, and Bogdan had much difficulty overcoming resistance on part of the local officials who seemed to compete with one another to create obstacles to settlement of even the slightest of matters. For this reason friendly relations with communal authorities were essential for persons engaged in agriculture. Such relations could be achieved through an exchange of services between parties according to the axiom, "If you help me, I'll help you, your relatives, and friends." In this way, a system of informal connections emerged which were valid throughout the economy of shortage (Wedel 1986).

Bogdan thus used a succession of loans to invest in the farm, to extend and furnish the house, and to buy a truck and equipment. In the 1980s his investments finally began to pay off and his income made him feel financially secure. His comfortable house of six rooms, designed by a well-known architect, aroused envy in many of his neighbors. The living-room furniture had been ordered in Swarzedz, the leather sofas and armchairs imported from Holland, and the TV and video systems from Germany. Bogdan preferred to rest in his hunting room where the place of honor belonged to a stuffed goshawk, its wings spread widely against a background of pheasants. In one of the corners, there was a stuffed heron balancing on one leg which watched over a collection of rifles and ammunition deposited in a safe next to its beak. That was the room where Bogdan met with his men friends who would discuss their work and future plans over drinks. The children's rooms in the first floor had been decorated according to the tastes of their small tenants.

An example of the third group is Cezary, a graduate of the agricultural faculty, SGGW AR[3]. His family had no farming traditions but he was encouraged to take up farming by a professor at the school. A bank credit allowed him to buy the farm and start a chicken-farm and a cherry orchard. He soon found his academic knowledge insufficient and was glad to use the advice of experienced farmers and his neighbors willingly helped the enthusiastic "townsman." Cezary was not discouraged by his initial failures, and constantly aimed at developing his farm. Several years later, his living standard was far from the initial situation. His large and modern house furnished in Scandinavian style, a modern kitchen, good cars, and holidays abroad represented a dream come true. Remembering the past, Cezary argues that he was much better than the locals at having his business settled with the commune authorities. First, because he knew the law and thus also his own rights. He would demand all that was due to him and execute his rights within statutory time-limits. The other factor that helped him was that he had been born in Warsaw. Local communist authorities had always been scared of "Warsaw" as the center of power. A person coming from Warsaw was believed to have connections, e.g., with the central authorities; improper treatment of such a person could mean trouble for local officials. Cezary argues that, although he had started from nought and based on nothing but credits, it took him several years only to achieve a standard he had never dreamed of. He fashioned his farm after what he had seen in the West. Before, he had always considered that impossible in Poland, but the course of events proved him wrong.

Concepts of the Good Life

Considering the discussion above, certain generalizations can be made about the three groups of rural entrepreneurs. In the first place the standard of living they achieved meant they lived a very different life from that of their parents. Still, they never showed off by throwing money around. In fact, they are exceptional in their careful calculation of the balance between consumption and production value. The reason for this was perhaps that their wealth had not been accumulated in a few months but resulted from long and planned activity involving a lot of self-denial and sacrifice. For this reason, they had no need to be conspicuous about their enhanced living standards. The farmers mentioned above were no doubt the elite, an informal group with whom they identified themselves as well. As elites in their respective neighborhoods, they stimulated village life and acted as forerunners of agro-technical novelties.

What are the features of the rural business class? Most certainly, they are men of enterprise with a lot of drive, and model organizers. They have a responsible attitude to work and require the same of their permanent and seasonal staff. They are aware of the importance of quality; with the emergence of competition, it gets more and more difficult to sell produce. Speaking of their plans for the future, they mostly focus on extending their production. Their aim is not just to survive, but they perceive their challenge to be constant development and improvement.

Such problems are usually discussed in the midst of friends, persons with a similar status. The meetings are private, accompanied by a cup of coffee or tea, cookies, and brandy. To most respondents, such occasions were not exactly business meetings but rather pleasant and relaxing events. Local news and scandals are also discussed, and the men joke a lot. The meetings are not the only shared aspect of this group's life. Sometimes they help one another, borrowing money, farming machines, or teams of workers. The group remains informal; its members do not join any official organizations.

The role of women in the sample families is diverse. For the most part, women are housewives only; they run the household, organize parties, and decide about purchases of furniture, rugs, and household equipment. Running the farm is exclusively the husband's responsibility. Of the sample nineteen families, only two women work as teachers. This, they argue, allows them to fulfill their own aims and aspirations and derive a lot of satisfaction from the job outside the home. The next and largest group of women not only run the household but also work in farming-related activities (e.g. supervising hired workers and organizing sales). In all the families, the wife is considered the husband's adviser. Yet during the men's meetings, her opinion is never quoted as that of the wife. Rarely any of the men ever state, "my wife tells me to ..."; at most, they might say "we have decided to ...". In some cases, the wife's opinion matters a great deal. Outside the family, though, it is the husband who makes the final decisions and the wife remains in the background.

Business investments enjoy priority over all other expenses, and in business matters the husband's opinion is conclusive. Household matters and plans, the organization of cultural activities, household provisioning, the children's education and upbringing are the women's domain. Still, of interest, all female respondents have a driving license and a car of their own. Consequently, as compared to other women, the wives of entrepreneurs are more independent in organizing their daily activities. During my interviews with the women, a lot of time was given to dress and fashion. The women read fashion journals and have many ideas to create their own style. Most buy their better dresses in Warsaw, at expensive stores. Their workday garments are casual. They attach a lot of importance to accessories and jewelry, and treat the interest in fashion as relaxation which helps them forget the daily routine. As one woman suggested:

> I love to visit a neighbor in the mornings, to have a cup of coffee and girls' talk. We tell each other what we've bought recently and what is worth buying, in terms of dresses, where it can be found and what it costs. We both have some rest and then off we go back to work.

In a sense, it is the women who determine their husband's style of clothing. They know about the latest suits and accessories and try to force them on their husbands. Here, however, the husbands often resist; they prefer their older suits and are usually reluctant to follow the latest fashion. To challenge this resistance on part of their husbands, female respondents buy fashionable garments for themselves and the children: " It helps me to buy nice things. It's great if you need a cheering-up. The things are actually trifles but they make my life, too." Women's favorite pastimes include reading of fiction, watching films (video cassettes mostly), and reading illustrated magazines, of the ladies' variety mostly.

Both men and the women among my respondents consider provisioning the family as an important issue. Generally, all family members meet in a large room, sometimes combined with the kitchen where they watch TV, read the press, receive guests and have meals. Great care is taken to serve elegant and "healthy meals." An important part of the daily routine even for these entrepreneurial families is thus the meal shared by the entire household, often a Polish-style "dinner" served at 2 p.m., or "supper" at 7 p.m. This offers the occasion to talk and tell one another about the latest news. Dinner usually consists of two courses, a soup followed by the main dish. In keeping up with Western trends three families stated that they had replaced meat with other products such as vegetables and vegetarian cuisine. Some younger couples now supplement Polish traditional meals with oriental dishes (Japanese, Chinese, Vietnamese). Additionally according to all of my respondents, alcohol was not consumed in excess in their households and people claim they seldom get really drunk at parties. Large and sumptuous parties, in fact, are infrequent and held only on occasions as weddings, christening, and children's first Holy Communions.

Considering their children, like parents everywhere most respondents would like their children to live better than themselves. Only a few respondents feel it proper to select their child's career for them but two believed that children ought to continue their parents' work and take over operation of the family farm. Should it prove impossible to maintain at least an average living standard through farming only, the children ought to find additional sources of income outside agriculture. Most respondents believe that children ought to both seek education in its own right but also train in a profession that will guarantee a reasonable level of subsistence. Two of the families mentioned the medical profession as the best choice for their children, two others considered psychology the best trade nowadays:

> The choice is self-evident as so many jobs are now open to psychologists. The trade's interesting enough and offers good money, too. You can set up a guidance center and earn your living quite well this way.

Some respondents also said that children could work outside agriculture provided the job gave them satisfaction. The concern for education is manifested in the parents' efforts to find a good school instead of sending the children to the one in the neighborhood. A large proportion of the children take extra lessons in a foreign language or music. Depending on their age, the children have household duties which are strictly executed. Younger children take care of a cat, dog, or rabbits or cultivate flowers in the garden. Elder ones tidy the house, help prepare meals or cook themselves. The eldest are treated as partners and have a say in all matters related to the farm. The parents see formation of the children's conscientiousness and diligence and their involved in the family business as an element of their preparation to life and education.

The Economic Crisis at the End of Socialism

The life assumptions of my sample families discussed above were severely challenged with the formal end of state socialism. In 1989, there was not only a breakdown in government but there was also a market crisis. Though the economy had moved closer toward a market system on the macro or national scale, capitalism in the Polish countryside proved a fake. Cheap credits were abolished and fuel prices raised to their economically logical level. At the same time the Polish market was invaded by great quantities of Western products (fruit, vegetables, diary products) even as the level of exports to the then-USSR collapsed simultaneously. The prosperity of 1970s quickly ended due to immense surplus production and the lack of markets for it. As a result none of my respondents found it possible to preserve the standard of living provided by their farms before the end of socialism. To preserve this standard, they now must undertake additional economic activity outside agriculture, nowadays a natural practice on many farms. However, their success during socialism provided them with some economic latitude in the transition.

Adam runs a transport firm, importing tangerines from Spain and distributing them all over the province and sometimes also the whole country. He has remained a local businessman, too. He continues to try to operate his orchard and the apples are sold to a food processing plant or alcohol distillery. Bogdan is wholesaler of fertilizers, pesticides and other chemical inputs though his cattle production is now considerably reduced. Cezary now is an owner of some pharmacies and he has reduced the expenditure on his orchards to the absolute minimum. He also runs a second-hand clothes shop where the wares are sold by the weight.

All my respondents said they still invested smaller or larger sums in their original production activities. In all cases, however, investments in the farms are being reduced and respondents even refuse to state explicitly how much longer they will continue to support their former production activities. They are preparing for the day when they give up their farms to remain as village inhabitants and rural businessmen. At present, their former lifestyles are also changing slightly. In particular they no longer evince feelings of security derived from their work. The difficulties of coping with the new market and economic situation are caused by uncertainty as to the possible economic decisions made by the succession of governments. The new business activities outside agriculture are treated as a necessary evil. Some consider the new activities in which they've entered (e.g. trading in second-hand clothes) to be detrimental to their status as respectable farmers. On the other hand, though, the new trade is much less absorbing than the respondents' original work and reasonable from the financial viewpoint, it still doesn't satisfy in the same way as agriculture. As one respondent said:

> I feel I'm growing lazy. Trade is nothing but profit, and it involves practically no risk; what cannot be sold today will certainly go tomorrow. What satisfaction can you derive from having sold a hundred pairs of trousers? This is business and nothing but business.

Or as another respondent said:

> A pharmacy is a profitable business; nothing to do, next to no risk, plenty of customers, and you can go on summer holidays. Still it's boring in a way.

As they talk of their new work in relation to agriculture my respondents tend to grow nostalgic. The money they earn fails to give them full satisfaction or recompense, perhaps because they have already grown used to having a lot of money. Earning money is not their main driving force and the reason for new economic activities. Yet some of my respondents are not really sure whether they would relinquish their present trade such as the pharmacy, trade in second-hand clothes, etc., even if the macro-economic situation were to change and make farming profitable again. Their "yes" is not really positive. One of them related and generalized his own experience as follows:

> I was into nursery-gardening once - what a toil. I decided to set up a small orchard of two hectares and I never returned to nursery-gardening. Today, I have an orchard of twenty-six hectares. Fruit-growing is easier and the effects are quicker. I know one thing; a person who tries to earn his living outside fruit-growing won't ever resume that trade.

Instead of a commitment to business *per se*, the respondents' system of values is oriented mainly to personal well-being, i.e. maintaining their good health, a happy family life, and above all their present standards of living. This latter is especially the focus today. To quote one of the respondents:

> I find it hard to get used to the situation where there's no money left in the drawer where we once used to keep cash. This is why you have to take up another trade not to drop too much below your standard.

Another stated:

> You have to start some additional trade; it would be a shame to lose what you've already gained. It's not just money that you lose; your whole life changes if you're poorer.

Thus, for the time being their new occupations serve only to enable their continued participation in agriculture, to which they remain committed due to its traditional meanings and cross-generational qualities.

Besides the economic transition to such new occupations, then, another most important challenge these emerging rural businessmen face is to overcome the psychological obstacles and conflicts they feel in the assumption of their new roles. The respondents' nostalgic attitude and long traditions of farming thus currently result in considerable stress during the transformation. Such stresses, in particular, differentiates our respondents from the so-called *nouveaux riches* who are perfectly happy at pecuniary gratification which they see as the aim in itself.

Related to these psychological issues, the changing economic circumstances of respondents have also produced change in the activities in which they engage outside work, for example during leisure time. Thus respondent families are joining new groups such as an art gallery in a small village on one of the region's lakes, which has developed into a club where people go for a wide variety of different activities. Here they can meet business colleagues and show off a little by driving a new car or wearing a new dress. During such meetings plans, projects and achievements are discussed, but the climate of such talks is still rather festive rather than business-oriented. One leaves a meeting relaxed and satisfied, convinced as to your own status in this specific community.

Related to Jacek Kurczewski's description of the middle class (Kurczewski 1994) my respondents clearly sense themselves members of Poland's developing middle class which makes their village residence somewhat incongruous to them. As middle class they see themselves as possessing a specific set of cultural traits including a definite work ethic, resourcefulness, and an ability to adjust to the new conditions of the Polish economy which confront them.. They are fully aware of these qualities which are, after all, among the determinants of the group to which they say they belong. Their awareness of affiliation to this group is very high, stressed and verbalized by nearly all. An interesting issue revealed during the interviews is the group's attitude to politics. Like the rural stratum from which they derive, but unlike the middle class to which they see themselves increasingly belonging, they keep their distance from political events and refuse to become actively involved in politics though many are formally members of the Polish Peasant Association. The sources of their knowledge of politics are TV and the press. Their lack of political involvement is perhaps explained by the contradiction they experience. That is, on one hand they approve the on-going democratic transformation of Polish society but, on the other hand, they vociferously criticize the new authorities who, they say, are incompetent and prone to making foolish decisions as to agriculture or privatization. Some respondents consider politics to be for people who want to make it to the top, or who "see to their own business". They suggest that for them to seek positions of authority would have little positive impact for improving the their region's agricultural situation. Thus they deprecate farmers who have become involved in politics: "They aren't farmers, they're fighters"

All respondents realize the current difficulty of improving the situation in agriculture. They know they can form associations and farmer lobbies to promote their own interests; but they know just as well that a change or return to the situation of the early 1980s is impossible today. Transformations in global agriculture involve a distinct shrinking of rural communities. Neither traditional nor highly specialized farmers can find a place for themselves in modern agriculture, and in any case all their numbers are bound to decrease with time. If it is to achieve some kind of market rationality agriculture will become more and more of an industry in Poland and there will be fewer and fewer persons employed in it. And with the rapid modernization of agriculture and its mass production of surplus the food producer's dignity will lose its former importance.

This situation implies a number of questions about my respondents' new role in society and the rules of conduct this will demand. Perhaps they will form a more clearly defined "business class" in the future; yet their business will not be the same kind of rural one which, from time immemorial, conferred the respect of one's neighbor and provided at least a small degree of satisfaction at the performance of your duties.

The context of this new situation is much broader than that discussed by respondents in interviews. Thus one can also discern other qualitative and quantitative changes not only in Poland but throughout east Europe. The production of surplus mentioned above, for example, has resulted in a few cases in farmers being paid for letting their land lie fallow, similar to the situation found in America. It has also contributed to the growth of mono-crop corporate-like production practices. These changes are naturally first perceived by leading traditional farmers such as our emerging business class and they are generally the first group to attempt to adjust to these new situations. It is therefore only natural when a prosperous fruit grower opens a denim stone-washing plant, and a potato magnate starts a transport firm. This in-between status of "farmer-cum-something else" is likely to remain until such trends as those above crystallize. What will follow, however, is open to speculation.

Notes

1. A renowned Polish furniture factory, using oak as its principal material.
2. DESA is a chain of antique stores.
3. Main School of Agriculture - Agricultural Academy.

References

Kurczewski, Jacek. 1994. "Siedem klas średnich." *Nowa Res Publica.* March, 1994.

Wedel, Janine. 1986. *The Private Poland: An Anthropologist Looks At Everyday Life.* New York: Facts on File.

About the Editor and Contributors

Daniel Bates is Professor of Anthropology at Hunter College, City University of New York. He has carried out field research in the Middle East on ethnicity, pastoralism, and rural land use. He is author of *Nomads and Farmers: The Yörük of Southeastern Turkey* (University of Michigan Museum of Anthropology), *Human Adaptive Strategies* (McGraw Hill), co-author of *Cultural Anthropology* (McGraw Hill) and *Peoples and Cultures of the Middle East* (Prentice-Hall), and co-editor of the journal *Human Ecology*. His current research concerns local politics and Moslem ethnics in Bulgaria.

Gerald W. Creed is Assistant Professor of Anthropology at Hunter College and the Graduate School of the City University of New York. He has conducted extensive fieldwork in rural Bulgaria, including nearly two years in the socialist era. Since 1992 he has been involved in an on-going project examining decollectivization and rural-urban interactions.

Hermine G. De Soto is research fellow in the Women's Studies Program and Women's Studies Research Center at the University of Wisconsin-Madison. She edited *Culture and Contradiction: Dialectics of Wealth, Power and Symbol* (Mellen Research University Press) and co-edited *The Curtain Rises: Rethinking Culture, Ideology and the State in Eastern Europe* (Humanities Press International). Forthcoming is *The Delayed Transformation: Experiences of Everyday Life in a Village in the Black Forest.* Her current research focuses on the transition from socialism to capitalism; gender issues and urban and rural change in Europe; and ethnic groups in Kazakhstan.

Andrzej Halasiewicz is a researcher and lecturer in the Department of Sociology at Nicolaus Copernicus University in Torun, Poland. He edited *The Peasant Issue or Peasant Problem* (Torun, NCU Press) and is co-author of *Agri-Business* (Tempus-Ellpid). His current research concerns variations in the response of rural farm and non-farm households to changing social and economic conditions and also with the revitalization and multifunctional development of the European countryside.

Chris Hann is Professor of Social Anthropology at the University of Kent, Canterbury, United Kingdom. Previously he taught for many years at the University of Cambridge. In addition to work in rural Hungary he has carried out fieldwork in Poland and Turkey. His main research interests include ethnicity and nationalism, and the many facets of modernization and restructuring in peasant societies, both Eastern and Western.

Radost Ivanova is Professor at the Institute of Folklore of the Bulgarian Academy of Sciences in Sofia. Her scholarly interests are oriented towards the studies of traditional culture and folklore, as well as the everyday life of modern Bulgarian society. She is the author of *Bulgarskata Folklorna Svatba* (Sofia, BAN), *Traditional Bulgarian Wedding* (Sofia, Svyat), *Epos-Obred-Mit* (Sofia, BAN). She has also written a large number of papers and reviews.

Andzrej Kaleta is a Professor in the Sociology Department of Nicolaus Copernicus University in Torun, Poland. He is the author of a number of books on rural sociology and on the problems of rural youth such as *Rural Sociology in Austria* and *Rural Youth as a Product of Disorganized Society* (both published at Torun, NCU Press). His current research concerns the revitalization of rural European communities based on peasantist traditions.

David A. Kideckel is Professor and Chair of the Anthropology Department at Central Connecticut State University. He recently published *The Solitude of Collectivism: Romanian Villagers to the Revolution and Beyond* (Cornell) and co-edited the *Anthropology of East Europe Review* special issue on "War Among the Yugoslavs: Anthropological Perspectives." Currently he is involved in a project analyzing the socio-political implications of privatization aid to transitional east Europe.

Jacek Kurczewski is former deputy speaker of the Polish *Sejm* and Director of the Institute of Applied Social Science at the University of Warsaw. He is author and co-author of numerous books and articles, including the co-edited *Family, Gender, and Body in Law and Society Today* (U. Warsaw) and most recently *The Resurrection of Rights in Poland* (Oxford). His current research concerns organizational aspects of the Polish transition to capitalism and the nature of voluntary associations in this process.

Christel Panzig is a social historian and rural ethnographer/sociologist. She is a former member of both the East German Academy of Agricultural Sciences and International Institute of Agriculture. Her research and publications focus on East German rural social history and women. Since unification she has directed research projects entitled "*Historical and Social Anthropological Studies: Continuity and Discontinuity of Mental Structures in East German Rural*

Society," and *"Transformations of Hegemonic Practices: Formation of Peasant Consciousness in East German Villages After 1945."*

Steven Sampson is a Research Fellow at the Institute of Anthropology, University of Copenhagen, Denmark. He is the author of *National Integration Through Socialist Planning: The Study of a Romanian New Town* (Columbia) and of numerous articles on various aspects of social change in Eastern Europe. He has done extensive fieldwork in Romania and Eastern Europe on planning, local elites, and the informal sector and has worked as a consultant in several European Community projects in Romania and Albania.

Carol Silverman is Associate Professor of Anthropology and Folklore at the University of Oregon and Director of the Russian and East European Studies Center. She has done fieldwork in Bulgaria, Macedonia, and Hungary, and with Roma in the United States. Her publications investigate gender, ritual, music, and the politics of culture among Balkan minorities.

Joachim Singelmann is Professor and Chair of the Sociology Department at Louisiana State University in Baton Rouge. He is the author of *From Agriculture to Services* (Sage) and co-author of *Das Ende der Kalassengesellschaft?* (Transfer Verlag). He also co-edited *Inequalities in Labor Market Areas* (Westview). His current research includes an analysis of socio-economic change along the Gulf of Mexico and a five year study of the transformation from socialism to liberal democracy in eastern Germany.

Joanna Smigielska is a Lecturer in the Faculty of Prevention, Resocialization, and Social Problems at the University of Warsaw. A specialist in rural sociology, she is the author of a number of articles on rural social relations, focussing on changes in rural markets.

Ildiko Vasary was a freelance writer and Honorary Research Fellow at University College, London. She did fieldwork in Hungary, most recently in 1990-1992, and was the author of an extensive number of publications including *Beyond the Plan: Social Change in a Hungarian Village* (Westview). She passed away last year.

Dennis Vnenchak is currently Visiting Professor of Sociology at the Nicolaus Copernicus University in Torun, Poland and Polish representative to the TEMPUS Project sponsored by the European Community, which concerns the development of East European democratic practice in the transition. He is the author of a number of books and articles on Polish society and culture, most recently *Lech Walesa and Poland* (Franklin Watts).